Newspapers of Maryland's Eastern Shore

BY DICKSON J. PRESTON

Wye Oak: The History of a Great Tree, 1972

Trappe: The Story of an Old-Fashioned Town, 1976

St. Luke's Parish: A History, 1978

Young Frederick Douglass: The Maryland Years, 1980

75 Years of Caring:
A History of the Memorial Hospital at Easton, 1982

Talbot County: A History, 1983

Oxford: The First Three Centuries, 1984

Newspapers of Maryland's Eastern Shore, 1986

Newspapers
OF MARYLAND'S EASTERN SHORE

by

DICKSON J. PRESTON

Published jointly by

THE QUEEN ANNE PRESS, QUEENSTOWN

&

TIDEWATER PUBLISHERS, CENTREVILLE

Copyright © 1986 by Tidewater Publishers

All rights reserved. No part of this book may be used or reproduced in any manner whatsoever without written permission except in the case of brief quotations embodied in critical articles and reviews. For information, address Tidewater Publishers, Centreville, Maryland 21617.

Library of Congress Cataloging in Publication Data

Preston, Dickson J., 1914-
Newspapers of Maryland's Eastern Shore.

Bibliography: p.
Includes index.
1. American newspapers—Eastern Shore (Md. and Va.)—
History. 2. American newspapers—Eastern Shore
(Md. and Va.)—Bibliography. I. Title.
PN4897.M233P7 1986   071'.521   85-40533
ISBN 0-87033-336-4 (Tidewater)

Published jointly by The Queen Anne Press, Queenstown, and
Tidewater Publishers, Centreville
Manufactured in the United States of America
First edition

Contents

	Illustrations	vii
	Publishers' Preface	xi
	Preface	xiii
	Acknowledgments	xvii
ONE	*Prelude: The Zenger Heritage*	3
TWO	*Beginnings: The First Shore Newspapers*	10
THREE	*First Flowering: The County Weeklies*	40
FOUR	*Civil War: A Shore Divided*	74
FIVE	*The Long Siesta: 1865 to 1923*	110
SIX	*Modern Times: Conflict and Survival*	145
SEVEN	*Today and Tomorrow: 1960 to 1985*	178
	Directory of Eastern Shore Newspapers	197
	Bibliographical Notes	257
	Index	261

Illustrations

Andrew Hamilton	6
Power of attorney granted by John Peter Zenger	8
Prospectus of James Cowan, June 3, 1789	11
Page one of *Maryland Herald and Eastern Shore Intelligencer*	14
James Cowan imprint, 1792	15
Advertisement from *Maryland Herald*, 1796	19
A fox hunt advertised, 1804	19
Earliest issue of *Apollo; or, Chestertown Spy*	22
Pamphlet published by Robert Saunders	25
Earliest issue of Easton's *Republican Star*	27
Pamphlet published by Thomas Perrin Smith	29
The "Sajou Brown"	31
Advertisements for steamboats, *Surprise* and *Maryland*	35
Obituary of Thomas Perrin Smith, 1832	37
Masthead of final issue of *Republican Star*	37
Announcement of sale of *Star*'s presses, etc.	39
Ad for men's tailoring, 1847	43
Early newspaper mastheads	44
Symbols of 1840 Whig presidential campaign	46
Early advertising featuring simple woodcuts	48
Patented cure-alls of the 1840s advertised	50
The *Cambridge Chronicle*, 1848	52
Ad illustrations, 1810 and 1850	53
The Somerset Iris and Messenger of Truth, 1828	55
Ads of slave buyers	57
Runaway slave ads	58

Ads in the *Centreville State Rights*, 1860	63
Mastheads of two Princess Anne papers	65
Trial of Editor Ricketts	68
Know-Nothing cartoon	71
Cambridge's *American Eagle*, 1856	73
John C. Breckinridge	75
John Bell	75
Presidential campaign cartoon, 1860	77
Centreville State Rights' announcements, 1860	78
"Dreadful conflagration," *Salisbury Sentinel*, 1860	79
Pro-South's *State Rights Advocate*	80
Illustration from *Uncle Tom's Cabin*	81
Announcement of Ordinance of Secession	83
Firing on Fort Sumter, *New York Herald* and *Easton Star*	86
Pro-Southern *Somerset Union*	87
Pro-Union *Somerset Herald*	87
Ads for Union volunteers	89
Announcement of *Kent Conservator* editor's arrest	93
Examples of *Easton Star*'s pro-Southern sentiments	95
Contemporary drawing of Battle of Gettysburg	95
Gettysburg as reported in pro-Union *Kent News*	96
Sharpshooter, May 14, 1864	100
Items from *Sharpshooter*	101
Cartoon of Lincoln's reelection campaign	105
Last Moments of President Lincoln	107
Reward for Lincoln's murderer	108
Kent News' report on murder of Lincoln	109
The *Crisfield Leader*	112
Trappe newspapers	113
Eastern Shore newspapers advertise themselves	115
Advertising page from Denton's *American Union*	116
Local news dominates page one	117
Editorial office of *Kent News*	123
Earliest known issue of *The Queenstown News*	126
Office of the *Free Press*, Greensboro	127

Staff of the *Easton Gazette*	129
An earlier office of the *Easton Gazette*	130
Easton Ledger staff	131
Samuel E. Shannahan	135
Baltimore department stores' ads	136
Easton Gazette features the automobile	136
Star-Democrat printing shop	137
Lorie C. Quinn	139
Dr. Edward J. Clarke	141
Wilson M. Tylor	141
Auto age in Easton	144
Salisbury Times newsroom in 1920s	146
Salisbury Times' first building	148
Max Chambers	153
Page one of *Salisbury Times*, December 5, 1931	157
H. L. Mencken's column in *Daily Banner*	159
Contrasting headlines	163
Fictitious radiogram in *Somerset News*	169
Editor Matthews thanks fellow journalists	169
Norman Harrington	172
Open house at *Easton Star-Democrat*	173
Maurice Rimpo	175
Opening of Bay Bridge	177
Easton Star-Democrat's composing room	181
Paste-up department, Salisbury *Daily Times*	181
E. Ralph Hostetter	185
Melvin Toadvine	185
Composing room of *Marylander & Herald*	187
Marylander & Herald pressroom	188
Marylander & Herald office	188
Salisbury *Daily Times* reporters at work	190
Newsroom of *The Daily Times*	191
Employee pasting up classified ads	191
High-speed Goss offset press	192
The Daily Times mail room	192

Publishers' Preface

"IN 30 years as a newspaper reporter and editor, I traveled to most parts of the world—South America, Europe, Asia, Africa, Canada, and all of the (then) 48 states—and covered every presidential campaign from 1948 to 1964. Also a few assorted wars, revolutions, scandals, strikes, epidemics, race riots, and whatever else was going on. Most of this was for Scripps-Howard Newspapers, for whom I was a Washington-based special correspondent from 1952 to 1966.

"Then I gave it all up to move to Talbot County, acquire a secluded bit of waterfront looking out over the Tred Avon River, take photographs of birds, and write about things that happened a long time ago . . ."

This was Dickson Preston's in-a-nutshell description of his own career, characteristically modest and facetious, an enormous amount unsaid.

After moving to the Eastern Shore, he ultimately became the undisputed historian of the area, constantly searching, inquiring, recording—and writing. His innate curiosity and his long newspaper experience served him, and his community, very well.

This history of newspapers on Maryland's Eastern Shore was commissioned in the late seventies by The Queen Anne Press. Preston's work was completed in 1981 but circumstances forced a postponement. Later, when publication was scheduled, Preston, already in declining health, moved quickly to bring the narrative current. He finished this task only a few weeks before he died in January 1985. The Directory, with only a few exceptions, however, is as he originally completed it in 1981. Although inevitably there have been additions and deletions to and from individual collections listed, the major change in the interim has been in the growth of the microfilm holdings at the Maryland State Archives. Preston mentions their program in his Preface, and it has continued vigorously since.

Although proud of his various books, Dickson Preston spoke of this as his major work. Both The Queen Anne Press and Tidewater Publishers are proud of their role in making it available.

Preface

AMERICA'S country editors and their county newspapers evoke a nostalgic era in the nation's past. Perhaps the editors were not great journalists in the modern sense, but they fulfilled their function: they mirrored faithfully the events and values of the communities they served, and they captured the essence of a time when the world was not yet so complex, when rural and small town standards still played a major role in American life.

On the Eastern Shore of Maryland county newspapers flourished as almost nowhere else. For the greater part of two centuries they were the region's only voice, and they bespoke it well. They were as insular and as stubbornly independent as the people whose lives and thoughts they chronicled.

These newspapers throve in a unique climate. Throughout the nineteenth century and well into the twentieth the Eastern Shore was virtually untouched by the outside world; it was a land overlooked, left stranded by the tide of westward expansion, unmarked by the waves of industrialization and urbanization which created the modern nation. The outlook of the Eastern Shore remained entirely rural. There were no dominant population centers, and consequently no reason to develop a dominant metropolitan press. Each of the Shore's nine counties, which altogether stretch a hundred and fifty miles, forming the eastern shore of the Chesapeake Bay, was an entity in itself, linked to the others only by a common need to present a united front against the outside world. Life was focused in the county seat towns and to a lesser extent in the even smaller towns and villages dotted through the countryside, rather than in any major city.

In this climate small newspapers, nearly all of them weeklies, bloomed by the dozens. Every county seat had one or more, and none made much effort to extend its influence or circulation beyond its county borders. They were county newspapers, pure and simple; and they were published largely by homebred, homegrown owner-editors whose viewpoints and standards were those of the communities in which they had their roots. Bigotry and narrow chauvinism existed side by side with warm generosity and a fierce pride in the Eastern Shore and all its products. Self-reliance was a necessity in a region with few outside resources; independence was a cherished virtue to a people who regarded everything and everyone from "beyond the Bay" with deep suspicion. The Baltimore dailies might presume to speak for the rest of Maryland, but on the Eastern Shore theirs was an alien voice. It was the country editors who spoke the language of the Shore.

Now all that is gone, or nearly so. The Eastern Shore, whether it likes it or not, has been brought into the mainstream of American life; television and the influx of population made possible by the great Chesapeake Bay bridge have ended its insularity. The country editors have also vanished, their county weeklies and small dailies bought up by corporate newspaper chains based outside Maryland. Almost without exception, the owner-editors with their strong local ties have been replaced by company executives and professional editors.

Whether these developments are good or bad is beside the point. The point is that they have occurred; the era of home-owned county newspapers and their homegrown country editors has gone the way of the country general store and the mule-drawn plough. Today's county weeklies may strive to retain some of the flavor of the past, but they are in reality interchangeable units in chain operations.

It is important, before it is too late, to chronicle the history of the country editors, to set down for the record the aspirations, attitudes, adventures, drudgery, failings, and devotion which gave meaning to their lives. That is why this book was written.

Just as the country editors have vanished, so in all too many cases have the volumes of newspaper files which represented their years of labor vanished with them. New owners, pressed for space or unconcerned about the Eastern Shore's "ancient history," have thrown away the early files of many papers. Hired outside editors or publishers with no local background often place little value on "dead" files which cannot sell advertisements or produce a profit. In the course of a move into a new building, twenty years of irreplaceable issues of the *Easton Star-Democrat* were tossed into the scrap heap. Numerous others have suffered the same fate. When Winifred Gregory, forty-five years ago, published her monumental work, *American Newspapers, 1821-1936*, she listed as extant the files of a number of Eastern Shore newspapers which have since disappeared as the papers changed hands or went out of business. Included were all issues of the *Crisfield Times* before 1908; the entire product of the *Eastern Shoreman*, published in Pocomoke City between 1889 and 1891; the *Eastern Shore Republican* from 1928 to 1935; the *Somerset News* before 1936; the Dorchester *Item* from 1894 to 1901; Hurlock's *Upper Dorchester News* from 1923 on; the *Centreville Times* files from 1851 to 1853; and the *Federals-*

burg Times starting with 1929. In other cases Gregory listed private collections of rare early papers which cannot now be located; and of course many Eastern Shore files had already vanished before she made her compilation.

Today no known copy survives of such early papers as *Freedom's Sentinel* or its successor, the *Queen Anne's Telescope*, Centreville publications of the 1840s; the *Freedmen's Journal*, a post-Civil War Chestertown paper published in the interest of newly emancipated blacks; the *Crumpton Gazette* or the *Crumptonian;* the *News Letter* or *Farm and Home* of Preston; the *Church Hill Air Line* or *Church Hill News;* the *New Era*, a Salisbury Republican Party organ of the 1860s; the *Union Reformer* or the *Temperance Banner*, pre-Civil War Elkton products; the short-lived *Social Journal* of Easton; or the *Worcester Spy* and *Worcester Palladium*, which reportedly were published at Snow Hill in the 1830s. Unless some source unknown has copies, all these are gone as if they never had been; we will never learn how they looked or what they stood for. In addition there are great gaps in the surviving files of even well-established papers, especially those of the lower Shore counties.

These are tragic losses; for early newspaper files are the life blood of local history. They provide a week by week record of inestimable value to historical or genealogical research. From them long forgotten controversies and personalities can be recreated with all their contemporary urgency and color; marriages, deaths, and other information sought for family genealogies can be ascertained; political and social attitudes and moral issues can be put in perspective. Without local newspapers, the history of the Eastern Shore cannot be completely understood or written.

But if much has been lost, much remains. Eastern Shore newspapers, especially the very early ones, have been preserved in a surprising variety of places. The directory section of this book is designed to provide a record of every surviving issue of every Eastern Shore newspaper known to the compilers, and exactly where each can be found by the researcher. It should be added that, while every effort has been made to make the directory as complete and accurate as possible, the editor and publishers are not responsible for errors and omissions in the information provided by the repositories. It also seems likely that some Eastern Shore newspaper collections may have been missed entirely; if so, the publisher would appreciate hearing about them for future reference.

Newspapers are fragile objects. They deteriorate rapidly when subjected to heat and humidity, or when handled too often. For that reason, owners of small collections would do well to arrange to donate them to larger repositories, which have facilities for storage under controlled conditions.

Even more important is microfilming, the only sure method of guaranteeing that files will be permanently preserved, and that original issues will not be damaged or destroyed by careless handling. Considerable microfilming of selected Eastern Shore papers already has been done through projects at the Maryland Hall of Records [now the Maryland State Archives], the Enoch Pratt Library, and the Maryland Historical Society. The Archives has indicated that it is willing to accept private collections temporarily on loan, if necessary, in order to microfilm them. Some publishers have made arrangements to have current and future editions put on microfilm.

However, much more microfilming is needed. A concerted effort to assure that all Eastern Shore newspapers, past and present, are made available on microfilm would be a contribution of tremendous value to the region's historical source materials. Only when that has been done can we be sure that the Eastern Shore of the future will be able to understand and appreciate its historic past.

Acknowledgments

LITERALLY hundreds of people have contributed in various ways to the making of this volume. My thanks go to all of them: library staff members, museum curators, historical society volunteers, newspaper editors, and other individuals who replied to queries with patience and understanding, and who aided my search for faded copies of long-forgotten newspapers.

Special thanks are due to the Wye Institute, which conceived the project and gave generous support and guidance throughout its realization; to Betty Dickinson of the Wye Institute staff for many helpful suggestions and comments, and for preparing the charts showing county newspaper histories in graphic form; and to the Institute's Margaret Gillespie, typist extraordinary.

Acknowledgments are also due to Norman Harrington, who took many of the photographs and contributed much information on modern Eastern Shore journalism from personal experience; Keith Harrington, Norman's able assistant; the late Charles J. Truitt, who shared with me his recollections of a lifetime; the late William B. Usilton III, editor emeritus of the *Kent County News*; Melvin Toadvine, editor of the *Daily Times* of Salisbury; Christopher N. Allan of the Maryland Hall of Records; the late Mary Starin, curator of the Talbot County Free Library's Maryland Room; Dr. Morgan H. Pritchett, Catherine Kennedy, and the entire staff of the Maryland Department at the Enoch Pratt Free Library; head librarian William B. Keller and the capable and helpful staff at the Maryland Historical Society; Albert V. Stant of the Queenstown Bank of Maryland, who performed heroic service in rescuing many issues of the *Queenstown News* from destruction; Woodrow T. Wilson, custodian of the files of the *Crisfield Times*; Joyce Ann Tracy, curator of newspapers, American Antiquarian Society; James P. Danky, newspaper librarian, the State Historical Society of Wisconsin; George Corddry, who provided valuable information from his manuscript history of Wicomico County; and my wife, Janet, who fielded errors with diligence and helped immeasurably with proofreading and other chores.

DICKSON J. PRESTON

Newspapers of Maryland's Eastern Shore

CHAPTER ONE

Prelude
THE ZENGER HERITAGE

SOME seventy years before the first newspaper appeared on the Eastern Shore of Maryland, two men who later would greatly influence the history of American journalism were residents of Kent County on the Eastern Shore. Just what their Maryland experiences had to do with events in New York which made them famous is anybody's guess. But it is a fact that John Peter Zenger, the "patron saint" of journalists for his role in establishing the basic concept of freedom of the press, gave his address as Kent County when he served as Maryland's public printer in the 1720s. And it is a fact that Andrew Hamilton, the attorney who defended Zenger so ably in his landmark libel trial that his words became part of the credo of American freedom, also lived in Kent County for several years.

These two simple facts have given rise to a good deal of speculative comment about Zenger and Hamilton among local historians. Much of it admittedly is at best unverifiable legend and at worst pure invention. Confident statements have been made, on little evidence, that Zenger operated a printing establishment in Chestertown for two years; that he and Hamilton must have known each other at that time; and that their Kent County friendship and Kent County experience somehow led to their association in the New York trial which struck a fatal blow at arbitrary government censorship of the press in America. Therefore—if only to set the record straight—it seems appropriate to begin a study of journalism on the Eastern Shore with a review of what is known, and what is not, about the two men and their stay in Maryland.

Factual information on Zenger is sketchy, though intriguing. We know that he was born in the Upper Palatinate of Germany in 1697, that he emigrated to New York with his family in 1710, and that he served an eight-year apprenticeship to learn the printing trade under William Bradford, New York's public printer. Records in New York indicate that by the age of twenty-three he had married, fathered children, and become a widower.

His name first appears in Maryland annals early in April, 1720, when he filed a petition with the General Assembly "praying that he may have the

Liberty of Printing the Laws for the Severall Countys the Provinciall Court and Upper and Lower house of Assembly." In brief, he was seeking the same post in Maryland as his former master held in New York—that of the colony's public printer.

It is worth noting here that the position was a transitional one in the development of journalism in the province. Maryland as yet had no newspapers, and the public printer performed a quasi-journalistic function by producing an official record of the doings of the courts and the legislature. When the *Maryland Gazette*, the colony's first newspaper, was launched in 1727 one of its primary aims was the similar one of providing official news of what was transpiring in government.

On April 12, 1720, both houses of the legislature approved Zenger's petition. He was instructed to bind his printed documents with leather and furnish copies to each of the twelve counties then existing in addition to volumes for the Provincial Court and the two houses of assembly. His official pay was to be seven hundred pounds of tobacco from each house for a total of fourteen hundred pounds, the equivalent of about twelve pounds sterling.

Because nothing bearing Zenger's imprint has survived, it is only by inference that historians conclude he did in fact print the laws enacted in 1720 and 1721. However, the documentation is substantial:

—At the end of the second 1720 Assembly session in October, the Lower House resolved "that the Printer be allowed five hundred pounds of tobacco for the Printing the Laws for the Countys &c . . . as last Sessions," a strong indication that he had printed those of the previous April.

—At the end of the August meeting of 1721, the Upper House resolved "that John Peter Zenger print the Body of Laws this Sessions [*sic*] as usual," again an indication that he had printed the laws of the two 1720 sessions.

By contrast, the often repeated assertion that Zenger set up his printing operation in Chestertown, Kent County, rather than in the more logical town of Annapolis, is based on only one piece of evidence. In the fall of 1720 he applied for Maryland citizenship; and on October 27 Governor Charles Calvert put his seal to "An Act for the Naturalization of John Peter Zenger of Kent County Printer & His Children." The only reference to Kent County was in the title. No residence was given in the body of the act, and nowhere was there mention of Chestertown, by that name or any other. Nothing was said, there or elsewhere, about where Zenger did his printing; nor does Zenger's name appear in any existing Kent County records. It has even been suggested that Zenger did not have a print shop, but took his work as public printer up to Philadelphia and set it into type at the establishment of Andrew Bradford, son of his New York mentor. Alternatively he might have traveled between Kent

County, where his children were, and Annapolis, where the job was. All that can be said from the single record is that in October, 1720, Zenger gave his residence as Kent County. Anything else is pure conjecture.

Wherever he lived and wherever he did his printing, Zenger certainly was gone from Maryland by the late summer of 1722. On September 11 of that year he married Anna Catharina Maulin in New York; and on November 1 the Maryland Assembly agreed that Michael Piper, master of the Free School of Annapolis, should be employed to print the acts of the legislature.

That is really all there is to know about John Peter Zenger in Maryland. He arrived sometime before April 12, 1720, and departed sometime before September 11, 1722. He served during three legislative sessions as public printer. He was recorded under date of October 27, 1720, as residing in Kent County. If he had not gone on to become one of the most celebrated figures in journalistic history, there would be no reason at all to examine his Maryland background except as a brief footnote in a dissertation on early colonial printers.

The evidence that places his equally celebrated defense attorney, Andrew Hamilton, in Kent County is far more abundant. Hamilton bought and sold land there over a period of nine years; he was specifically named as living on an estate called Henberry, six hundred acres near the head of the Chester River, in 1713; and he represented the county in the Maryland legislature in 1715. His daughter Margaret, born in 1709, who married the mayor of Philadelphia, and his son James, born in 1710, who became governor of Pennsylvania, almost certainly were born in Kent County.

A native of the British Isles, probably Scotland, Hamilton emigrated to the Virginia Eastern Shore shortly before 1700. He practiced law and married there before moving to Kent County. On March 26, 1708, he purchased Henberry; and a deed dated May 6, 1713, records his purchase of about three hundred additional acres adjoining "the Plantacon whereon the sd Andrew Hamilton now lives."

In 1715 he was elected as a Kent County delegate to the Lower House of the Maryland Assembly; but his service there was brief and undistinguished. He was in fact fined for tardiness and was absent during most of the session. Late in 1715 he moved to Philadelphia, where he represented the Penn family in legal matters and, along with other posts, performed lengthy service as speaker of the Pennsylvania House. He sold Henberry in 1717, ending all connection with Kent County.

Thus there is no real reason to suppose that the two men ever met in Kent County. Their times of residence did not overlap; Hamilton lived there from 1708 to 1715, Zenger at most from 1720 to 1722. Indeed, it seems likely that their paths never crossed before Hamilton, as a renowned Philadelphia lawyer,

Andrew Hamilton. (Courtesy New-York Historical Society)

was prevailed upon to defend the obscure Zenger in the 1735 New York City libel trial which became a landmark case in American legal history.

Nevertheless, their common Maryland experience cannot be dismissed as mere coincidence. Most significantly, both were exposed there to the same ferment of liberal and even revolutionary ideas which they later espoused with such dramatic effect in New York.

Maryland in the early 1700s was in fact ahead of New York, and most of the other colonies, in defying the arbitrary powers assumed by appointed governors from England. During Hamilton's years as an Eastern Shore lawyer, and Zenger's term as public printer, the record was filled with sharp exchanges between governors, who insisted they had absolute authority, and the elected representatives of the freemen, who insisted that ultimate power rested in them and in the English common law. This was the identical issue which came to a head in the 1735 Zenger trial, and which provided a springboard for the American Revolution forty years later.

Maryland's defiance reached a peak in 1722, when the elected Lower House tartly told Lord Baltimore that the colony was not to be treated as " a conquered Country," that its people were entitled to the rights and privileges of the common law of England, and that "whoever shall advise his Lordship or his successours to govern by any other Rules of Government, are Evil Counsellors Ill-wishers to his Lordship . . . and intend thereby to infringe our English Liberties." When Lord Baltimore insisted that he and, through him, his appointed governors had veto power over English statutes, the House bitterly protested that such power would reduce the people of Maryland "to a State of Villianage [sic] and Slavery," their so-called freedom resting on nothing more than "the precarious terms . . . of your Lordships pleasure."

It was this defiantly democratic spirit, rather than any mythical personal relationship, that Zenger and Hamilton took with them from Maryland; and it was in this sense that their common Maryland background can be said to have had an important influence on the events which later occurred in New York City.

The 1735 libel trial itself can be summarized briefly. Zenger, after his return to New York, set up shop as a book publisher and master printer. In 1733 leaders of the "popular party," which represented the freemen and the old Dutch settlers, financed him in starting a newspaper, the *New-York Weekly Journal*, in opposition to the dictatorial policies of Royal Governor William Cosby. Although Zenger had little say in the paper's editorial content, which was supplied by a group headed by attorney James Alexander, he was held responsible for its repeated diatribes against Cosby and his supporters. In November, 1734, acting under an edict granting him control over printing presses in the province, the governor ordered offending copies of the *Journal* to be burned by the public hangman, and had Zenger arrested and jailed without bail.

For his trial, which took place August 4, 1735, Alexander's group secured the services as defense attorney of Hamilton, undoubtedly the best-known lawyer in the colonies. The specific charge was that Zenger had published "false news and seditious Libels . . . to traduce, scandalize and vilify . . . his Excellency the said Governor, and the Ministers and Officers of Our said Lord the King." Hamilton built his case around a bold challenge to this wording. Nothing printed in the *Journal* had been either false or seditious, he argued, since it was the truth—and truth was a perfect defense against a charge of libel. Furthermore it was up to the jury, rather than either the pro-Cosby judge or

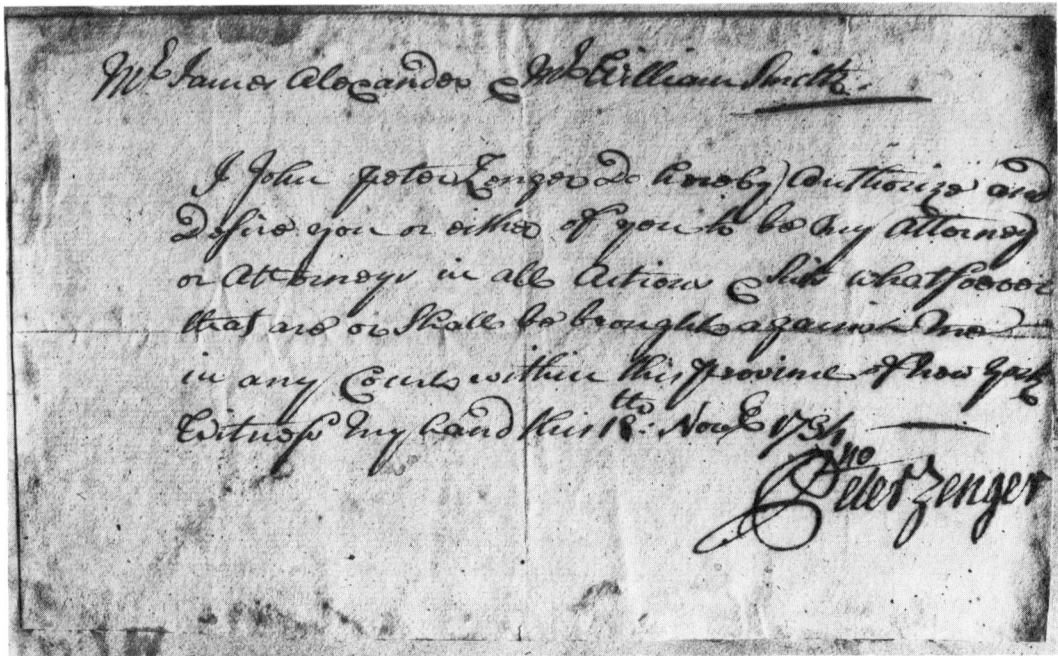

Power of attorney granted by John Peter Zenger after his arrest. (Courtesy New-York Historical Society)

the royal governor, to determine the facts in the case. These two concepts, contrary to then-prevailing legal precedent both in England and America, would provide the basic foundation on which freedom of the press would rest in future years.

But Hamilton went much further than a mere attack on government censorship in New York. In a peroration which would be printed and reprinted throughout America—and even in England—for the next half century, he told the jury their duty was not simply to decide on the facts in this case, but to "support Liberty . . . against lawless Power" wherever the two forces clashed.

> The question before the Court and you, Gentlemen of the Jury, is not of small or private concern, it is not the Cause of a poor Printer, nor of *New York* alone, which you are now trying; No! It may in its Consequence, affect every Freeman that lives under a British Government on the main of America. It is the Cause of Liberty; and I make no Doubt but your upright Conduct, this Day, will not only entitle you to the Love and Esteem of your Fellow-Citizens; but every Man who prefers Freedom to a Life of Slavery will bless and honour You, as Men who have baffled the Attempt of Tyranny; and by an impartial and uncorrupt Verdict, have laid a noble

Foundation for securing to ourselves, our Posterity, and our Neighbours, that, to which Nature and the Laws of our Country have given us a Right,—the Liberty both of exposing and opposing arbitrary Power (in these Parts of the World, at least) by speaking and writing Truth.

When the jury brought in a verdict of "Not Guilty," there were loud huzzas in the crowded New York City Hall. Zenger was freed the next day and later, after Cosby's death, was made public printer both of New York and New Jersey as compensation for his ordeal. Hamilton was honored at a dinner, given a public salute by the guns of the ships in New York harbor when he sailed for Philadelphia, and presented the Freedom of the Corporation by the Common Council of New York. Both were regarded as heroes throughout the colonies, and Hamilton's eloquent words were quoted wherever men gathered to talk of liberty and independence. As historian Gouverneur Morris later put it, the Zenger trial "was the germ of American freedom, the morning star of that liberty which subsequently revolutionized America."

Such is the story of how two men who had once lived in Kent County on the Eastern Shore of Maryland went on to strike a powerful blow for freedom of the press, and for all the liberties which Americans hold precious. Cold examination of the facts may indicate their Kent County experience had less significance than fond partisans of the Eastern Shore would like to believe. But certainly Eastern Shore journalism owes much to them. The Zenger-Hamilton heritage of fearless independence, of "speaking and writing Truth" without regard for consequences, set a high standard for the Eastern Shore newspapers which followed, and for the country editors who produced them.

CHAPTER TWO

Beginnings
THE FIRST SHORE NEWSPAPERS

JAMES COWAN, in the spring of 1789, was a young man of big dreams and small experience. He had in abundance the brash optimism of youth, and he had some other assets: he was newly fledged as a journeyman printer; he was affianced to Miss Jane McHurd of Anne Arundel County; and his ambition was to start a newspaper in a new territory, where he could be a pioneer. But he also had some liabilities: trained as a printer, he knew almost nothing about the writing and editing end of the newspaper business; and he seems to have been equally ignorant about the Eastern Shore of Maryland, where he proposed to start his newspaper.

He was not a native Eastern Shoreman; that much seems certain. Speculation has him born in Pennsylvania, and serving his apprenticeship in Philadelphia under the same Bradford family of printers from whom John Peter Zenger, seventy years earlier, had learned his trade; but both suggestions are based on nothing very substantial.

What we do know for sure about James Cowan begins with his appearance in Annapolis. On May 28, 1789, he married Miss McHurd in Anne Arundel County; and on June 3, he announced in a printed prospectus that he intended to start a newspaper, designed to serve the entire Eastern Shore, at the town called Easton, or Talbot Courthouse, in Talbot County.

The prospectus, addressed "To the Public," reveals something of Cowan's youthful enthusiasm as well as his ignorance of Eastern Shore geography. It opened with lofty sentiments, discussing the "infinite importance to every free people, that they should be accurately and speedily informed of the measures of government . . . to form a just idea of their rights and interests," and asserting that only a well-conducted newspaper could fill this need.

But the citizens of Maryland's Eastern Shore, Cowan continued, did not have a newspaper. "Public prints have by no means had a general circulation among them." A few "gentlemen of information" subscribed to outside papers, "but rarely have they reached the interior and great body of the people."

Therefore, Cowan believed, "a paper established at Easton, commonly called Talbot Court-house, would, in a great degree, put it in the power of the

Eastern Shore to obtain every public information by a ready and cheap communication. [The] paper would reach the interior parts of each county—and hundreds who would not choose to take more expensive and distant prints, might profit by their communications. To the lower and more inland counties, a press at Easton would be, as a source from which political intelligence might diffuse itself, of the highest consequence."

On this reasoning, he proposed to establish a weekly newspaper to be published at Easton, "as soon as five hundred subscribers can be procured."

Cowan's opening premise was sound enough: the Eastern Shore, with a third of the state's population, did lack a newspaper of its own, and the few subscribers to the papers from Philadelphia, Baltimore, and Annapolis were chiefly gentlemen of education and means.

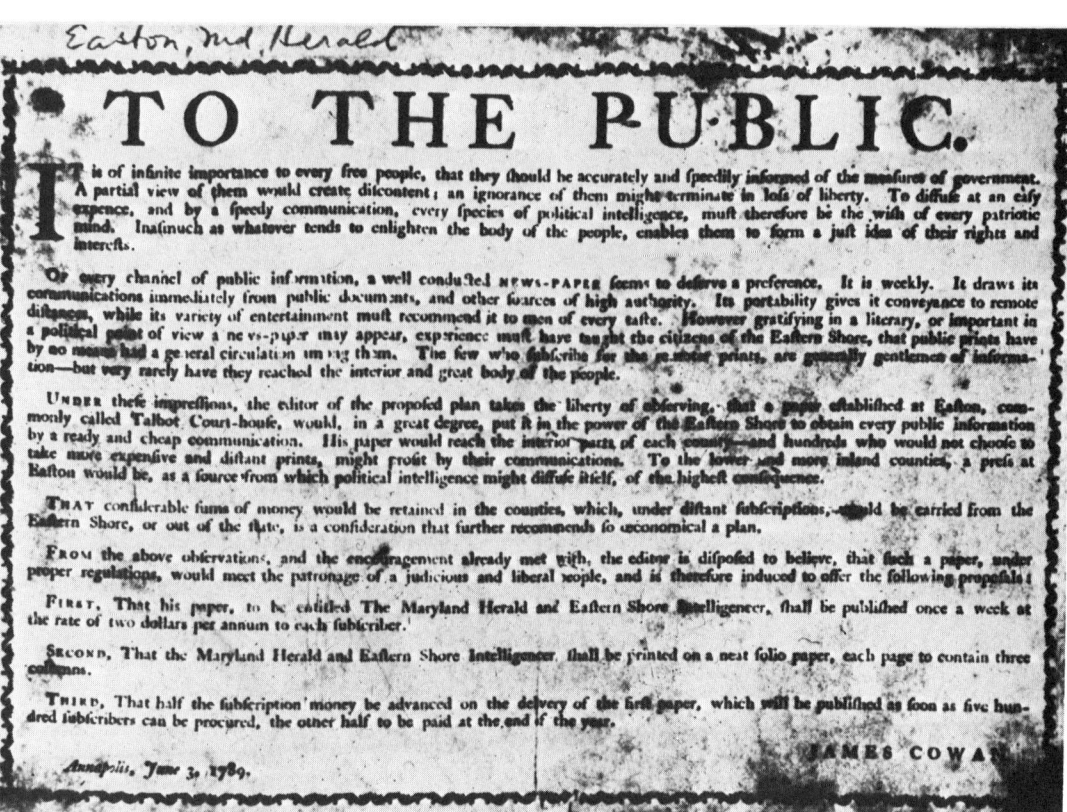

In this prospectus, published June 3, 1789, James Cowan announced his intention of starting an Eastern Shore newspaper. (Courtesy Maryland Historical Society)

However, he was clearly unaware of some basic facts about the Eastern Shore. It had no "great body" of people in the "interior parts," hungry for public information and political enlightenment. It was, as it always had been, made up largely of tidewater plantations linked to the outside world and to each other by water. The inland farms being opened up to wheat production were for the most part operated by tenant farmers, many of whom could not sign their names, let alone read a newspaper. As for the "lower and more inland counties"—by which he presumably meant Caroline, Dorchester, Somerset, and Worcester—their principal centers were all on navigable water, and were as accessible by boat from Baltimore or Annapolis as from Easton. The few roads were barely passable, and there were even fewer bridges.

Easton, which because of its central location was considered the "little capital" of the Eastern Shore, was just beginning to emerge as a true town. Before the Revolution it had consisted of only a few houses, taverns, and artisans' shops straggling along the main road near the redbrick courthouse, built in 1712. It had not been laid out as a town until 1786, nor given the name of Easton until December, 1788. When Cowan announced his proposed newspaper, it did not even have a town government—the first commissioners would not be elected until March 21, 1791. There was talk of erecting a new courthouse, but nothing had been done about it.

Cowan no doubt was influenced by the supposition that Easton was a sort of Eastern Shore Annapolis, or soon would become one. It is true that the Maryland Assembly had assigned the general courts for the Eastern Shore to Easton in December, 1788, a few months before he issued his prospectus, and that the Shore's land office and treasury were located there. There was even gossip around Annapolis that the legislature would meet in alternate years in Easton, talk made more plausible when, in December, 1789, the Assembly agreed to pay five-sixths of the cost of building a large new Talbot County courthouse. But nothing ever came of the idea of Eastern Shore sessions of the legislature.

Nor did Cowan ever get the five hundred subscribers at two dollars a year his prospectus called for. Nevertheless, he persisted. In March, 1790, he advertised in the *Maryland Gazette* for "a lad of good character and capacity . . . as an apprentice to the printing business, on the Eastern Shore." And on Tuesday, May 11, the inaugural issue of the *Maryland Herald and Eastern Shore Intelligencer*, the Eastern Shore's first newspaper, appeared on the streets of Easton. It would have no competition until 1793, when the *Apollo* was announced in Chestertown.

The front page of that first issue of the *Herald* was taken up almost entirely by Cowan's "salutatory"—a statement of his aims and hopes as his beloved "only child" was "ushered to the world." Cowan admitted that he had little talent as a writer, and his rambling, convoluted style confirms it; but he was evidently deeply concerned with the ethics of journalism.

On the touchy question of freedom of the press, then being debated as the thirteen states considered whether to adopt the Bill of Rights with its First Amendment prohibition against "abridging the freedom of speech or of the press," he hedged his bet slightly. He strongly defended the right of any citizen to speak, or write and publish, his opinion of public men and their *public* actions; but he was not sure how far this extended to their private lives and characters. He was puzzled by "the extreme difficulty of drawing a precise line between liberty and licentiousness," and invited essays from readers on "this delicate and important subject."

For himself, writing in the third person, he solemnly pledged his "honour and reputation . . . to maintain a strict impartiality, never to refuse or grant to one side that which he would refuse or grant to the other," and "never to debase his paper by making it the vehicle of slander." His aim was "to avoid, above all things, the confounding of authentic facts with uncertain rumour, or vague surmise." His "ardent wish" was to provide "every benefit of the press without any of its abuses."

Articles from readers must be signed if they reflected, even indirectly, on any individual's private character. But he stopped short of saying he would not accept them, a failure on Cowan's part which would later land him in deep trouble.

Unhappily, Cowan was soon to deviate from the very precepts he had so earnestly espoused. He became the first Eastern Shore editor—though not the last—to violate his own standards, and to let his editorial columns be used for slanted political propaganda and slanderous attacks on the private, as distinguished from public, lives of local individuals. He even initiated the practice of charging space rates for signed statements in which irate writers traded insults and insinuations with each other. Eventually this became a major source of revenue.

From the beginning, it was evident that Cowan was operating on a shoestring. He apologized to his readers for printing his first issue with "worn" and "inferior" type, and said he hoped to acquire a new set within two months, after which the *Herald* would "be published, not only in a more beautiful and perfect letter, but on a larger scale." This hope was not realized for nearly ten years. Meanwhile he made do with what type he had, sometimes printing long articles entirely in italics, sometimes using different sizes and fonts on the same page, sometimes reducing the size of his sheets. His circulation at the start was only about three hundred, and never rose much above that. Nor did he apparently

[Vol. I.]   THE   [No. 1.]

MARYLAND HERALD,
AND
EASTERN SHORE INTELLIGENCER.

TUESDAY, May 11, 1790.

TO THE PUBLIC.

AFTER a variety of unlooked-for difficulties, THE MARYLAND HERALD and EASTERN SHORE INTELLIGENCER, is at length ushered to the world. It is natural for its editor to feel that kind of solicitude which agitates the breast of a *fond parent*, on the first introduction of an *only child* on the great theatre of public life. It is not therefore merely in conformity to custom, that he commences with an humble address in its behalf.

To descant fully on the uses of a news-paper, if his abilities were even adequate to the subject, would be a needless undertaking. The secret friends of tyranny and usurpation, and all those who dread the spirit of free inquiry, dare not openly attack the press. They endeavour to effect their purpose by employing the powers of ridicule against news paper productions, and news-paper intelligence, and expatiate freely on the few partial inconveniences resulting from their abuse. But the most exalted characters in America, on every suitable occasion, have been the warmest advocates for public prints. They perceive how essential it is to the preservation of freedom, that the people should be speedily informed of the measures of government, and obtain every species of political intelligence. And there is no friend to the dignity of human nature, who would not cheerfully submit to a trivial inconvenience, to which sometimes the best of men may be exposed from public prints, when he reflects on their influence in the prevention of crimes, the excitement to laudable acts, the diffusion of knowledge, and the consequent establishment of equal liberty on the basis of equal rights.

But to afford every benefit of the press without any of its abuses, should be the ardent wish and constant aim of the conductor of a news paper.

That public prints have by no means had a general circulation on the Eastern Shore, must be universally admitted. A great deal of important political intelligence has never reached the great body of the people at all; and when sometimes by accident they obtain it, it comes either with so many additions, or such mutilation, that they would be better without it altogether. The few subscribers to remote prints may not, indeed, derive much information from the establishment of a press at Easton. But the editor conceives that he will render an acceptable service to them, as well as to their less opulent or enlightened countrymen, if, by the successful prosecution of his plan, he shall afford those advantages which are enjoyed by our citizens in almost every other corner of the United States. That they may be enabled, in some measure, to decide how far he deserves that encouragement on which he relies for subsistance, he solicits their attention to his plan.

It is his intention, in the first place, to inform them of every important transaction in our own government, and of every thing which materially concerns them in the general government, and to give them an account of every other remarkable occurrence which he shall be able to collect. He will be careful to mention, occasionally, the source of his information, and to avoid, above all things, the confounding authentic facts with uncertain rumour, or vague surmise. He will not profess that which is not in his power to perform. From his situation, it will be impossible to obtain a great number of original interesting articles. He must depend greatly on other prints; and presumes that he shall answer the purposes of the greater part of his subscribers just as well as if they were furnished with the prints of New-York, Pennsylvania or Baltimore.

When times are dull, and foreign countries, as well as this great and extensive continent, shall be barren of incident, he will endeavour to supply the place of news by selections from those authors who have best blended amusement with instruction. The ingenious essays of his own countrymen, and particularly of his neighbours, will be received with gratitude; and unless some extraordinary circumstance shall otherwise require, will be published in the order of their reception. He will, in short, strive to gratify every class of readers, and to please every denomination of men.

One principal use of a news-paper is to spread the advertisements of individuals, respecting their various concerns; these he will insert on the same terms which are observed by the printers of Baltimore.

The most arduous part of his undertaking is to act properly with respect to controversy and satire. He pledges his honour and reputation, at all events, to maintain a strict impartiality, and never refuse or grant to one side that which he would refuse or grant to the other. Whenever he shall think himself bound to insert a piece containing strictures on an individual, or even the most distant unfavourable allusion to private character, the writer must not expect that secrecy which is due to the author of a general essay. It is, however, his fixed determination, whatever security or indemnification may be offered, never to debase his paper by making it the vehicle of slander. It is equally his desire to maintain the true freedom of the press. If at any time he shall appear to deviate from his avowed principles, let candour reflect on the extreme difficulty of drawing a precise line between liberty and licentiousness. It is a task which requires talents far superior to his; and it would afford him singular satisfaction to be presented, at his outset, with an original and masterly essay on this delicate and important subject.

At one of the most critical stages of the late war, the legislature of this state thought proper to inflict penalties for seditious speaking or writing. It was, assuredly, the most enlightened policy which dictated the following restriction:

——"Provided, that nothing herein before contained shall be taken or construed to preclude or prevent the exercise of the right "of any citizen of this state to speak, or write and publish, his opinion and sentiments of the acts or proceedings of the legislature, or "the executive, or of the *public* conduct of any of the members thereof, or of any person in the judicial department, or holding any "office in this state, it being the wish and desire of this assembly to encourage a free inquiry into the *public* conduct of every person "entrusted by the people, as the best means to ____ the freedom of this republic, and the good and faithful conduct of its trustees and "servants."——Acts of May session, 1781, ____, sec. 5.

The continuance of the act being limited to the duration of the war, it has long since been suffered to expire; but the right herein declared can expire only with our freedom.

The editor has been constrained, by necessity, to make use for the present of types not a little worn, and perhaps inferior to those of many other American news-papers. He expects, in the course of two months, to be furnished with a new set; and if he should be happy enough to meet with reasonable encouragement, the Maryland Herald, &c. shall be published, not only in a more beautiful and perfect letter, but on a larger scale.

It will, from this time, appear in Easton on every Tuesday morning.

He begs leave to return his most grateful thanks to all those who in any manner have contributed to his plan; and he most earnestly requests those gentlemen who have taken the trouble of procuring him subscriptions, to make their respective returns as early as may be, with convenience to themselves.

JAMES COWAN.

LONDON, Feb. 1.

A war seems now inevitable: The full establishment of our marine, the purchase and equipment of the tenders in the river, and the completion of every estimate laid on the table of parliament, unequivocally declare it. What kind of war this country may be engaged in, time only can discover; but as a naval one, it is not likely to be of a very extensive nature. A fleet in the Baltic, and another in the Mediterranean, will probably be all the force that is necessary.

ever find the "lad of good character" he had sought as an apprentice; a letter from an admirer noted in 1791 that "the printer of the Herald . . . is at once compositor—collator—selector—searcher—worker of press—and devil." The writer went on to belabor the public for their "lethargy" in failing to support an Eastern Shore press, and urged them to give it something more than good wishes. The *Herald* attracted few advertisers despite its low rates of three weekly insertions for a dollar. Easton in the 1790s did not yet have many merchants, and some of those did not pay their printing bills. Cowan had

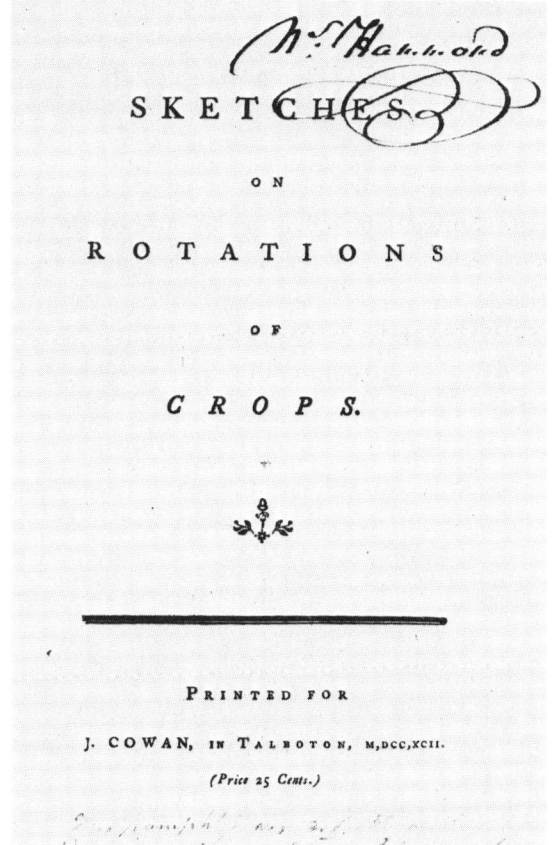

James Cowan imprint dated 1792. The "sketches" in this pamphlet were by John Beale Bordley of Wye Island. (Courtesy Maryland Historical Society)

Opposite, page one of the first newspaper ever published on the Shore, the *Maryland Herald and Eastern Shore Intelligencer* for May 11, 1790. (Courtesy Maryland Historical Society)

repeatedly to insert notices urging those who owed him money to pay up. Even to maintain the paper—much less support his family—he had to practice "rigid economy" and supplement his income by printing pamphlets and broadsides, and selling everything from books to groceries at his newspaper office.

His financial woes were eased somewhat when, on February 15, 1792, he was named postmaster; but this in turn increased the pressure on him to abandon his proclaimed impartiality in politics. The appointment was at the hands of President Washington's supporters, who controlled the national government and, in the sharpening partisanship of Washington's second term, were beginning to be called Federalists because they favored a strong federal system. Their opponents, the Republicans (later the Democrats), rallied behind the banner of Thomas Jefferson. Cowan, an admirer of Washington, was naturally inclined to the Federalist viewpoint; and most of his subscribers were well-to-do and conservative "gentlemen planters" who considered Jefferson a wild-eyed radical. Gradually the *Herald* began more and more openly to endorse the Federalist cause.

From a journalistic standpoint, however, his worst troubles stemmed from the delight Eastern Shoremen took in lambasting each other in public print as soon as they had a newspaper of their own in which to do it. Although he had pledged himself never to let the *Herald* become a "vehicle of slander" nor to confuse facts with "rumour or vague surmise," Cowan permitted his reader correspondents to do exactly that, and they fell to with a will. Soon the columns of the *Herald* were filled with controversies, political and personal, some of which went on for months and were couched in crude and vulgar terms, and with deliberately insulting notices and cards. It is difficult to believe today that a newspaper would publish a paid announcement that "John Turner of Easton, is a coward," or that Richard Lyons (a Methodist preacher from Somerset County) "perverts the truth." But Cowan did, to his short term profit and eventual sorrow.

It was part of his general bad luck that he came upon the Talbot County scene at the same time as Jacob Gibson, a salty and pugnacious character who was undoubtedly one of the champion letters-to-the-editor writers of all time. For a quarter of a century, Gibson kept his fellow Eastern Shoremen entertained, amused, enraged, and scandalized with a constant barrage of ridicule, satire, tirades, invective, accusations, and even satirical poetry directed against his numerous political and personal enemies. A powerfully built man who kept in shape by his work as a "practical"—as distinguished from "gentleman"—farmer, he also engaged in many public fist fights—most of which he won.

An ardent Jeffersonian Republican and a great admirer of the French, from the Revolutionists to Napoleon, Gibson despised all Englishmen, all Federalists, and James Cowan, although not necessarily in that order. He insisted on calling himself "citizen Jacob" and gloried in having the common touch, in contrast to his aristocratic (and Federalist) foes. At one point he replied to his critics:

> If citizen Jacob is that great fool you all wish the people to believe, how comes it his writing calls such a host of you into the Herald to answer him? . . . If he had been educated at college, at the expense of the poor like you aristocrats, he would make you bawl where you now only grunt.

In 1793, and again late in 1795, Gibson was accused of private peccadilloes to which he replied with great vigor and vulgarity in the *Herald*. The 1793 case involved a charge that he had "accidentally" sheared a neighbor's sheep with his own, and sold the wool at a profit. The 1795 affair was more serious; he was actually indicted by the grand jury for allegedly using a half bushel measure that was smaller than standard in measuring out his wheat for sale. The resulting furore ran on for months in the *Herald*. Gibson called his accuser, among other things, "an unprincipled rascal" motivated by "villainy and a malicious heart." The reputation of at least one woman was smeared by the vilest sort of innuendo, and leading Talbot Countians were openly slandered.

Finally Cowan, who had done nothing to halt the abuse of his editorial columns, issued a lame apology to readers who complained. He blamed the whole thing on politics, which was probably accurate, since Gibson's accusers were Federalists and his defenders Republicans. "To conduct a public paper at all times in a manner which shall admit the warmth of Party-Disputes, and yet be free from indelicacy of language, is in certain circumstances scarcely practicable," Cowan said. His own "severe indisposition" had prevented him from passing on what was published, and he hoped his readers would understand.

Eventually Gibson was acquitted of the false measure charge, and the affair blew over. But Cowan did not change his weak-kneed policy of publishing practically anything his correspondents were willing to pay for. Gibson remained the chief offender; he estimated in 1802 that he had paid Cowan at least four hundred dollars for signed articles published in the *Herald*. But others also took up the cudgels. Residents of Caroline, Queen Anne's, and Kent counties, with no newspapers of their own, used the *Herald* and its later rival, the *Republican Star,* to air their private grievances; and at times the columns of both papers were filled with personal insults involving men fom Chestertown, Denton, Centreville, and even Dover, Delaware.

Meanwhile, Cowan himself abandoned all pretense of political neutrality. By 1799 his paper had become an outright tool of the Federalists. Its front pages were filled with lengthy articles, culled from other Federalist papers, viciously attacking the Jeffersonians and all they stood for. As Gibson later revealed,

Cowan let Federalist correspondents publish anonymous articles free of charge, while billing the opposition for use of his columns.

At this juncture a young Virginian, Thomas Perrin Smith (of whom more later), arrived in Easton and founded an opposition newspaper to support the Jeffersonian cause. He called it the *Republican Star; or, Eastern Shore Political Luminary;* and almost from its first issue in August, 1799, it outstripped the *Herald* in popularity. Republicanism was rapidly gaining ascendancy on the Eastern Shore even among the well-to-do planters who had been Cowan's initial backers. Within a year Smith was able to boast that he had four hundred subscribers, more than the *Herald* had ever had. When Smith was awarded the postmastership in 1801, as a reward for his vigorous support of the newly elected President Jefferson, it was almost the last straw for Cowan.

By 1802 the *Herald* editor was in desperate financial straits. He was deeply in debt and, from all reports, drinking heavily. His dream had turned into a nightmare. To try to make ends meet he had turned the *Herald* office into a sort of general store: among items he listed for sale in October, 1802, were text books, prayer books, Bibles, Walker's gazetteer, children's books, hymnals, Greek texts, Chesterfield's letters, fiction (*Romance of the Forest, The Beggar Boy, Maid of Hamlet,* etc.), sealing wax, wafers, ink powder, ink stamps, pen knives, writing paper, copy books, and "groceries in general."

In his desperation, he applied for a license to sell retail liquor; and by the bitterest of coincidences the county court justice assigned to rule on his petition was his old nemesis and archenemy, Jacob Gibson.

Just at this time, the *Herald* was publishing a series of anti-Republican articles which were particularly offensive to the hot tempered Gibson. One, a crude satirical burlesque entitled "The Grand Caucus," lampooned prominent Talbot County Jeffersonians under thinly disguised pseudonyms. Gibson was cast as "Squire Mush-o Justice," a bubble-headed nincompoop who talked in simplistic generalities. Edward Lloyd, the county's richest man but a Republican in politics, was called "Lord Cock-de-doo-dle doo" in derision of his passion for cockfighting.

If this weren't enough, Cowan published on October 12 a lengthy front-page article, reprinted from the *New York Evening Post,* denouncing the "Jacobins"—by which were meant the Jeffersonians—in blunt terms as traitors, atheists, and power-hungry men with "designs against the freedom of their country." The author accused them of "fraud and artifice," "open falsehood," "calumny," "preposterous promises, operating on unwary ignorance," and assorted other crimes. Gibson, who prided himself on being an American "Jacobin," could hardly miss the application to him.

When Cowan appeared before Gibson seeking approval of his liquor license, the justice—undoubtedly with smug inner satisfaction—turned him

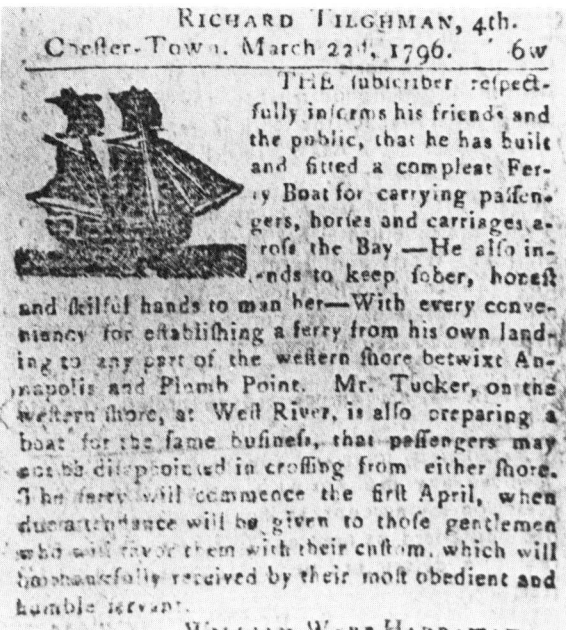

Left, Advertisement for Haddaway's Ferry, from the *Maryland Herald* of March 22, 1796, was one of the earliest ads to carry an illustration. *Right,* Fox hunting was a popular sport in the early 1800s.

down unless he could get letters from "neighbours of repute," testifying to his character. Cowan indignantly refused, charged Gibson with political motivation, and in the next issue of the *Herald* published a vicious attack on Gibson's alleged private as well as public character.

This was too much for the explosive Gibson, who responded both with his fists and his pen. He marched into the *Herald* office and knocked Cowan down, or, in Cowan's words, "in the true spirit of a Jacobin way-lay'd me, and brought my head to the ground before I knew the assassin was near me." Gibson then wrote an account of the affair, published in the *Republican Star* of October 26, 1802, which for sheer viciousness was probably the most remarkable statement ever published in an Eastern Shore newspaper. It was anything but a credit to editor Smith that he permitted so savage an attack on a fellow editor, no matter what their differences, to appear in the *Star.*

After listing his essentially petty reasons for refusing the liquor license, Gibson proceeded to take the hide off Cowan in an unparalleled burst of venomous prose:

> Mr. Cowan wishes the public to believe that I am actuated by political revenge . . . If I had any revenge to be gratified, every person would think me a glutton not to be satiated with his fast approaching destruction, a noted drunkard, of bankrupt circumstances, and friends "if ever he had any," worn out, his securities mulcted with his debts to the general government of money received . . .
>
> I know of no general character Mr. Cowan has; he is known as a partisan printer to the Federalists who now hate him as a pest to them, and speak of him on all occasions as poor lazy Cowan; and by the Republicans he is only known to be despised. With all these reasons . . . I declare to God my mind is in the fullest manner impressed, that Mr. Cowan is unworthy of a benefit under a law made intentionly for honest, fair-dealing men . . .
>
> I challenge him or my greatest enemy to charge me with one act that has violated the laws of my country, except in chastising supposed insults; and I will have him and all others to take notice, that from this day forward, I will not withhold the same chastisement from him or any other person that hereafter attempts to implicate my character . . . if the author of any anonymous publication is not given up [i.e., made public], I shall take the printer for the author and treat him accordingly. So help me God.

The effect on "poor lazy Cowan" was devastating. His weaknesses had been publicly exposed, his financial troubles ridiculed, even his fondness for the bottle laid bare in print. It was a cruel thing to do to any man. How much Gibson's letter may have hastened Cowan's "approaching destruction" cannot be estimated, but it must have had a considerable influence. Henceforth Cowan was a laughingstock, not only in Easton, but on the entire Eastern Shore.

Within two years, he was forced to close down the *Herald;* and in the same issue (November 13, 1804) in which he announced the suspension of the paper, Cowan inserted a terse notice: "The Editor of this paper is under the painful necessity of informing his Creditors that he shall apply to the next Legislature of the State of Maryland for an act to relieve him of his debts." This was the procedure then followed for declaring bankruptcy.

Of the circumstances which had brought about his downfall, he wrote bitterly (as usual in the third person):

> The greater part of those who had been his patrons, but who now differed from the opinions which he maintained upon political subjects, withdrew their subscriptions from his paper; and some of them (if they may not be charged with having attempted it) would have been pleased with the destruction of his press and the ruin of his family.

That may have been a final veiled thrust at Gibson, who certainly was not displeased with the destruction of Cowan's press no matter how he felt about "the ruin of his family."

Whether Cowan was jailed for his debts, an ancient practice then still in vogue in Maryland, is not clear. His name was among those of nearly a hundred persons listed in "An Act for the Relief of Sundry Insolvent Debtors" passed by the Legislature January 20, 1805, whose petitions to be discharged from their debts were "found reasonable."

Under the bankruptcy laws of the time, he was required to surrender to his creditors all his property except for clothing and bedding; to publish an announcement of his condition in the *Star* (this appeared for three weeks beginning July 2, 1805); and to appear before the county court, including Associate Justice Jacob Gibson, at a hearing which took place on Monday, August 12.

After that the name of James Cowan vanishes from the records. Nothing is known of his later life—where he went, what he did, what happened to his wife, or when, where, and how he died. It was a sorry ending, in obscurity and ignominy, for the man who, with such high hopes and ideals, had founded the first newspaper ever published on the Maryland Eastern Shore.

In Chestertown, the Shore's second newspaper had appeared briefly and died a dozen years earlier, also in circumstances that were less than happy.

Coeditors Robert Saunders, Jr., and George Gerrish launched the *Apollo; or, Chestertown Spy* in March, 1793, as a semiweekly, to appear each Tuesday and Friday. Both were young men who had trained as printers. Circumstances suggest they may have met in Philadelphia, and that they had not known each other long before they set out on their Eastern Shore venture.

Saunders was probably the son of Robert Saunders, a Harford County, Maryland, planter, and the older brother of John Saunders, who also became a printer. If so, he was twenty-one years old and a newlywed at the time he went to Chestertown. On March 4, 1793—just a few weeks before the *Apollo* first appeared—the marriage of Robert Saunders, "printer of Baltimore," to Elizabeth Bancker was reported in the *Philadelphia Minerva*.

Gerrish reportedly was a native of Nova Scotia who had served his printing apprenticeship in Halifax. He was a good-looking young man with black hair and hazel eyes, rather round shouldered, about five feet, ten inches tall, with two scars on his forehead—or so he was described later when he was wanted as a horse thief.

The earliest issue of the *Apollo* which has survived was dated Tuesday, March 26, 1793, and labeled "Vol. I, No. 3," which leads to the supposition that

Vol. I.]   THE   [N°. 3.

Apollo; or, Chestertown Spy.

rice, single, 4d.]   TUESDAY, March 26, 1793.   [Per Annum, 18/9.

To the PUBLIC.

THE first Number of the APOLLO, &c. is now submitted to the perusal of its enerous Patrons, with the pleasing ho:, that it will merit their approbation an support.

he extraordinary marks of applause, wi. which the inhabitants of this, and the counties adjacent, received the proposal for this undertaking, *claims our warmest acknowledgments*: But the best return we can make is, we presume, to render th APOLLO sufficiently entertaining and instructive, by presenting the public with the latest and most important Foreign and Domestic Occurrences.

The APOLLO, &c. is intended to be comprised of original and extracted Essays, nral, political, historical, commercial, a icultural, philosophical, &c. Poetry, .necdotes, and Abstracts of Foreign and Domestic Occurrences, which may serve to give the Public a just idea of the prosperity and political situation of our own and other countries. To this end the Editors earnestly solicit the assistance of the learned, in this and the neighboring counties, who wish the prosperity of their fellow-citizens.

The Editors return their sincere thanks for past favors, and hope from their Experience in, and unremitting Attention to Business, to merit their future Patronage.

CONDITIONS.

I. It shall be printed with a handsome Type, and on a fine sheet of Crown Paper, to contain twelve columns of Letter-Press.

II. It will be put to press every *Tuesday* and *Friday Mornings*, and delivered to subscribers in town by the hour of nine the same morning, provided nothing material should occur.

III. At the end of each Session of Congress, the proceedings shall be printed in a pamphlet, and delivered to subscribers *gratis*; the convenience of having them in an octavo volume is much superior to that of having to refer, on every occasion, to a file of newspapers.

IV. The price of this Paper will be *Two Dollars and an Half* per annum---the one alf to be paid on delivery of the first aper, and the other half at the expiraon of nine months.

*** Advertisements not exceeding a quare will be inserted three times for *One Dollar* and those of a greater length in proportion; for the fourth, and every insertion afterwards, *One Fourth of a Dollar.*

PREJUDICE.

AMIDST the black cloud of vices which infest mankind, none more degrades the person, or is more detestable in its consequences, than prejudice. It is antipathy to intelligence---deaf to the gentle voice of reason---it forces from the mind that sensibility, which cannot delight in the misfortune of others. Miserable must that person be, who bars from his determinations the benevolence of candor---He is destined to grovel in the mud of ignorance, and plunges himself by a voluntary leap, below the horizon of rationality. Miserable must a state soon be, if her legislators consult not the best advantage of their constituents; but predetermined by the dogmatisms of self interest exert their influence only in such measures as run parallel with so partial a cause. Prejudice can deny the innocent amusements of the stage--banish *Melpomene* and her more jocal sister to some hospitable state---expelling with them the milder virtues. Are seminaries for literary improvements, beyond the reach of this vice? With reluctance we answer---far otherwise. Even those who are invested with authority in such noble institutions can disrobe themselves of candor---can open the doors of their souls to partiality, and perhaps without one sting of remorse---without the visage of plausibility, debar a youth from the advantages of an establishment, which placed them in a seat of independence, not to abuse so great a privilege, but to diffuse knowledge with liberal hands---to attend to merit; not to the dictates of prejudice---to encourage exertions in the pursuit of science; not to strike a damp on laudable ambition---to burnish the characters of the sons of literature; not unfeelingly, unjustly to cast a dash on good reputation, nor thrust a dagger into the bosom of sensibility. Such actions are the horrid retinue of prejudice. May every enlightened mind despise the groveling vice, and rise superior to a dread of its votaries.

THOMAS BRUFF,
GOLD and SILVERSMITH,
At his Shop in Chestertown, near the Printing-Office.

MAKES and repairs Plate, Jewelry, and other Gold and Silver Work, of the most fashionable and approved Patterns: Particular Attention will be paid to the Elegance, as well as Strength of Workmanship, the greatest Punctuality observed: And as he sells for ready Cash, and the Prices so reduced, as to put it out of the Power of any Person to furnish such Articles upon better Terms.

N. B. Cash given for old Gold and Silver.
March 19, 1793.

GEORGE BYERLY,
(Lately from Philadelphia)
Has opened a STORE on Bowly's Wharf, and opposite to the Sign of the Turk, Baltimore,
Where he has for Sale, on the lowest Terms,
WHOLESALE and RETAIL,

OLD London Particular, London Market, and York Madeira Wine, of the first quality, and fit for immediate use; Ditto Sherry, or Paxaretta, Wine, in quarter-casks; Ditto Port, Lisbon, Malaga, Teneriffe, and Muscadine Wine; Ditto Cogniac Brandy; Wine Bitters, of a superior quality, of his own manufacturing; Old Jamaica and Antigua Spirits, of an excellent quality; West-India Rum; Hyson and Souchong Tea, of the best quality; Loaf and Muscovado Sugar; Coffee; Pepper; Allspice; Nutmegs; Mace; Cloves; and Cinnamon; Cayan Pepper and fine Mustard; Pearl Barley; Almonds; Raisins; and Currants; Anchovies; Capers; Olives, &c. &c.

He is determined to keep a complete Assortment of the best Liquors; and flatters himself from the knowledge and long experience he has had in the Wine Business, to give full satisfaction to those who please to favor him with their Custom, Liquors sent out by him, and not approved of will be exchanged.

*** Captains of vessels and others, may be supplied with Liquors bottled at the above Store.

March 16, 1793.

PETER KIRKWOOD,
GOLD and SILVERSMITH,
In the Shop adjoining where Mr. Piper formerly lived,

TAKES this Method of informing his Friends in particular, and the Public in general, that he now carries on his Business in all its various Branches; and flatters himself, that from his Attention to Business, and the Elegance of his Work, to merit the Favors of the Public. He returns his sincere Thanks to those Ladies and Gentlemen, who have hitherto favored him with their Custom, and hopes, that from the Cheapness of his Work, and Punctuality in Business, to merit a Continuance of the same.

N. B. The highest Price given for old Gold and Silver.

Chestertown, March 22, 1793.

Pursuant to the last Will and Testament of JOHN BROWN, Esq. *(deceased)* will be Sold on the 15th day of April next, at Church-Hill, by Public Vendue, Ninety ACRES of

Excellent WOOD-LAND,

Lying on each side of the Main Road, leading from Chestertown to Church-Hill. The Terms will be made known on the Day of Sale by the Subscriber, who the Executrix of John Brown, Esq. has empowered to sell and dispose of said Land.

JOHN LAMBERT WILMER.

Queen-Ann's county March 20, 1793.

R A G S.

CASH, and the highest Price, given for clean Cotton and Linen RAGS, by the Printers hereof.

the founding date was March 19. But this is by no means certain. The March 26 issue carried an announcement that "the first Number of the APOLLO, &c. is now submitted to the perusal of its generous *Patrons*, with the pleasing hope that it will merit their approbation and support." That could be taken as an indication that the March 26 paper was the first actually published, and that the numbering was a typographical error. The question will never be resolved unless an earlier issue turns up, which at this late date seems most unlikely.

In appearance, the *Apollo* was a more attractive paper than Cowan's *Herald*, its only Eastern Shore rival. It was well printed with new type on excellent paper, and showed evidence of careful proofreading. The youthful editors promised that on publication days it would be "delivered to subscribers in town by the hour of nine the same morning," unless some "material" mishap should occur. They also promised, rather rashly as it turned out, to provide without charge a separate pamphlet at the close of each session of Congress containing a summary of its proceedings. The *Apollo*'s price was to be two dollars and a half per year, half in advance, or four pence per single copy. Advertising rates were one dollar for three insertions "not exceeding a square" (about two by two inches), and twenty-five cents per issue thereafter. Advertisements of greater size were priced proportionately higher.

All signs pointed to success—or so it must have seemed at the beginning. Subscription payments flowed in at an encouraging rate, and a number of advertisers took space in the early issues. In any case, Chestertown in 1793 appeared to be a better bet than Easton for starting a paper. It was the largest town on the Eastern Shore, and had become its busiest port with the decline of Oxford in Talbot County. As early as 1774 an English visitor, George Chalmers, had described it as having two hundred houses. Potential advertisers included two silversmiths, a tavern and billiard room, a saddlemaker, a watchmaker, a hat store, boarding houses, and several merchants who sold groceries, dry goods, drugs, liquors, and other items. The March 26 issue even had an ad from a Baltimore dealer who offered fine wines, spirits, rum, loaf sugar, pepper, spices, mustard, almonds, raisins, anchovies, capers, olives, and other imported delicacies at his store "opposite the sign of the Turk" on Bowly's Wharf.

Chestertown was also the Shore's cultural center as the seat of its only institution of higher learning, Washington College, founded in 1782. The town

---

Opposite, earliest known issue of the *Apollo; or, Chestertown Spy*, dated March 26, 1793. (Courtesy Maryland Historical Society)

boasted a dancing school operated by a Mr. Curley, who in his spare time sold chandeliers and gave lessons in the French language; a singing school which staged vocal concerts; and a drawing school for boys and girls conducted by "Mr. Boudier, painter." Twice during the year 1793 a troupe of professional performers visited Chestertown to present programs of rope dancing, tumbling, singing, pantomimes, and clown acts.

To capitalize on this cultural atmosphere, the *Apollo* editors announced their paper would publish "original and extracted essays, moral, political, historical, commercial, agricultural, philosophical, &c." Also "poetry, anecdotes, and abstracts of foreign and domestic occurrences, which may serve to give the public a just idea of the prosperity and political condition of our own and other countries." They especially solicited "the assistance of the learned" who might want to contribute essays.

It was an ambitious project; but it soon suffered a rude jolt. Sometime during the weekend of April 13-14, the handsome George Gerrish vanished, taking with him all the money thus far received in advance subscription payments. On April 16 Saunders announced tersely, without giving a reason, that "the partnership of Gerrish and Saunders is dissolved," and that henceforth he would be sole editor and publisher. Not until the end of the year did he reveal what had happened; on December 31 he published a notice saying what everybody in town already must have known, that Gerrish's only purpose in helping establish the newpaper had been "to induce people to subscribe, receive their money, and make off."

In the interim, Saunders had struggled valiantly to keep the paper afloat despite the loss of six months' revenues. In July he changed its name to the more prosaic *Chestertown Gazette*, a hint that the high-flown title of *Apollo; or, Chestertown Spy* may have been Gerrish's idea in the first place.

But he never recovered from his partner's perfidy. In the December 31 issue, after reporting what had happened, he admitted he could not afford to provide the promised pamphlet containing the proceedings of Congress, "as the expense attending it would be nearly equal to two-thirds of the subscriptions." He begged his friends' indulgence, blaming his financial problems on the disappearing Gerrish, and promised to continue his efforts to deserve their patronage.

However, no issue of the paper has ever been found with a date later than December 31, 1793. So it appears that, despite his promise, Saunders had to cease publication on that date, or shortly afterward. He did manage to continue his printing business in Chestertown at least for a time; a pamphlet entitled "An Act to Regulate and Discipline the Militia of this State" bears the date 1794, and the inscription: "CHESTERTOWN: Printed by Robert Saunders, Jun. at his Printing Office in High-street."

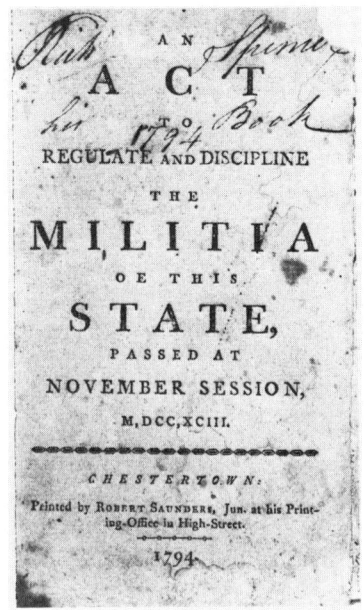

Pamphlet published by Robert Saunders at his Chestertown printing shop in 1794. (Courtesy Maryland Historical Society)

What happened to him after that is uncertain. From 1794 through 1805 a Robert Saunders resided in New York City, where he was recorded as a paper manufacturer, and later as printer and publisher of two newspapers, the *Diary* and the *Time Piece*. There is no way of knowing if this was the same Robert Saunders, although it appears likely.

As for Gerrish, his later career seems to have followed the pattern he set when he absconded from Chestertown. His name next turns up in Reading, Pennsylvania, where on October 14, 1796, a "G. Gerrish" was listed as a partner with Jacob Schneider in publishing the weekly *Impartial Reading Herald*. Later "Georg Gerrisch" was involved in publishing the German-language *Adler* in Reading.

On June 19, 1797, the following advertisement appeared in the *Maryland Journal* of Baltimore:

PRINTERS TAKE NOTICE!!!
One Hundred Dollars Reward

Was stolen from the subscriber about the 4th instant, by a certain George Gerrish, a black full-blood mare, 4 years old . . . Said Gerrish is a native of Nova Scotia, he served an apprenticeship to a printer in Halifax, and has been engaged in that business, in many printing-offices on the continent, he is a well-looking young man, about 25 years of age, 5 feet 9 or 10 inches high, round shouldered, his head stooping, black hair, two scars above one of his eyes, which are hazel coloured. It is supposed he is gone toward Richmond, Kentucky, or Boston . . . The last time he came to my house, he told me that he had been last in Baltimore, but was now going into partnership with a Mr. Wilmer, at Havre de Grace.

(signed) Robert Harris

"Mr. Wilmer" probably was the Reverend James Jones Wilmer, who had been associated with the *Eagle of Freedom* in Baltimore and in 1797 was conducting schools in Havre de Grace and other Maryland towns. There is no record that he ever went into partnership with Gerrish. However, a definite link between the Gerrish or Gerrisch of Reading was provided in the *Weekly Advertiser* of Reading on October 16, 1798. An anonymous correspondent asked a person addressed as "Mr. Arrogance" whether it was true that he was

> the intimate acquaintance of George Gerrish, who was formerly the partner of Schneider, and who married an innocent young woman in this place, and borrowed a horse of a worthy citizen here, which it was proved he never meant to return, and on whose head a reward of 100 dollars was offered for horsestealing in Maryland.

There is, of course, no proof that all these George Gerrishes were the same person. But it is asking a lot from coincidence to insist that, in the thinly populated Maryland and Pennsylvania of the 1790s, there were two different printers by the same name, one of whom helped himself to his partner's money while the other helped himself to his friends' horses.

With the expiration of the *Chestertown Gazette*, as Saunders had renamed the *Apollo*, Chestertown was once more without a newspaper. There is no reason to believe a printing office remained in the town after Saunders left in 1794; no imprint of pamphlet or handbill identified with Chestertown after that date exists. It would be thirty-one years before the *Chestertown Telegraph*, Kent County's second newspaper, was established.

Thomas Perrin Smith, who founded the Eastern Shore's third newspaper, the *Republican Star* of Easton, was a man of far different mold than any of his predecessors. He was not a printer, but something of an intellectual with an inquiring turn of mind which gave him an advantage in the editorial end of publishing. However, he was also a good practical businessman. Above all, he was lucky—or perhaps farsighted—in selecting Easton as the town in which to launch his career. As the nineteenth century started, it was beginning to fulfill the promise Cowan had foreseen for it a decade earlier. It rapidly outstripped Chestertown. Soon, in addition to district and federal courts and various state offices, it would have the Shore's first bank, its first brick hotel, its most progressive business leaders, its first home-financed steamboat. Thus it became not only the Eastern Shore's best source of official news, but its business, political, and social center as well. Until the rise of Salisbury and Cambridge after the Civil War, it would remain without a serious challenger. That helps to explain why, for a quarter of a century after Smith arrived, Easton had the Eastern Shore's only newspapers, and long after that had the most widely circulated ones.

A native of Virginia, Thomas Perrin Smith was born January 17, 1776, the second of five children of Perrin and Margaret (Wishart) Smith, both descendants of early Virginia settlers. He came to Easton in the spring of 1799 with his brother George Wishart Smith, who was looking for a farm to buy. But Thomas Perrin did not appear to have had any particular career in mind. At twenty-three, he was still seeking his niche in life. Almost certainly he had not been trained as a printer, nor had any experience at a newspaper, for he later complained of the difficulty of hiring competent printers to do this work for him.

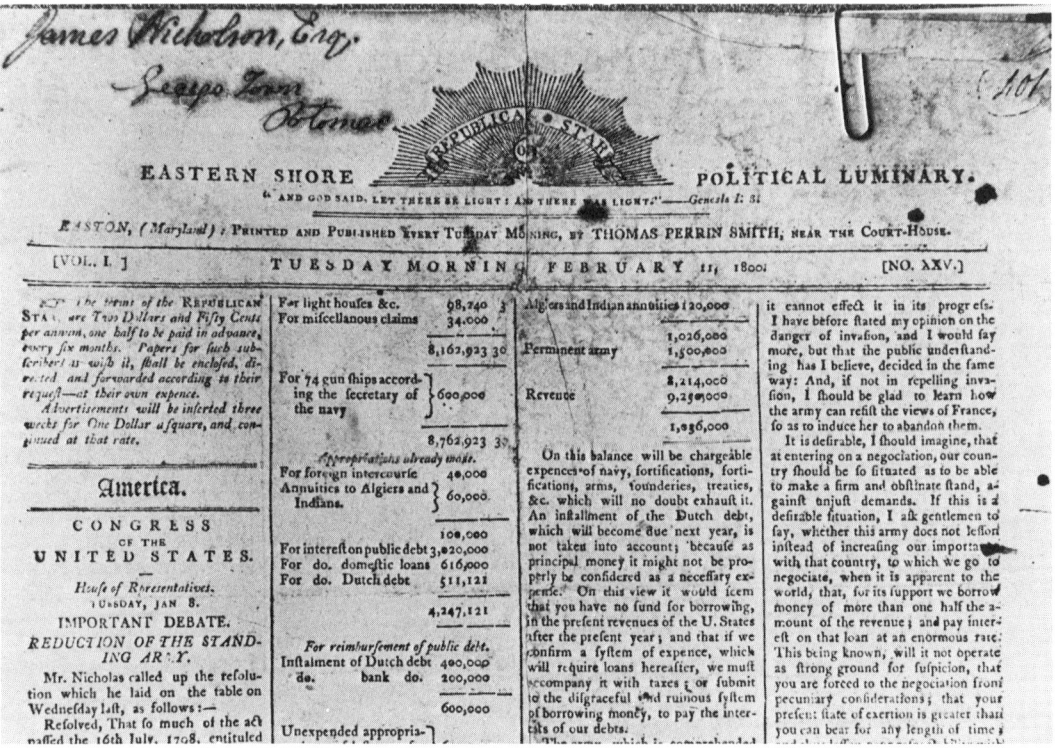

Earliest surviving issue of the *Republican Star* of Easton. (Courtesy American Antiquarian Society)

He soon became aware of the Federalist bias of the *Herald*. Just as Cowan had been a youthful admirer of George Washington, Smith from his childhood had been imbued with the liberal republicanism of Thomas Jefferson, the leading intellectual and most original thinker of the time. He was a Jeffersonian and proud of it; and with the 1800 presidential election fast approaching, local Jeffersonians were looking for a man to edit a newspaper which would counterbalance the *Herald*. When a "number of citizens" urged him to start such a paper, he quickly accepted and—undoubtedly with financial help from backers of Jefferson—launched the *Republican Star; or, Eastern Shore Political Luminary* in August, 1799. The first issue probably appeared on Tuesday, August 27, although this is not certain since no copy of the inaugural paper has survived.

From the beginning, the *Star* frankly declared its partisanship. It was out to help get Thomas Jefferson elected president, and Smith made no bones about it. In his words, "having from my infancy been reared upon the principles which I still profess, I at once proclaimed them to the world, that the citizens who might tender me their patronage should not be deceived by a false and delusive idea of impartiality." If that was a thrust at Cowan's pretense of being neutral, it was a popular stand with most Eastern Shoremen. They tended, as they still do, to regard a political neutral as a sort of mental eunuch. The *Republican Star* was just what its name implied, a Republican (i.e., Jeffersonian) paper; you could admire it or hate it, but you knew where it stood.

Even so, Smith kept his hand out to his political opponents, some of whom were undoubtedly potential advertisers. As he said in his first anniversary issue, August 19, 1800, "I did not, and hope I never shall, lose sight of the high esteem in which I hold men who are friends to their country tho' ever so much opposed to me in politics."

Other Republican editors greeted with delight the advent of a Jeffersonian newspaper on the Eastern Shore. On September 3, 1799, Alexander Martin commented in the *Baltimore American:*

> A newspaper has been commenced at Easton, on the Eastern Shore of this state, by a gentleman of the name of T. P. Smith—it is entitled "The Republican Star," and from the talents and spirit of the editor, excites strong expectations of benefitting the good cause.

(Incidentally, that is the earliest mention on record of the *Star* and of Thomas Perrin Smith as its editor, since no issue earlier than that of February 11, 1800, appears to have survived. Dr. Samuel A. Harrison, in his history of Talbot County newspapers published in the *Easton Star* in the 1870s, said there was no evidence that Smith really was the first editor of the paper; but he was not aware of the *American* item.)

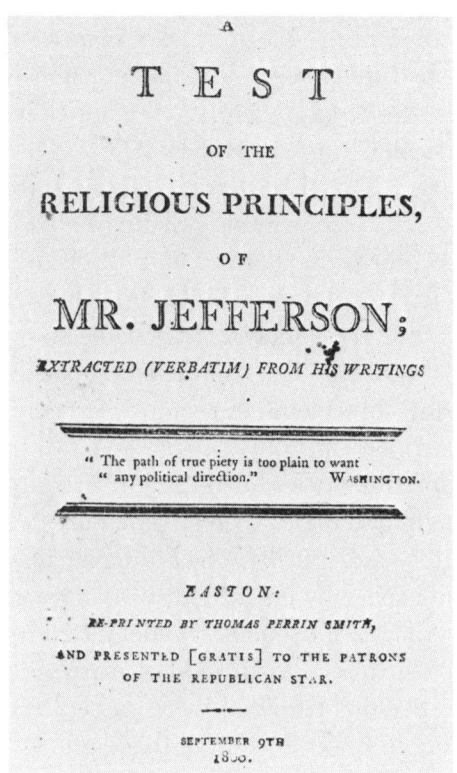

Pamphlet published by Thomas Perrin Smith defending the religious beliefs of his hero, Thomas Jefferson. (Courtesy Maryland Historical Society)

Martin's "good cause," of course, was Jefferson's election as president; and when that occurred Smith's personal "good cause" benefited with it. His paper became the official organ for publication of government laws and documents, which helped sell subscriptions; and on June 27, 1801, he replaced Cowan as Easton postmaster. This was a political plum of considerable monetary value which in the early days nearly always went to the editor of the paper which supported the winning presidential ticket. Smith kept the postmastership for nearly a quarter of a century, finally resigning on October 8, 1825.

The *Star*'s first office was a small structure on the west side of Washington Street, two or three doors north of Federal. Here the paper was printed, the post office was conducted, job printing was done, and books were offered for sale. On September 9, 1800, Smith produced his first separate publication, a six-page pamphlet entitled "A Test of the Religious Principles of Mr. Jefferson," which was offered free to *Star* patrons. It was in reality a piece of campaign propaganda designed to answer charges that Jefferson was an atheist, and to smear President Adams, who was seeking re-election, as a man who favored government support of an established religion—a doctrine which had been anathema to Eastern Shoremen since pre-Revolutionary days, when they were taxed to support the established Anglican Church in Maryland.

On November 15, 1803, Smith announced that the *Star* would move two doors farther north on Washington Street, into a new frame building he had erected as a home, not only for his paper and the post office but for himself and his sister, Ann, who kept house for him. A few years later he built a brick house on the same site and moved the frame structure to the rear as a back wing. Both houses are still standing; the brick house is (1982) the home of the Chesapeake Bay Yacht Club, and the frame one is quarters for its feminine counterpart, the Harbor Club.

As the years passed, Smith became something of an institution in Easton. He was described as a man of medium height and build, with large features, a ruddy complexion, and a bearing of dignity and gravity. According to Dr. Harrison, his scrupulously neat dress, and especially his ruffled shirts, "were long remembered by Easton residents." A lifelong bachelor, he delighted in poking gentle fun in the columns of the *Star* at the institution of marriage. Items about weddings involving some ridiculous situation were carried no matter where they had occurred. An example is a collection of three reports printed one after the other in the *Star* of June 4, 1805:

> Married at Limerick (Eng.), Mr. Thomas Kelly, aged 89, to Bridget Madican, aged 14 years. [Actually this must have taken place in Ireland, not England.]

> —At London, the Earl of Ormond to Miss Clarke, daughter of Price Clarke, Esq. This lady, who is only sixteen, has a fortune of eighteen thousand pounds, in cash, and a clear estate of eighteen thousand pounds per annum.

> —At Butterwicke, Lincolnshire (Eng.), Mr. T. Wood, of that place, to Mrs. Dobson, of Staxton. The united age of this happy couple is one hundred and sixty three years. She is the bridegroom's fifth wife, and he is her third husband.

On more serious matters, Smith showed himself to be both a responsible editor and a solid member of his community. He was the first Eastern Shore editor to publish substantial amounts of local nonpolitical news, and the first to campaign for civic improvements.

One of his long-term projects was to secure fire protection for Easton, which had no fire engine and where even the town pumps, the only source of water in an emergency, often were not in working order. The *Star* of January 25, 1803, published an item about an Easton house fire, to which Smith appended this comment:

The "Sajou Brown," a trained monkey, was advertised in Easton's *Republican Star*, November 9, 1802.

We are, by the arrival of almost every mail, shocked with details of destruction by FIRE, in various parts of the nation; and at the same time have to witness the helpless situation of the town of Easton, with more than one-half of her public pumps out of order! Citizens of Easton, remember that when the dreadful sound of "FIRE" rebounds in your streets, it will be too late to insist on your commissioners having the pumps repaired.

After that the *Star* carried numerous warnings of potential disaster if fire were to hit the principal business district along Washington Street, where Smith had his home and office. In the words of a letter published April 2, 1805, "in all human probability the whole street would be in a short time enveloped in flames; the honest and industrious merchant and mechanick ruined; and this now happy and flourishing village rendered the scene of desolation and despair." Predicting Easton might become "a heap of ashes," Smith called editorially for a town meeting to organize some form of "security of property against fire." But nothing was done.

The somber warnings came true early on Sunday morning, February 28, 1808. A disastrous fire wiped out four buildings on north Washington Street, and only heroic efforts by volunteer bucket brigades saved the frame structure which housed the *Star*. Smith, who had spent the hours from 3:00 A.M. until sunup lugging printing and post office materials to a place of safety, reported angrily in Tuesday's edition that as a result of the town "having no Engine, and [being] otherwise unprepared with weapons of defense, the risque and labour became more than doubly severe . . . It is with the utmost difficulty that the Editor is able to issue the paper this morning." He expressed his gratitude toward "those gentlemen who so politely exerted themselves in his behalf" and—in a noteworthy acknowledgment for that time and place—thanked especially "the People of Colour, many of whom behaved with . . . spirited firmness, during the calamity."

As usually happens, the disaster succeeded in arousing action where Editor Smith's warnings had failed. Within days, a fund of $1,005 was raised to buy a fire engine, and on April 20 a volunteer fire company which included most of the able-bodied males of the town was organized.

In national affairs Smith continued to support President Jefferson; here, too, he was not content merely to print the news, but urged action on the local level. When Great Britain angered Americans in 1807 by insisting on its right to search and seize American vessels on the high seas, one of the underlying causes of the War of 1812, the *Star* called for an indignation meeting in a statement which is a classic of bombastic chauvinism:

> Your independence, the legacy of the heroes of '76, has been attacked by a band of sea robbers and pirates. You are now called upon to assemble around the standards of your country and adopt measures that will convince the cowardly assassins that we are descendants of those heroes who once drove them from our country, and that we are willing and ready to do it again or perish with our constitution.

With Brigadier General Perry Benson, a hero of the Revolution, in charge, the called-for meeting was held at the Easton courthouse shortly afterward. There is no hint that England's leaders were impressed by the defiant resolutions adopted on that occasion. But, as James C. Mullikin points out in his *Story of the Easton Star-Democrat*, "it cannot be doubted that when the War of 1812 finally broke out, part of the intensely patriotic attitude of the Eastern Shore toward the government can be attributed to the influence of the *Star*." And Editor Smith backed his words with action; when a British fleet threatened St. Michaels in August, 1813, he helped defend the town by serving as a private in the militia company commanded by his brother, Captain George Wishart Smith.

After the demise of the *Herald* in November, 1804, Smith—as proprietor of the Eastern Shore's only newspaper—inherited the same problem that had plagued Cowan: the tide of insults and invective which Shoremen directed at each other. For example, the *Star* of August 27, 1805, carried this paid notice:

> For reasons satisfactory to my mind, I publish and declare William Barroll, Esq., of Chestertown, to be a SCOUNDREL.
>
> T. M. Forman

Two weeks later came Barroll's reply:

> As that *contemptible fellow*, Thomas M. Forman, has thought proper to publish me in the Star as a "SCOUNDREL," I now call upon him for those "reasons satisfactory to his mind" which caused him to take such an unwarrantable liberty with my character—after that the world shall see who is the scoundrel.
>
> William Barroll

For the next several issues, Forman, Barroll, and their friends engaged in a lively argument over personal matters which must have mystified most readers of the *Star*.

Going on at the same time was another feud which involved a dozen men, most of them from Kent County, and finally embroiled even editor Smith himself. It started as an exchange in which James Page accused Richard Hatcheson of besmearing the reputation of a young lady, and Hatcheson reported that Page had "a wicked heart and a weak head." Soon others were drawn in. William Spencer was described as "a man equalled by none in villainy and cowardice," except for his brother Jervis Spencer; and a detractor said of the two Spencers, along with Dr. James Sykes: "Nature blushes to acknowledge, among her progeny, this trio whose hearts are fraught with every villainy and vice . . . and whose souls shrink from the very idea of virtue and honor."

Eventually center stage was occupied by Luke Howard and Dr. Alexander Stuart, who had not even been involved in the original dispute. On August 27 the *Star* published a statement by Howard, directed at Dr. Stuart, which started off, "Now, thou lying varlet . . ." and went on from there, with free use of such choice words as "culprit," "driveler," "scoundrel," and "arch demon" to characterize the doctor.

By this time Smith had had enough. In the *Star* of September 17, he scolded the disputants, not for their violent language, but for boring his readers:

> Gentlemen . . . who are engaged in personal quarrels, ought to know that the public are totally uninterested in their disputes, and believe that the columns of a newspaper might be much better filled, either by foreign news, or by essays on political, agricultural, or philosophical subjects.

Therefore, once the current disputes were finished, he would "no longer hold himself bound to publish anything merely of a personal nature." If two parties insisted on "a war of ink and paper," he would be "very happy to accommodate them with handbills."

With this statement, Smith apparently thought he had made his editorial position clear. But he soon found out he was wrong. Early in November, Dr. Stuart marched into the *Star* office, brandishing a copy of Howard's remarks and demanding that Smith publish a refutation signed, not by Dr. Stuart, but by the editor himself. When Smith refused, explaining that he was only a "neutral party" and didn't know anything about the facts in the case, Dr. Stuart angrily replied that he would sue the editor and threatened, according to Smith, "that his weight and influence in the state would crush him." Smith's account concluded: "On Saturday last, the sheriff of this county served a writ on the Editor, at the suit of Dr. Alexander Stuart, of Kent County, with the name of Nicholas Hammond, Esq., as counsel." Hammond was Easton's leading attorney, president of the recently established local bank, and an ardent Federalist, so that his name on the suit carried even more weight than Dr. Stuart's did.

Eventually the doctor's temper cooled and the suit was dropped; but Smith continued to have problems with irate correspondents. He never did fully carry out his editorial pledge to eliminate personal controversies, and on occasion indulged in them himself. In 1808 he accused a prominent Talbot Countian, identified only as "Mr. XYZ," of false pretenses in supporting James Monroe for president when he really favored a Federalist, Charles Pinckney of South Carolina. According to eyewitnesses, "Mr. XYZ" marched into the *Star* office and presented a paper which he demanded that the editor sign. Smith refused, whereupon "said Z struck said Smith several times with a small whip, which the said Smith returned with his fists." The witnesses jumped in to prevent further damage.

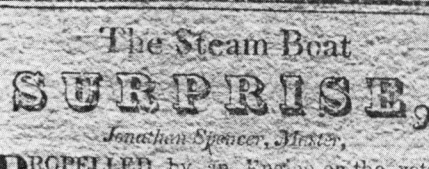

Left, The *Surprise*, the Eastern Shore's first steamboat, began operations in 1817. *Right*, Second steamer to serve the Shore was the *Maryland*, financed and built by local capital in 1818.

When a new opposition paper, the *People's Monitor*, appeared in Easton in 1809, it complicated matters for Smith still more. He felt constrained to provide a public forum to persons of his own party who wished to answer remarks printed about them in the Federalist *Monitor*, even if the original insults had not appeared in the *Star*.

In July, 1809, the *Monitor* printed some disparaging remarks about Maryland Governor Robert Wright of Queen Anne's County and his son, the hot-tempered and controversial Gustavus W. T. Wright. The younger Wright challenged *Monitor* editor Samuel B. Beach to a duel. Beach declined to fight. Smith then permitted Wright to use the *Star*'s columns to denounce Beach as a "base coward and lawless slanderer." Like his 1802 publication of Jacob Gibson's vicious attack on Cowan, this was harsh treatment of a fellow editor; but it was in line with the no-holds-barred journalism of the time.

Since Gustavus Wright and his father were Democratic-Republicans, as the Jeffersonians now were beginning to be called, Smith gave young Wright a free hand in denouncing his enemies in print. During that same summer, the *Star* published another missive by Wright castigating Vachel Keene, describing him as "a young pettifogger of Easton," and calling him a "poltroon and puppy" because like Beach he had refused to fight a duel. At issue, according to Wright, were remarks Keene had made about Wright's relations with "those villains Hanson and Livermore, of Baltimore," who were otherwise unidentified. Wright said he accosted Keene on an Easton street and "struck him several times across the face with a rattan," but Keene refused to accept the challenge and instead retreated to a nearby house, where he armed himself with a pistol. Under the dueling code then in vogue, this made Keene a "poltroon," or so Wright declared.

As the years passed, the ardor of the Eastern Shore's hot-blooded young blades gradually cooled. Dueling, already illegal in Maryland, went out of style, and so did the practice of conducting personal vendettas in the newspapers.

Smith's main concern in his later years was to maintain the *Star* in the dominant position it had gained when it was the Eastern Shore's only newspaper, with wide circulation throughout the area. The opposition of the *People's Monitor* was not difficult to overcome; founded as a Federalist Party organ, it arrived on the scene (January 14, 1809) just as the Federalists were dying out as a national political force. But with the advent of the *Easton Gazette*, edited by the capable Alexander Graham, in December, 1817, the *Star* faced real opposition for the first time. The *Gazette* would remain in the field, much of the time as Talbot County's leading newspaper, for more than a hundred years. Later came additional inroads on the *Star*'s position from the *Eastern Shore Whig*, founded in 1828, and the host of county weeklies which sprang up about the same time throughout the Shore.

Politically, Smith remained true to his Jeffersonian principles; but the liberalism of the 1790s was the conservatism of the 1820s. After the election in 1828 of Andrew Jackson, whom the *Whig* had supported and the *Star* opposed, the *Star*'s circulation and influence steadily declined. The old Republican Party was now the Democratic Party; and the Age of Jackson, with its aggressive national policies and crude exploitation of the spoils system in government jobs, had replaced the Age of Jefferson, when the dictum that "the best government is the least government" was widely believed.

Thomas Perrin Smith died May 2, 1832, at the age of fifty-five, and the *Republican Star* died with him. He had been the living embodiment of the *Star* for thirty-three years, the first Eastern Shore editor to whom the word "great" might be applied, and one of the few of that caliber it has ever had. He had established many precedents for journalism on the Shore, and had overcome financial and political obstacles which would have destroyed a lesser man.

PRINTED AND PUBLISHED EVERY TUESDAY MORNING
BY
Thomas Perrin Smith.

TERMS

Two Dollars and Fifty Cents per annum, payable half yearly in advance.—No paper can be discontinued until the same is paid for.

ADVERTISEMENTS are inserted three weeks for *One Dollar*, and continued weekly for *Twenty-five Cents* per square.

OBITUARY.

The Editor of this paper, THOMAS PERRIN SMITH, departed this life on Wednesday night last, the 2d inst. after a severe illness of a week, in the 56th year of his age.—Mr. Smith was a native of Virginia, and came to this town about the year 1799, and established the REPUBLICAN STAR, of which paper he was the publisher and proprietor from that period until the day of his death. By diligence, industry and frugality, Mr. S. had acquired a very comfortable independence; but with a kind of parental fondness, he still continued the publication of the "Star" after its avails had ceased to be important to the support of himself and family.

Mr. Smith had never married, but was blessed with an affectionate and amiable sister, whose unvaried care and tenderness was devoted to her brother with almost unexampled fidelity. Mr. S. discharged the various relations he held to society and to his family in the most laudable manner. He was an excellent citizen, and an obliging neighbour—as a brother he was tender and affectionate, and as a master he was kind and indulgent. His remains were interred in the Episcopal burying ground at White Marsh Church, on Friday afternoon.

In consequence of the death of Mr. Smith, it has been found impracticable to do more this week, than issue this half sheet. It is hoped the patrons of the "Star" will receive it with indulgence.—This occasion is embraced to inform them, that as yet, no definitive conclusion has been adopted in regard to the continuance of this paper—It will therefore be published as usual until some arrangement shall have been made, and which, when made, will be announced to the public.

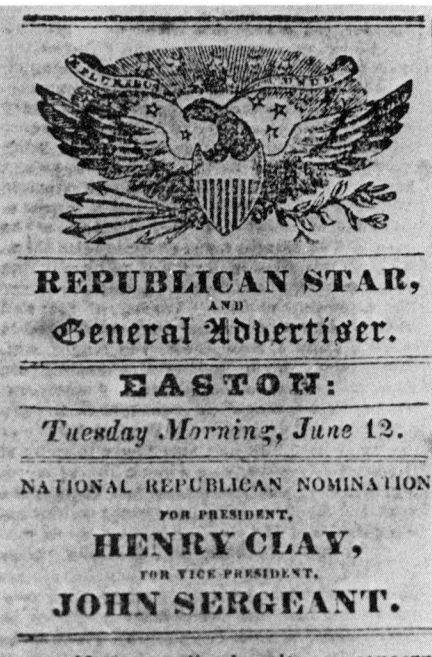

Left, Obituary of Thomas Perrin Smith, in the *Republican Star* of May 6, 1832. *Above*, Masthead of the final issue of the *Republican Star*, dated June 12, 1832.

The *Star* of May 8 printed his obituary on page one, with a black border around the page, but the inside pages were completely blank. Smith's trustees continued publishing the paper for six weeks after his death before announcing, in the issue of June 12, 1832, that it would be discontinued. That was the final edition of the Eastern Shore's first successful newspaper.

At a public sale held shortly afterward, the *Star*'s presses, type, and office furnishings were bought by Mrs. Rachel Green, mother of John D. Green, who had been the *Eastern Shore Whig*'s first editor but had resigned his post in 1830. Mrs. Green had also owned the press and type used to print early issues of the *Whig*. Now she hoped to launch her errant son, who reportedly had problems with alcohol, on a new publishing venture which was announced but never became reality. Her role in these behind-the-scenes activities is not altogether clear; but the scanty records indicate she may have been, in fact if not in name, the Eastern Shore's first—and perhaps its only—woman newspaper publisher.

PUBLIC SALE.

BY Order of the Orphan's Court of Talbot County, will be sold at Public Auction, on WEDNESDAY the 20th day of the present month, (June) at the late residence of Thomas Perrin Smith, Esq. deceased, in the town of Easton, all the PERSONAL ESTATE of said deceased, (except the Bank Stock and Negroes) consisting of a large quantity of very valuable

Household & Kitchen Furniture.

THE WHOLE STOCK OF BOOKS,
(Some of them very valuable.)
BLANK BOOKS STATIONARY, &c.
IN THE STORE.

Three Printing Presses,
AND ONE STANDING PRESS,
ALL THE TYPES,
FURNITURE & FIXTURES,
For Newspaper and Job Printing,
IN THE OFFICE OF THE
"Republican Star,"

Which, to a man with a small capital, would be a handsome investment, the Paper having a good list of Subscribers, with a good share of Job and Advertising Business.

ALSO,—One CHARIOTTEE & HARNESS, nearly new, one GIG & HARNESS, 1 HORSE, 4 COWS, BACON, LARD, and various other articles too tedious to enumerate.

The terms of sale will be a credit of 6 months on all sums over five dollars, by the purchaser or purchasers giving note with approved security, bearing interest from the day of sale, for all sums of and under five dollars the cash will be required. Sale to commence at 9 o'clock, A. M. Attendance given by
JOHN STEVENS, Adm'r.
of Thomas Perrin Smith, deceased.
june 5   w

☞ NOTICE.

ALL Persons indebted to the estate of Tho's. Perrin Smith, Esq. late of Talbot county deceased, are requested to make immediate payment, as indulgence cannot be given; and all persons having claims against said estate will please to present them for settlement as soon as possible.   JOHN STEVENS, Adm'r.
of Thomas Perrin Smith, dec'd.
may 22   w

Announcement of the sale of the *Star*'s presses, type, and fixtures after Smith's death. The equipment was purchased by Mrs. Rachel Green, who hoped to start a new paper with her son John as editor.

CHAPTER THREE

First Flowering
THE COUNTY WEEKLIES

FOR thirty-two years between 1790 and 1822, Easton had the Eastern Shore's only newspapers except for the brief and disastrous experiment in Chestertown. Then came a sudden flowering; all up and down the peninsula, weekly papers burst into bloom like violets in the spring sun. By 1831 every one of the eight existing Shore counties had one or more newspapers, and with the establishment of the *Caroline Advocate* at Denton in 1834, there was at least one in every county seat.

These journalistic ventures came in quick succession: the *Cambridge Chronicle* (1822); the *Elkton Press* (1823); the *Centreville Times* (1824); the *Chestertown Telegraph* (1825); the *Somerset Herald* of Princess Anne and the *Snow Hill Messenger* (both 1827); and the *Caroline Intelligencer*, published in Hillsboro (1831). Along with Talbot County's three papers, they represented every county on the Shore: Cecil, Kent, Queen Anne's, Caroline, Dorchester, Somerset, and Worcester. (Wicomico County was not carved out of Somerset and Worcester counties until 1867. Salisbury, then located in Somerset County, but later to become the Wicomico County seat, produced its first paper, the *Sentinel*, in 1859.)

The reasons behind this sudden flowering were part politics and part economics. In the presidential years of James Madison and James Monroe, there had been so little political controversy that the period (1809-1825) has come down in history as the Era of Good Feelings. But as Monroe's second term ended, so did the harmony the young nation had enjoyed for nearly two decades. America was having growing pains; politically it was splitting into warring camps divided on vital issues—conservatives versus radicals, North versus South, East versus West. New political alliances were formed as factional infighting ripped apart Jefferson's old party, the Democratic-Republicans. From the shattered remnants of the Federalists rose a new and vigorous conservative party, the Whigs. In the election of 1824 four major candidates sought the presidency: John Quincy Adams, the New Englander; Andrew Jackson, hero of the radicals and the newly developing West; William Crawford, spokesman for the South; and Henry Clay, the Great Compromiser. The voting was so close that the election was thrown into the House of Representatives, where Adams won with Clay's help although Jackson had the most popular and electoral votes.

In the next few years the country was torn by these factional disputes; and the Eastern Shore was no exception. Every splinter group wanted its own local voice: the Jacksonians, the emerging Whigs, the old-line Jeffersonians, the pro-South conservatives. The easy way to obtain one was to start a newspaper; used presses and type were cheap, and young men willing to act as editors even cheaper. For an investment of a few hundred dollars, a newspaper could be put into operation. During the campaign it would roll out weekly editions praising its candidates and lambasting the opposition; and then, if the faction which had started it lost the election, it would in all likelihood quietly vanish.

At the same time the county seat towns, in a modest way, were becoming centers of commerce. Not all the newly created newspapers failed. There was even reason to hope that a young man who was willing to work day and night, and whose wants were small, could make a living as a small town job printer and newspaper editor. The example of Thomas Perrin Smith, who had started with nothing and risen to be a substantial man of affairs, with a brick town house and a directorship on the board of the Farmers Branch Bank of Easton, must have inspired many a youthful editor elsewhere on the shore.

The cost of operating a printing and newspaper shop at that time was minuscule. The hand presses which were in universal use on the early Eastern Shore newspapers were simple devices not much changed since Johann Gutenberg first devised a printing press in 1450. They consisted of two upright beams with a heavy platen, or piece of iron, suspended between them. The printer laboriously set the type by hand, plucking each character out of a case (capitals in the upper case, and small letters in the lower one, which accounts for the origin of those terms) and placing them in a line. The lines were locked into a form. The forms for pages one and four were placed on the flat bed of the press and inked with a hand roller. A sheet of paper was laid on them, and the printer pulled a lever. The platen descended and pressed the paper against the inked type—hence the word "press" itself. When sufficient sheets for the entire run had been printed on one side, the type for pages one and four was replaced by that for pages two and three. The sheets were turned over, the pressing process repeated, the papers folded in the middle, and the "four-page" edition was ready to go.

This continued to be the standard operation for Eastern Shore newspapers long after Frederick Koenig of London developed a revolving cylinder press, driven by steam, in 1812. When John H. Emerson purchased a horse tread press in the 1830s and moved his printing shop from Centreville to Denton, where he published the *Pearl*, it was considered an important technological development. By substituting the motive power of a horse walking continuously on a treadle for the arm power of a man, the horse tread press conserved both time and energy. More advanced devices, such as the vastly improved power-driven Hoe presses, perfected by 1840, made no dent whatever on the Eastern Shore. They could print twenty thousand sheets per hour; but who needed that in an area where a weekly circulation of one thousand was something of a miracle?

Newsprint, though superior in strength to today's wood pulp paper, was also inexpensive. Many Eastern Shore weeklies carried standing advertisements offering to buy old rags. These were converted locally into a paper which, while rather coarse and grayish, far outlasted the cheaper, mass-produced wood pulp paper which arrived in the 1870s.

Composition—the setting of type and laying out of ads—was the most time-consuming part of the process; and even this was not as laborious as it might seem. Many advertisements ran on from month to month without change, so that the only composition each week was preparing the few new ads and setting into type the essays, political screeds, and other items, culled from big city dailies, which constituted most of the editorial content.

On most Shore papers, local reporting was virtually unknown. Except in the event of a major fire, storm, or other disaster, the only local news was in the form of announcements of meetings, weddings, and deaths. Almost invariably the newspaper was a one or two man operation. The editor acted as publisher, printer, ad taker, bookkeeper, newswriter, and sometimes even sweeper-up. If he was lucky and could afford it, he might have an assistant to help with the printing, and perhaps a boy, called a printer's devil, who was apprenticed to learn the trade in exchange for six to eight years of unpaid or poorly paid labor.

It was not an easy life, nor one suited to those who sought leisure and luxury. Consider the valedictory of John D. Green as he resigned the editorship of the *Eastern Shore Whig* of Easton in 1830. He was giving it up, said Green, "because my profession and I cannot agree. She, like a young bride, requires too much court. I could give her either all day or all night, but both I never can nor never will give."

Lewis Caton put the problem in different words when in 1835 he offered the *Borderer*, a Snow Hill paper, for sale after editing it for only a little more than a year. Possession would be given immediately, on accommodating terms. Caton was reticent about why he wanted to sell, but he made it clear that no loafers need apply. "A young man of industrious habits," he wrote, "possessing a thorough knowledge of the business, and who would devote his undivided

Ad for men's tailoring, 1847.

attention to the duties of the office," could soon make the paper "a source of revenue." That was a backhanded way of saying that publishing a newspaper required both skill and hard work.

Caton got his man; the *Borderer* closed down in September, and early in October J. W. Welch came out with a new Snow Hill paper, the *Worcester Sentinel and Farmers' and Mechanics' Shield*. But Welch, like Green, may have proved unwilling to pay "court" to his bride all day and all night. At any rate, the *Sentinel* soon went out of business.

Many of the early papers bore proud names, fitting emblems of their patriotism, philosophy, or politics. It was an age of bombast; if scare headlines had not yet been invented, newspaper titles carried their own pointed messages: *Freedom's Sentinel*; the *American Eagle*; the *Maryland Censor*; the *Worcester County Shield (and Spirit of the Whig Press)*; the *Kent Bugle*; the *Temperance Banner*; the *State Rights Advocate*; the *Union Reformer*; the *Jackson Picket Guard*; the *Denton Pearl*; the *Aurora*; the *Intelligencer*; the *Mechanic*; the *Inquirer*; the *Borderer*; the *Telescope*; the *People's Press*; the *People's Monitor*. Perhaps the most charming name of all was the *Somerset Iris and Messenger of Truth*, a Princess Anne paper that bloomed in 1828 and died in 1829, and the most unusual, though in a later era, Chesapeake City's *Chesapeake Chesapike*, named, as its publisher proclaimed, "for a fighting fish of the Bay."

THE AMERICAN UNION.

VOL I. DENTON, MD., TUESDAY, NOVEMBER 13, 1860. NO. 18.

WORCESTER COUNTY SHIELD.

SNOW HILL (MD.), TUESDAY, NOVEMBER 18, 1851.

American Eagle.

E PLURIBUS UNUM

A FAMILY NEWSPAPER:—Devoted to Local, General and Foreign News, and the Dissemination of American Principles.

VOL. 2, CAMBRIDGE, MD., WEDNESDAY MORNING, OCTOBER 22. 1856 NO. 25.

AMERICAN EAGLE

R. S. TALL, EDITOR AND PROPRIETOR.

POETRY.

MY MOTHER

A TEMPERANCE STORY.

THE DREAM

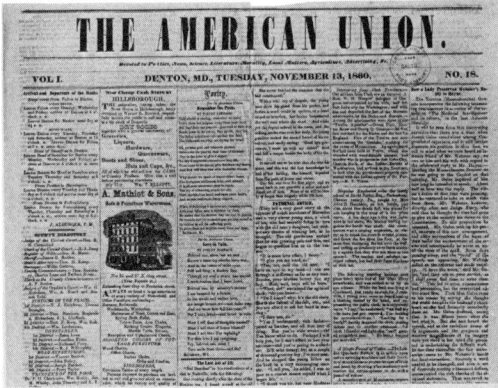

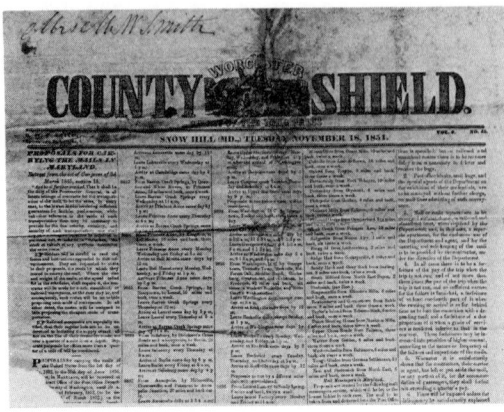

Patriotism and pride were the hallmarks of early newspaper titles.

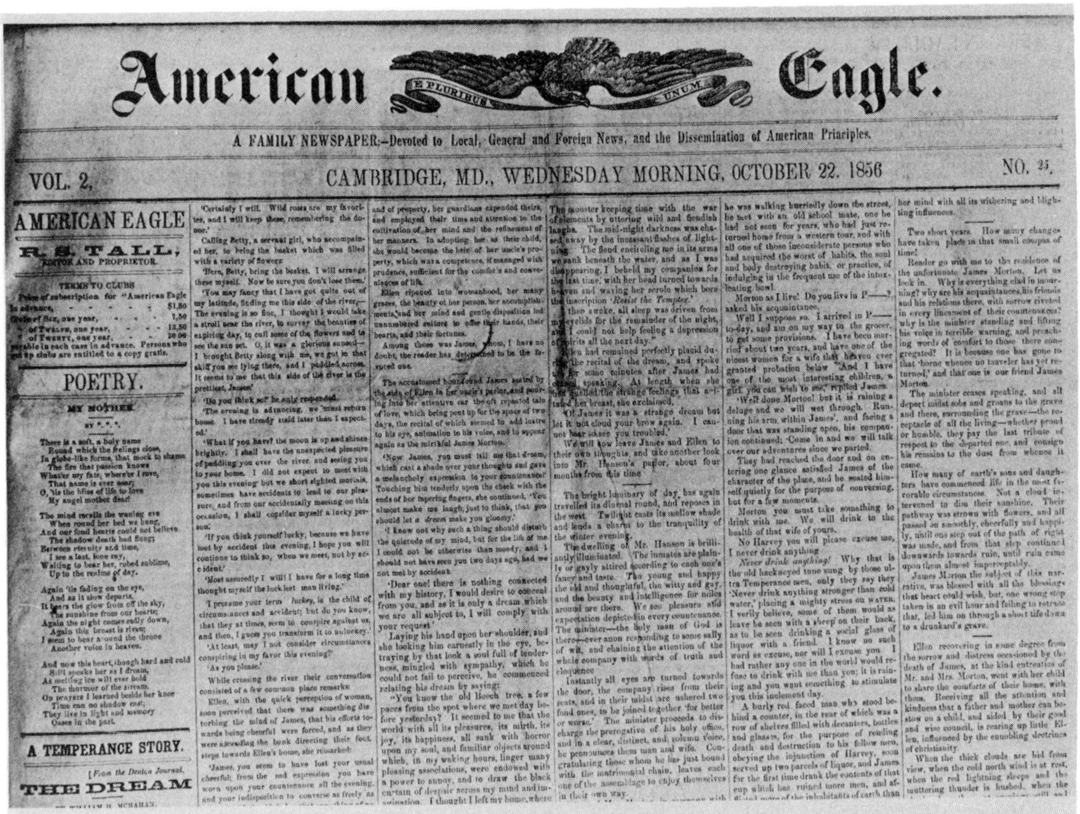

Most of these soon succumbed, to be followed by others which in their turn perished. But a few survived, though under different names. The *Centreville Times* (1824) lives on in the *Queen Anne's Record-Observer;* the *Eastern-Shore Whig and People's Advocate* (1828) is now Easton's daily *Star-Democrat;* the *Chestertown Telegraph* (1825) became the *Kent Bugle*, which metamorphosed into the *Kent News* and eventually the *Kent County News*. The *Denton Journal* (1847) lasted more than a century; and the *Cecil Democrat*, born in 1834 as the *Cecil Gazette and Farmers' and Mechanics' Advertiser*, finally gave up the ghost in 1981 after 147 years of existence.

Only the *Cecil Whig*, of all the Eastern Shore's early newspapers, has never changed its name since the day it was first published in August, 1841. There is a feeling of rocklike solidarity, of roots firmly fixed in the past, about a newspaper which in 1981 proudly bears the name of a political party which died in 1854. Perhaps that helps account for the *Whig*'s survival.

In the rapidly shifting kaleidoscope of national politics during the turbulent 1820s and 1830s, some editors found themselves embarrassed when the name emblazoned on their paper's masthead came to stand for an opposition political faction. It is well to keep in mind that the Republican Party of Jefferson's time became the Democratic Party under Jackson, and that today's Republican Party did not exist until the 1850s. Thus the *Cecil Republican* of 1832 could be succeeded by the *Cecil Democrat* a decade later without the slightest change in basic policies.

A classic case in point is that of the *Eastern-Shore Whig* of Easton. Despite its name, it was not a Whig paper like the *Cecil Whig;* in fact, it strongly supported Andrew Jackson and the radical wing of the Democratic Party. When it was founded in 1828, the old-line Federalists and other conservatives had not yet organized themselves into the national Whig Party. The name was chosen to stress its liberalism, in honor of the Revolutionary War Whigs who had opposed the Tories.

But as the 1830s progressed, the word "Whig" became associated with everything the publishers of the *Eastern-Shore Whig* despised in politics. For nine years after the *Republican Star* succumbed with the death of Thomas Perrin Smith, the *Whig* was the only voice in Talbot County for the Jacksonian Democrats—and yet it bore the name of the party which bitterly opposed the Democrats.

Editor-proprietor George W. Sherwood finally found a way out of the dilemma when fire destroyed the *Whig* office and all its equipment March 22, 1841. The paper was out of business for a month, and when it finally resumed publication April 20, it had a new name as well as a new appearance. Sherwood described it as "a weekly paper to be styled the 'Eastern Shore Star' to supply

A log cabin and barrel of hard cider were symbols of the 1840 Whig presidential campaign. When the *Cecil Whig* was founded the next year, it was first published from a real log cabin built in Elkton as a campaign promotion. (Courtesy Library of Congress)

the place of the 'Whig.'" He gave the first issue the label of "Volume I, number 1" to emphasize the idea that this was an entirely new paper, and said he hoped the change in title would "in future, prevent confusion."

Thus the *Eastern Shore Star*, predecessor of the present *Star-Democrat*, rose out of the ashes of the *Eastern-Shore Whig* and not the old *Republican Star*, which had died nine years earlier. Sherwood may have hoped to capitalize on the fond memories Talbot Countians had of Smith's *Star*, but he did not revive it. In fact, he had turned down a request by the late editor's sister, Ann

Smith, who helped finance his new equipment, to resume the name *Republican Star*.

As Dr. Samuel A. Harrison said in his history of Talbot County newspapers published in the 1870s, the *Star* of his day was "by no means the successor of the *Republican Star*, except that it came after and is of the same political faith and similar name." By the same token the present-day *Star-Democrat* is descended from the *Eastern-Shore Whig* of 1828 and not the *Republican Star* of 1799.

Nor can much credence be put in the claim the *Kent County News* exhibits at the top of its front page to be "a direct descendant of the Chester Town Spy, established in 1793." In the Chestertown case, there was a gap of at least thirty-one years (1794-1825) during which the town had no newspaper.

The oldest Eastern Shore newspaper in terms of continuous existence is probably the *Queen Anne's Record-Observer*. It grew out of the *Centreville Times*, which was established July 17, 1824, according to an article in *The Eastern Shore of Maryland and Virginia* (1950), a three-volume history edited by Charles B. Clark. On July 26, 1864, this account continues, the *Times* was purchased by William W. Busteed and Charles T. Loveday, "who published it thereafter under a black title-head reading 'The Observer.'" In 1936 the *Observer* was merged with the *Queen Anne's Record* to form the present paper, the *Queen Anne's Record-Observer*.

If this account is correct—and there is no reason to doubt it—the *Record-Observer* predates both the *Kent County News* and the *Star-Democrat* in direct descent from an earlier paper.

Politics may have been the life blood of Eastern Shore newspapers during their early flowering; but politics didn't pay bills or buy groceries. For income the hard-pressed editors relied principally on job printing and secondarily on advertising, with subscriptions running a poor third as cash producers.

The ads were of all sorts: notices of sheriffs' sales, or auctions of the property of deceased persons; reward offers for runaway slaves; announcements of the sailing schedules of packets or steamboats, and of the schedules of stages; listings of the "splendid" merchandise just imported from Philadelphia or Baltimore for sale at low prices by local merchants; offerings by hatmakers, watchmakers, tanners, blacksmiths, silversmiths, innkeepers, wood cutters, slave buyers, owners of stud horses, shoe stores; want ads for wet nurses, cooks, or overseers; notices that husbands would no longer be responsible for debts of wives who had left their bed and board; statements of dissolution of partnerships and of new stores opening up "at the stand formerly occupied" by a vanished merchant. As reflections of the life and color of the times, they are far more rewarding than the few drab bits of local news items which occasionally got into the papers.

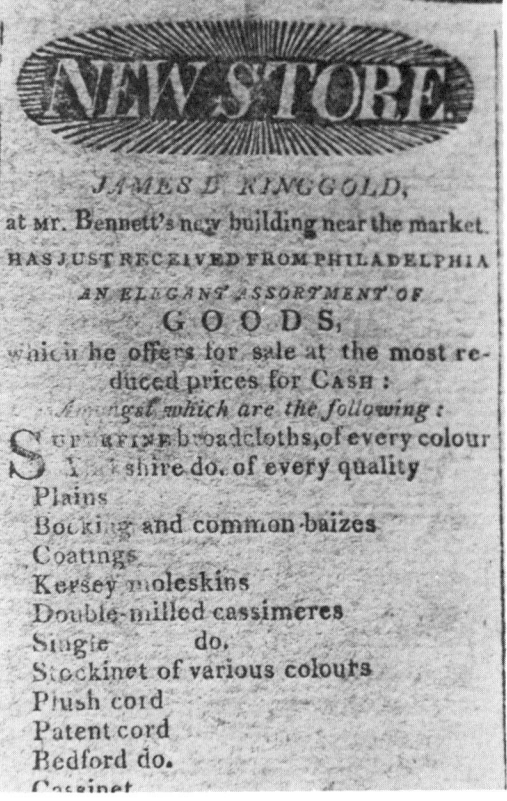

Early advertising featured simple woodcuts.

For many years, however, patent medicine advertising provided the bulk of their newspaper revenue for most Eastern Shore editors; indeed, it is difficult to see how some of them could have survived without it.

Some of these ads were sponsored by local druggists. Others were provided in ready-made form by the proprietors and, once printed up, could be inserted month after month with no additional cost for composition. Thus they were doubly welcome.

The claims made for the remedies they promoted were so preposterous as to verge on criminal fraud. An ad for Holloway's pills, "wonderful in cases of dropsy," listed thirty-five different ailments they could cure, ranging from sore throats to fits, venereal disease, consumption (tuberculosis), scrofula or King's evil, and ulcers. They sold for thirty-seven and one-half cents a box.

Advertised at the same time was Dr. Houghton's Pepsin, a "true digestive fluid or gastric juice" prepared from the fourth stomach of the ox following "directions of Baron Leibig, the great physiological chemist." According to the ad, Dr. Houghton's Pepsin was "a truly wonderful remedy for indigestion, dyspepsia, jaundice, liver complaint, consumption and debility." Best of all, it contained "no alcohol, bitters, or acids"—just plain old ox stomach extract.

Dr. Lockward's "celebrated anti-dyspeptic elixer" was a "certain cure for dyspepsia, liver, bilious, and nervous complaints; jaundice, general debility, lowness of spirits; and diseases incident to females." Hamilton's essence of mustard was even more effective; it cured "acute and chronic rheumatism, gout, palsy, lumbago, numbness, white swellings, chilblains, sprains, bruises, pain in the face and neck, &c."

Local merchants sold—over the counter—such drugs as opium and laudanum, an opium derivative which was very effective in keeping small children quiet and contented. It was many years before Eastern Shore parents discovered that in giving their youngsters laudanum, they were turning them into youthful dope addicts.

Also advertised were other fine products: Hahn's "true and genuine corn plaisters, speedily removing them root and branch without giving pain"; and Hahn's genuine eye water, "a sovereign remedy for all diseases of the eyes"; genuine Persian lotion, "celebrated among the fashionable throughout Europe" as an invaluable cosmetic in removing freckles, pimples, inflammatory redness, scurfs, ringworms, sunburn, and prickly heat; and sovereign ointment for the itch, an "infallible remedy" which could be "used with the most perfect safety by pregnant women." Dr. LeRoux's patented Indian Vegetable Specific was guaranteed to expel "the venereal poison, however deeply rooted in the constitution," without the dreadful side effects which often accompanied the use of mercury.

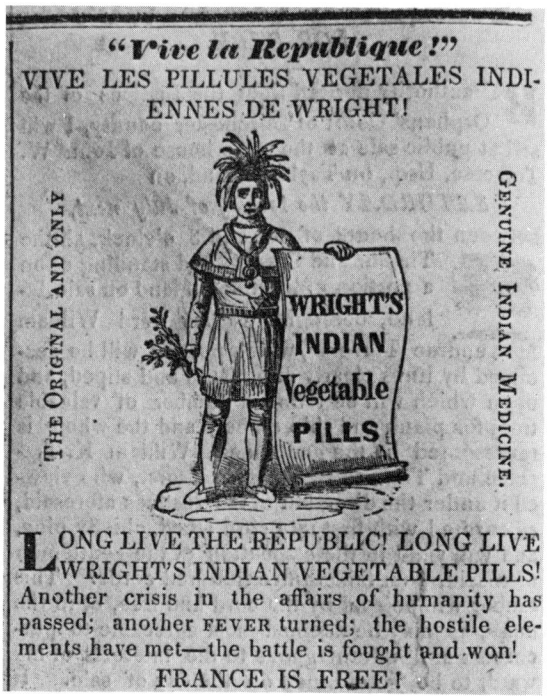
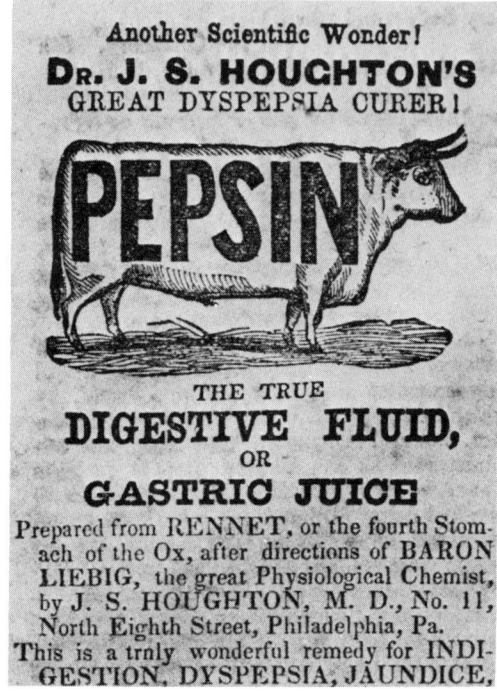

Patented cure-alls of the 1840s may not have been the miracle medicines their makers claimed, but they were a wonderful source of revenue for Eastern Shore editors.

The listing could go on and on. Editors considered it none of their business to police the claims made in the advertisements they published; and at that, the patent medicines of the day were probably less harmful than the bloodletting by means of leeches which was still a standard practice for most Eastern Shore physicians.

Nor was an editor's conscience likely to be troubled if his editorial moralizing contradicted his advertising. The *Eastern-Shore Whig*, for example, printed on page one of its October 10, 1835, issue this stern stricture entitled "Drunkenness":

> Drunkenness expels reason, drowns the memory, defaces beauty, diminishes strength, inflames the blood, causes internal, external, and incurable wounds, is a witch to the senses, a devil to the soul, thief to the purse, a beggar's companion, a wife's woe, and children's sorrow, makes a strong man weak, and a wise man a fool;

he is worse than a beast, and is a self murderer, who drinks the other's good health, and robs himself of his own.

In the same paper were ads for William H. Groome's store, with its fine stock of "Old Madeira wine, Gold and Pale Sherry, Tenerif and Port, J. Spirit, Old Rye Whiskey, &c"; for the tavern of Solomon Barrett, whose "bar is well stocked with the choicest liquors"; and for the Farmer's & Citizen's Retreat, in the most fashionable part of Easton, Elijah McDowell's Union Tavern, Solomon Lowe's Easton Hotel, and Henry C. Middleton's New House of Entertainment in Centreville, all of which emphasized their well-stocked bars in their advertising.

Life moved at a leisurely pace, and news of the "outside world"—by which was meant anything beyond the bounds of the Eastern Shore—was slow to trickle in. There were no wire services, no radio or television, no instantaneous transmission of information about wars and disasters. Europe must have seemed a million miles away. The roundabout means which foreign intelligence reached the Shore is reflected in an item published in the *Snow-Hill Messenger* on January 4, 1831:

> It is reported on the authority of a passenger who lately arrived from Europe, that he saw an extra issued from the office of the *London Courier*, that Russia had actually declared war against France.

Nothing further was said about the alleged war in subsequent issues, although there were reports from time to time on the revolution in France during which Charles X was forced to abdicate and Louis Philippe became king. These came in the form of one or two sentence items reprinted from New York dailies.

The dominance of the Methodist church, especially on the lower Shore, was evidenced in articles with a strongly moralistic tinge. The *Worcester County Shield and Farmers' Manual*, another Snow Hill paper, took a firm stand in 1846 against "theaters and bowling saloons," of which there couldn't have been too many in the village of Snow Hill. It also listed, among agencies of the devil, infidelity and the Universalist church, a New England sect which not only rejected the Methodist doctrine that only those who were "saved" could go to heaven, but favored the abolition of slavery.

The sad decline in moral standards since George Washington's day was noted by the *Cambridge Chronicle* of September 23, 1843. It warned of impending doom unless "extravagance and idleness ... luxury and dissipation" disappeared from the American scene. As a case in point, the *Chronicle* told readers:

> When Washington was president, his wife knit stockings in Philadelphia, and the mothers made doughnuts and cakes between Christmas and New Years. Now the

Cambridge Chronicle of 1848.

married ladies are too proud to make doughnuts, besides they don't know how, so they even send to . . . some . . . French cake maker, and buy sponge cakes for $3 a pound.

This proved, in the *Chronicle*'s view, that the United States might soon go the way of Sparta, which had lost her preeminence in ancient Greece "the moment luxury was introduced." Whether Spartan ladies had forgotten how to make doughnuts was not made clear.

High fashion, another Methodist target, was also viewed with alarm. The *Somerset Herald* in 1840 reported in grim detail on the death of a young lady who had been lacing her corset so tightly that she could scarcely breathe. "When she went to a doctor complaining of breathing difficulty it was already too late," the *Herald* mourned. "She was a large, healthy person, and was ignorantly led by the desire to please, to sacrifice her life at the shrine of fashion, and the prevailing idea of beauty of form. She was said to be of amiable disposition and correct moral habits, otherwise."

In the same vein, the Snow Hill *Borderer* reported in 1834 the story of a young man who wore such tight pantaloons when he called on his betrothed that his legs looked like "the handles of a wheel barrow tilted on end." The girl's mother took a horrified look at his skinny legs and chased him away, so that the engagement was broken off. The tale was presented as a warning of the dangers of following current fashions to extremes.

Like most other Shore papers, the *Borderer* devoted much space to the temperance movement, a favorite Methodist crusade. On May 11, 1834, its entire front page, and part of the second, were given over to the text of an address which had been delivered by Gordon M. Handy before the Worcester County Temperance Society at the Snow Hill Methodist Episcopal Church. Handy favored temperance.

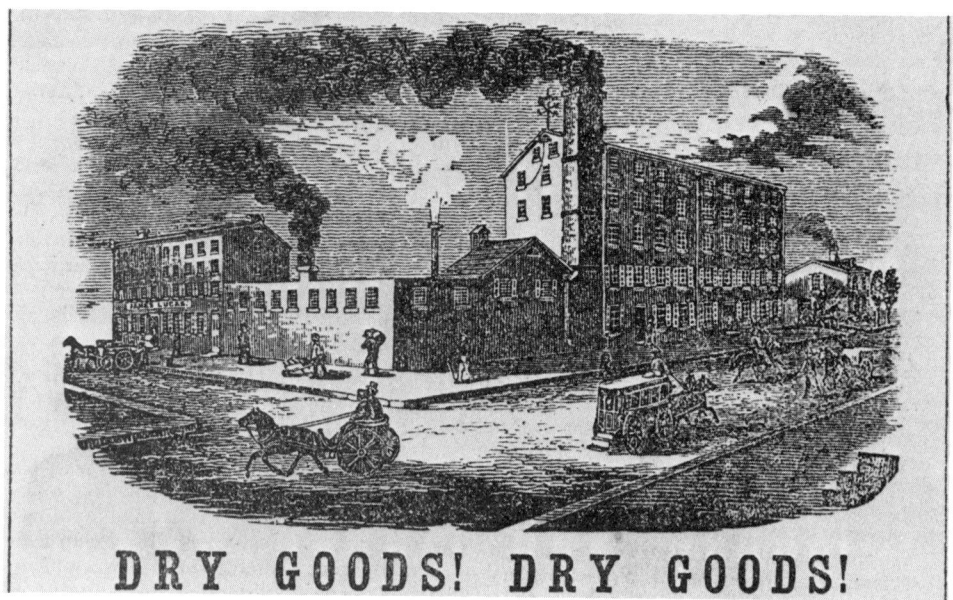

THE UNION TAVERN.

THE subscriber has opened a *Public House* at Easton, in those commodious buildings lately erected at the corner of Washington and Goldborough streets. He solicits public patronage, and invites the attention as well of the gentlemen of Talbot, whose business or pleasure may call them to town, as of all travellers.

No exertions shall be wanting on the part of the subscriber for the accommodation of those who may favor him with their calls; and he trusts that the assurance, which, he flatters himself, the character he has sometime maintained in the line of his business must afford, will be amply fulfilled by his unremitted endeavors to please and gratify his customers.

Dinners or suppers will be prepared for select parties of gentlemen, on the shortest notice, and in private apartments.

Particular attention will be paid by the

Ad illustrations improved in quality as the nineteenth century progressed. Compare the detail in the dry goods ad, from the 1850s, with the crude hotel picture of 1810.

In Snow Hill, even the Fourth of July took on an antiwhiskey flavor. According to the *Borderer*, on the morning of the Fourth in 1835 the townspeople assembled at the Presbyterian Church for a reading of the Declaration of Independence by Walter P. Snow (for whose family the town was named) and a patriotic oration by George R. Smith. In the afternoon they met again, this time at the Methodist Church, where James L. Vallandigham orated on Temperance "in his usual happy and impressive style."

Other than temperance reports and an occasional article on such good causes as the duties of the Sunday School teachers, almost the only local news carried in the *Borderer* concerned the great fire of November 24, 1834, in which forty houses, the Worcester County courthouse, eight stores, two hotels, and other structures were destroyed. "Never! No, never, can we forget the night of the 24th of November last," editor Lewis Caton wrote in a review of the past year published February 8, 1835. "Time may roll on in its usual course. New events may occur—but the eventful night with all its attendant and terrific horrors, can never be erased from the minds of those who witnessed them."

The disaster received widespread attention in the "outside" press, and donations to help rebuild Snow Hill flowed in from many areas. The Maryland General Assembly authorized the county to borrow $10,000 to build and equip a new courthouse. Over a period of weeks the *Borderer* reported receipt of $4,500 from the citizens of Philadelphia, $1,670 from Baltimore, $291 from Lancaster, Pennsylvania, and $216 from Salisbury, plus additional gifts from the Methodist churches in Smyrna, Delaware, and Elkton, and from individuals in Drummondtown, Virginia, Georgetown, Delaware, Easton, and Princess Anne. The final total was $7,859.95.

Despite its colorful name and its noble-sounding slogan ("Be Just and Fear Not—Let All the Ends Thou Aim'st at, be thy Country's, thy God's, and Truth's"), the *Somerset Iris and Messenger of Truth* was strictly a political sheet, founded for the sole purpose of supporting John Quincy Adams against that "dangerous" radical, Andrew Jackson. In issue number one, June 13, 1828, the editor declared political war on "doctrines which are believed by a large portion of the community, to be dangerous to the constitution and the liberties of our Republic," and on an individual (Jackson) "destitute of all proper qualifications for the civil head of this country." Ensuing issues carried almost nothing except slanted articles pointing out Adams' virtues and Jackson's deficiencies.

Nevertheless, its proprietors, owner Joseph Smith and printer George Brown, took the high road in discussing their newspaper. Its symbol pictured a suitably draped lady sitting on a rock, with flowers in front of her and a rainbow over her head. The word "Iris," they pointed out, referred not to the flower but to the rainbow, the proverbial sign of a covenant God had made with Noah. "In

Above, Despite its noble name, the *Somerset Iris and Messenger of Truth* was a political hack sheet promoting the 1828 candidacy of John Quincy Adams. When Adams lost to Andrew Jackson, it went out of business. *Left*, The "Iris," depicted here, was a rainbow symbolizing God's covenant with Noah.

its stupendous sweep, this glorious Bow, encircling the earth and heaven, is an emblem of the universal empire of 'truth.'" They hoped "that our Iris will not only be the harbinger of our country in the political storm which is now raging, but will continue, for years to come, the MESSENGER OF TRUTH to an enlightened, a reflecting, and a virtuous community."

Alas for these splendid aims; Jackson won the election, and the *Iris*, like John Quincy Adams, faded from the scene.

As its name implied, the *Democrat and Dorchester Advertiser*, established in Cambridge in 1845, was another paper of pronounced political views. In his prospectus editor John T. Taylor claimed that "the want of an independent and fearless advocate of the principles and policy of the Democratic Party in Dorchester County, has been deeply felt and lamented by the Democracy of the Whole State." He called on Democrats of the Eastern Shore, and particularly of Dorchester, to lend him a helping hand at a cost of only two dollars a year.

The *Democrat* succeeded where the *Iris* had failed. The Democratic Party became dominant in Dorchester County politics; and the newspaper which spoke for it, with some name changes and a couple of mergers, survived for more than one hundred and twenty years.

On one hot political issue, all Eastern Shore newspapers of this era were agreed. Slavery must not be tampered with; the institution was as sacred as prohibition or loose-fitting clothes. Abolition, as noted earlier, was an invention of the devil. And those who criticized the domestic slave trade, in which thousands of Eastern Shore blacks were torn from their homes and families and shipped to the Deep South, were either evil or misinformed.

As the Cotton Kingdom expanded in the 1820s, slave buyers in large numbers spread throughout the Shore, where black field workers were in surplus supply. Their offers of "Cash for Negroes" appeared in almost every Eastern Shore newspaper, and brought ready responses from hard-pressed farmers caught in the agricultural depression which followed the War of 1812.

However, many Eastern Shore slaveholders, sincerely concerned about the welfare of the blacks they owned, were reluctant to sell them for shipment out of Maryland, where slave conditions were said to be better than in the Deep South. The newspapers carried reassuring articles designed to soothe such fears. For example the *Cambridge Chronicle*, in its issue of Christmas Day, 1830, reprinted with evident approval a lengthy piece from a Mississippi paper, the *Natchez*, describing in glowing terms the treatment of blacks sent there from more northerly areas.

> In many respects their condition is bettered by the change . . . The people are considerate and humane; slaves for the most part work no more, nor harder than thousands of white people do in the old states, and as numbers do here. They are

> # CASH,
> ### AND THE HIGHEST PRICES GIVEN FOR
> # NEGROES,
> by the Subscriber, who has just received in addition to his former stock, a fresh supply of that much wished for article *CASH;* which he is willing to change for Slaves, on the most favourable terms to the owners.
>
>   JOSEPH B. WOOLFOLK,
> *Aug.* 6   at S. Lowe's Tavern.

Ads by slave buyers seeking blacks for shipment to the Deep South ran regularly in Eastern Shore newspapers.

well clothed and housed, they are properly attended to in sickness, if occasion requires they have the best medical attendance—they are well fed, sometimes live sumptuously; at particular seasons they have their frolics and balls, sing and dress, and dance, and whirl about on one leg equal to any stage player or palace dancer about the city of Washington. As to any acts of cruelty inflicted upon them, no more cases occur here than among the white people in other countries toward each other, and when this happens, they who inflict are not rendered popular by it—quite the contrary.

The writer invited any Northerner who doubted him to visit Mississippi. There he would see Negro housing "that would ornament the banks of the Delaware or the Potomac; and in our towns, particularly on Sunday, he would observe dozens . . . as fat and as sleek, and as full or airs and graces, and many of them as good for nothing, as some hundreds of our white brethren of the Atlantic cities."

Blacks might have told a different story; but in 1830 blacks were not writing articles to be published in the *Cambridge Chronicle*.

Runaway slave ads from the 1840s.

Another example of the attitude toward slavery appeared in the *Worcester County Shield*, which reported in gleeful detail the story of a Northerner who had been tarred and feathered in Lexington, Kentucky, for writing a letter critical of slavery. The article, reprinted from the *Louisville Courier*, quite obviously approved of the action. It said the Kentuckians felt "that this man who had been received and hospitably entertained, was guilty of great wrong." A party of two hundred went to his lodgings, took him to the courthouse yard, removed all his clothing, covered him with pitch from head to toe, shaved his head, and "nicely planted" the contents of several bags of feathers in the pitch. "He was then set loose, and charged to go and sin no more." After trying unsuccessfully to remove the stuff, "he left on the morning train."

In the climate of the times, most Eastern Shore whites would have found this very amusing. It was exactly what they believed critics of slavery deserved.

Another major concern in those same years was the perennial question of whether the Eastern Shore should secede from Maryland and unite with Delaware, to which it was naturally linked by geography. This was considered no joking matter; the notion of a united peninsula had great appeal for many Eastern Shoremen. It had surfaced as early as 1776, when Shore delegates made an unsuccessful attempt to include the right of secession in the first Maryland Constitution. It was fired up again in the 1820s by the Shore's disgruntlement over having to help pay for costly internal improvements, such as the Cumberland Road, the Chesapeake and Ohio Canal, and the Baltimore and Ohio Railroad, which the Eastern Shore claimed were solely for the benefit of the Western Shore and Baltimore.

When the Delaware Legislature in 1833 formally proposed a merger, the Maryland press reacted with vigor. The *Baltimore American*, speaking for the Western Shore, heaped ridicule on the proposal. Not content with having two United States senators whose votes, representing seventy thousand people, could neutralize the wishes of New York's two million, the *American* said, little Delaware now "grows ambitious . . . She has therefore cast longing eyes upon the territory of her neighbors—the Chesapeake Bay is her Rhine, and the Eastern Shore of Maryland what Belgium is to France . . . Delaware is stretching her hand over a territory twice as large and one-third more populous than herself."

But the *Easton Gazette* thought the proposition was worth serious study. It should be treated with "attention and respectfulness," and due consideration given to the effect it would have on both shores, "whether beneficial, injurious, or neutral." And a letter published in the *Gazette* undoubtedly expressed the feelings of many Eastern Shoremen. The writer, who identified himself only as "H. H.," enthusiastically embraced the idea.

> . . . I have long contemplated this union and amalgamation as a most desirable political change, calculated greatly to advance our own interests, whilst those of our Fellow Citizens on the Western Shore would not receive the slightest preju-

dice, if indeed we may be permitted to judge from their frequent assertions of our being on them a tax and a burden; and surely if this be the case, they will be the last to object to that which is so evidently to their own advantage.

The writer, later identified as Henry Hollyday, a prominent Talbot County attorney and landowner, went on to assert that the interests of the Eastern and Western shores were "often totally dissimilar and not infrequently conflicting. On the policy of Internal Improvements alone there is an almost impassable barrier between them." The Western Shore, he jeered, required great expenditures to make transportation and navigation feasible, while on the Eastern Shore "nature has most bounteously provided for us navigable streams and moorings for our craft at almost every man's door."

Despite the opposition of Baltimore, the proposal came close to winning approval by the Maryland General Assembly. Resolutions to implement it were passed by the House, forty votes to twenty-four, with a surprising number of Western Shore delegates in favor, but were killed in a Senate committee by a single-vote margin.

That stopped the secession movement for the time being. However, the Eastern Shore remained bitter over the Western Shore's growing dominance, particularly the burgeoning wealth and influence of Baltimore. When a proposal was advanced later in 1822 for a vote reform convention "to distribute the powers of government more equally among the inhabitants of the State," the *Easton Gazette* virtually roared with indignation. The reformers' real aim, said the *Gazette*, was "to produce a revolution in the State."

> The counties on the Eastern Shore and the small counties on the Western Shore are to become the victim and prey of the large Cities and Counties on the Western Shore, [and] the people of the former will be made "hewers of wood and drawers of water" to serve the wealth and power and haughtiness of their lusty, over-grown neighbors, who, insatiate of power as they are of wealth, seek now to devour all around them.
>
> . . . If there is a man on the Eastern Shore so dead to shame as to join these destroyers of our peace and safety, let him be known, that the people may avoid him as an infectious leper.

The reform move was dropped (although it would come up again), and the Eastern Shore appeased by appropriation of one million dollars to help build the proposed—but never completed—Eastern Shore Railroad down the spine of the peninsula. The political imbalance of which Baltimore complained, whereby one of the two United States senators was required by law to be from the Eastern Shore, and the smaller counties had relatively far more strength in the Legislature than the larger ones, would continue on the books for many years.

Eastern Shore secession came up again in 1842, when Worcester County delegate Levi Cathel brought up a bill in the House "to authorize the Eastern shore to attach themselves [sic] to the State of Delaware," provided Delaware and the United States Congress approved. This time an Eastern Shore editor played a leading role. Western Shore delegates wanted the measure to take effect only when and if the Eastern Shore pledged to pay its share of the huge state debt. Cecil County delegate Amor T. Forwood, hot-tempered editor of the *Cecil Democrat*, countered with an amendment calling on the state to give the recently completed Chesapeake and Delaware Canal outright to the Eastern Shore, with "all the right, title, claim and interest of the Western Shore . . . forever."

The result was deadlock, and Cathel's bill got nowhere. Tragically, Forwood was shot to death by a rival Elkton editor a year later in a dispute which arose in part over the same issue, as described later in this chapter.

But the secession movement lived on. It came up again at the Constitutional Convention of 1851, where Thomas Holliday Hicks of Dorchester County called for a statewide referendum on the right of the Eastern Shore to unite with Delaware "if they shall hereafter judge it for their interest to do so."

Most Eastern Shore newspapers applauded. Not so, however, Thomas K. Robson, the ardently proslavery young editor of the *Easton Star*. He feared a union with Delaware would throw the Eastern Shore into the orbit of Wilmington, which as he saw it was a hangout of abolitionists and a harbor for runaway slaves. Would the "bigoted partizans" such as Hicks, he asked, have the Eastern Shore "rush into the wedded embraces of Abolition Wilmington in preference to continuing an affectionate fellowship with Democratic Baltimore?" That led him into assertions which must have startled many readers familiar with the Shore's repeated efforts to gain the right of secession:

> We positively deny that there is any disposition on the Eastern Shore to secede from the Western Shore . . . The heart of every Eastern Shoreman pulsates with the true Maryland feelings—an ardent love of his state—and nothing could induce the people here to withdraw from the "Old Maryland Line." Indeed, secession of any kind is regarded as treason; and the worst of traitors are those whose infernal malice would prompt them to divide the State of Maryland.

Curiously, both parties to this debate completely reversed their views on secession when it became a national rather than a regional issue ten years later. Hicks, who favored the right of Eastern Shore secession in 1851, played a decisive role as governor in blocking Maryland efforts to secede from the Union in 1861, and was angrily denounced by Southern sympathizers on grounds he had been a secessionist himself when the interests of the Eastern Shore were at stake. Robson, who called secessionists "the worst of traitors" in 1851, became so passionate an advocate of Southern secession in 1861, that eventually he was exiled to Virginia for the duration of the Civil War.

At any rate Hicks' proposal, like the others before it, was defeated by Western Shore opposition; and the question of Eastern Shore secession has never received serious consideration since 1851, although it has been brought up again and again—sometimes in jest, sometimes in anger—whenever Eastern Shoremen felt themselves oppressed and frustrated by big and bossy Baltimore.

The practice of horsewhipping or otherwise chastising erring editors appears to have died out in recent years, replaced by the more civilized libel suit or retraction demand. It was not so in the days of Eastern Shore journalism's first flowering. Irate readers who took offense at editorial comments were so quick to respond with buggy whips, fists, or even guns that a pistol in the editor's desk drawer became a standard part of a newspaper's equipment.

Even John Peter Zenger, who might be described as the great-uncle of Eastern Shore journalism, was not immune to threats of violence. After he left Kent County and became editor of the *New-York Weekly Journal,* an article he published so insulted a member of the Governor's Council that he threatened to take to Zenger with a walking stick. Thereafter, it is recorded, Zenger went about his printing duties armed with a sword, a spectacle which afforded his rival publisher, William Bradford, much public amusement.

James Cowan, the Shore's first editor, was also the first to feel the sting of an irate reader's fists, when Jacob Gibson knocked him flat with one punch. Thomas Perrin Smith, Cowan's successful rival, was lashed with a buggy whip. Samuel B. Beach, editor of the *People's Monitor* of Easton, was challenged to a duel, and publicly labeled a "base coward and lawless slanderer" because he did not accept the challenge.

Thomas J. Keating, fiery editor of the *Centreville State Rights,* also was challenged to a duel, by George M. Russum. Russum disliked Keating's strongly pro-secessionist sentiments in the Civil War. Keating refused to duel, but in a caustic letter published in his paper informed Russum he could always be found at his newspaper office if his adversary wanted action.

Thomas E. Martin, editor of the *Worcester County Shield,* offered to fight the editor of the *Somerset Union* for insinuating that Martin was an "outsider"—as crowning an insult in 1857 as it was later. The *Union* had described Martin as the "imported editor" of the *Shield,* charged him with being "an habitual dealer in personalities alike contemptible and indecent."

"We are an Eastern Shoreman by birth and education, and in feeling Marylander all over," the *Shield* editor shot back. "We stand on our own 'dung

PROF. L. MILLER'S HAIR INVIGORATOR.

AN EFFECTIVE SAFE AND ECONOMICAL COMPOUND,

For Restoring Gray Hair to its original color without dyeing, and preventing the Hair from turning grey; for preventing Baldness and curing it when there is the least particle of vitality or recuperative energy remaining; for removing Scurf and Dandriff, and all cutaneous affections of the Scalp; for Beautifying the hair, imparting to it an unequalled gloss and brilliancy, making it soft and silky in its texture and causing it to curl readily.

THE great celebrity and increasing demand for this unequalled preparation, convince the proprietor that one trial is only necessary to satisfy the discerning public of its superior qualities over any other preparation at present in use. It cleanses the head and scalp from dandriff and other cutaneous diseases; causes the hair to grow luxuriantly, and gives a rich, soft, glossy and flexible appearance, and also where the hair is loosening and thinning, it will give strength and vigor to the roots, and restore the growth to those parts which have become bald, causing it to yield a fresh covering of hair.

There are hundreds of ladies and gentlemen in New York who have had their hair restored by the use of this Ivigorator, when all other preparations had failed. L. M. has in his possession letters innumerable testifying to the above facts, from persons of the highest respectability. It will effectually prevent the hair from turning gray until the latest period of life; and in cases when the hair has already changed its color, the use of the invigorator will with certainty restore it to its original hue, giving it a dark, glossy appearance. As a perfume for the toilet and a hair restorative it is particularly recommended, having an agreeable fragrance; and the great facilities it affords in dressing the hair, which, when moist with the invigorator can be dressed in any required form so as to preserve its place,

T. J. KEATING,
ATTORNEY AT LAW,
CENTREVILLE MD.

WILL give faithful attention to all business entrusted to his management, in Queen Anns, Kent, Caroline and Talbot Counties. Feb. 10, 1860.

G. P. Keating,
ATTORNEY AT LAW,

HAVING located at Towsontown, Baltimore county, Md., for the practice of his profession, will give strict and prompt attention to any business entrusted to his care in Baltimore city or county. Feb. 10, '60.

T. B. Quigley,
ATTORNEY AT LAW,

HAVING located in Centreville, will practice in the Courts of Queen Anns Kent, Caroline and Talbot Counties and give strict and prompt attention to all business entrusted to his care.

☞ Office formerly occupied as the Post Office. Dec. 6. 2859—y

MEDICAL CARD.
DR. J. A. HOLTON,

OFFERS his professional services to the citizens of Centreville and vicinty for the treatment of Disease in its various forms, and will promptly attend to all who may desire his aid and exert himself to the best of his skill for the cure of all invalids for whom he may be calledt to prescribe.

He can always be found at his residence on Commerce Street; below Water Street, when not professionally engaged. feb. 2, '58.

DENTISTRY.

J. T. TWILLEY, SURGEON DENTIST,

HAS removed to the office on Lawyer's Row formerly occupied by Dr. C. H. Emory, where he may always be found ready to attend to the duties of his profession, except

Lawyers, doctors, and dentists advertised alongside patented hair restorers in the *Centreville State Rights* of 1860.

hill'; and we defy our brother to show that we ever indulged in 'personalities' of any sort, unless we had been previously assailed . . . If our usually amiable brother will be satisfied with nothing less than a war of that sort, we will await his leisure with patience, and perhaps gratify his groveling ambition."

For sheer melodrama, however, nothing in Eastern Shore history—or in the history of American journalism, for that matter—can top the showdown in Elkton in 1843 between the editors of the *Cecil Whig* and the *Cecil Democrat*. Rival editors who felt like killing one another have been common enough; and there have been some brisk fist fights. but it is doubtful if anywhere else in journalistic annals can be found a case quite like the one in which Palmer C. Ricketts of the *Whig* shot to death Amor T. Forwood of the *Democrat*—and, what's more, got away with it even though the whole town saw him do it.

The argument started over a political issue—Forwood's stand as a delegate to the Legislature of the previous year against paying off the state debt—but it soon became intensely personal. Ricketts charged, in the vituperative style of the time, that the *Democrat* spoke for a party whose deeds were "evil, . . . foul, deceitful and black," and that Forwood showed "a vast deal of greenness in his editorial capacity." In ensuing exchanges such words as "falsehood," "fool," and "liar" were hurled back and forth. Forwood chided Ricketts for his lack of independence; Ricketts compared Forwood with a "young goose."

In the *Whig* of August 26 came the topper. Ricketts said of the *Democrat* of the preceding week;

> Some thing we had written was garbled, misrepresented and falsely quoted, and an attempt was made at criticism and ridicule. There are few things more ridiculous than the idea of the Democrat perpetrating criticism. A paper in which more philological errors are committed, or the editorial [content] of which is more insipid and puerile, is probably no where printed.

That did it. Forwood, who had a reputation for emotional outbursts, flew into a rage. He allegedly told friends "he'd cowhide Ricketts as sure as there was a God in heaven, if Ricketts didn't kill him" first, and that he would cut off Ricketts' ears with a pair of scissors. An even more sinister rumor was that he had vowed he and Ricketts "both could not live in the world together." It was freely predicted around Elkton "that one or the other . . . would be in hell before the week was out." Ricketts armed himself with a Colt six-shooter, and prepared for the worst.

On Tuesday, August 29, according to witnesses, Forwood waited on the porch of the post office at noon, the time Ricketts habitually went to pick up his morning mail. Forwood was carrying a heavy walking stick. But Ricketts didn't show up that day; perhaps forewarned, he started for the post office, then turned back.

Two long-vanished Princess Anne papers. The *Village Herald*, founded in 1827, and the *True Marylander* were united to form the *Marylander and Herald*.

On Wednesday morning, Ricketts wrote later, he spotted Forwood in the main street, wearing a linen coat with a weight dangling in a side pocket. "I believed it to be a pistol with which he intended to shoot me, and I believe it still," Ricketts asserted. Ricketts put his own revolver in his pocket, and carried it with him when he finally started for the post office.

Elkton's main street, on which the post office stood, was alive with visitors that morning. Many were Democrats, friends of Forwood, in town for a party convention at Dehaven's tavern; others were onlookers attracted by the gossip that the Ricketts-Forwood showdown was at hand.

They were not disappointed. While Forwood was standing on the porch of Dehaven's tavern talking to fellow Democrats, Ricketts walked up to the post office and entered. As he collected his mail, postmaster Adam Whann noted that he picked it up with his left hand, keeping his right hand in his pocket. Forwood saw him go in, rushed across the street to the *Democrat* office, emerged with a cane in his hand, and stepped up onto the post office porch just as Ricketts came out the door.

The two men were face to face at last. The time was almost exactly noon—High Noon at Elkton—on Wednesday, August 30, 1843.

As nearly as it can be pieced together from the often contradictory testimony of witnesses, what happened in the next thirty or so seconds was this: there were angry words. Forwood brandished his cane, then sprang at Ricketts, grabbing his right wrist and pinning his hand in his pocket. They struggled, and stumbled into the street. Four shots rang out. Forwood threw up his hands, declared "I'm a dead man" or "I am killed," and staggered toward Dehaven's tavern. Ricketts walked rapidly down the street in the opposite direction. Amid shouts of "arrest him!" and "seize the murderer!" Sheriff Edward L. Foard sped down the street after Ricketts, who submitted to arrest after being assured Foard would protect him from mob violence.

Inside Dehaven's tavern, Forwood lay on the floor in extreme agony. A friend stripped off his linen coat, and if there were weapons in its pockets, they were quietly removed. A witness later testified that when he examined the coat, the contents of the pockets were only a handkerchief, pencil case, penknife and a plug of tobacco. A doctor found a single-barrelled pistol in the pocket of Forwood's pantaloons, and set it aside without looking to see if it was loaded. It quickly disappeared.

The stricken man's three wounds (one shot had missed) were dressed, and a ball was extracted from his right shoulder. He was placed on a bed, where he lay for the rest of the day and evening, in extreme pain but for most of the time conscious and talking volubly. He "couldn't stand" the things Ricketts had written about him. He had never meant to shoot him, but wanted to fight him with his fists. Ricketts was a "cowardly rascal" for firing his gun so often; but Forwood forgave him and hoped God would forgive him. That night Forwood sank into a coma, and about 9 o'clock he died.

Ricketts lost no time in getting his side of the story into print. In Saturday's *Whig*, edited from his jail cell, he published a lengthy account stressing his claim that he had acted in self-defense. Forwood had sprung upon him, carrying a heavy stick; while they wrestled, "the exertion fired the pistol." Even after that, Forwood had continued to attack and Ricketts, retreating, fired three more shots. "No man, God knows, can regret the occurrence more than we do, yet no man we venture to assert would have done otherwise than we did," Ricketts wrote.

The *Democrat* told a different story. Under the heading, "A HORRIBLE DEED!!!," its new editor, T. M. Coleman, insisted that it was Forwood who had acted in self-defense. While the two men were talking, this version maintained, Forwood had seen Ricketts attempt to draw a pistol from his pocket, and had seized him by the arm to prevent it. "Ricketts jerked his arm from Mr.

Forwood's grasp, and stepped back and fired." An accompanying eulogy, edged in black, described Forwood as "a generous and noble hearted young man; cut down in the flower of his youth, and in the full spring-tide of his hopes."

Ricketts was charged with three counts of manslaughter, since doctors could not be sure which of Forwood's three wounds was the fatal one. For the next eight weeks he continued to edit the *Whig* from his jail cell; he had hundreds of visitors, many of them, as he wrote afterward, ladies whose "kind hands and warm hearts" did much "to light up the gloom of our prison." Sheriff Foard and his family treated him as an honored guest.

The trial, which began October 26, was a series of triumphs for the defense from start to finish. At the beginning, the judges ruled prospective jurors could be seated even if they had expressed an opinion on the case; later they barred the prosecution from presenting any evidence on the articles in the *Whig* which had enraged Forwood, and which might have shown malice on Ricketts' part.

Before a crowded courtroom, witness after witness for the prosecution told varying, often contradictory stories of what they had seen and heard. One witness said Forwood had challenged Ricketts to throw aside his arms and fight him "like a gentleman," and said he had distinctly heard the click of a pistol being cocked in Ricketts' pocket before Forwood seized his wrist. No one else could confirm that. Others claimed that before firing the last shot Ricketts had taken deliberate aim, and had then said: "There, d—n you, you s— of a b—, I've killed you at last!" This was firmly denied by several defense witnesses, who swore that Ricketts had never used profanity in his life. The defense witnesses gave uniform accounts, all insisting that Forwood had been the attacker, and that Ricketts had acted in self-defense.

After hearing thirty-five witnesses over a period of three days, the jury got the case at noon on Saturday, October 28. Four hours and twenty minutes later they returned with their verdict: not guilty on all three counts.

"Mr. Ricketts rose in his place, and was instantly surrounded by many friends, who shook hands with him, congratulating him on the result," reported the Baltimore *Sun*, which devoted more than six columns of space to the trial. "On leaving the court house, he walked to the . . . dwelling of the Sheriff, to take leave of the family, accompanied by perhaps three hundred gentlemen of the town and neighboring country."

Had justice really been done? It is impossible to say now, except to note that the prosecution's case was badly handled and was crippled by adverse rulings from the bench. In effect it was Forwood, not Ricketts, who had been on trial; and he was not there to defend himself.

At any rate, most Cecil Countians were delighted with the result. Ricketts continued as editor and publisher of the *Whig*, except for a brief absence, until his death March 8, 1860. "He died," wrote George Johnston in his 1881 *History*

The *Cecil Whig* of November 4, 1843, devoted nine columns to the trial of editor Palmer C. Ricketts for the slaying of Amor T. Forwood.

of Cecil County, "respected by all, and deeply regretted by a very large portion of the community in which he lived."

If editorial homicide was the big news of the era in Cecil County, it was bigotry and its political effects which attracted the most attention at the other end of the Shore. No history of Eastern Shore journalism would be complete without consideration of the peculiar cult called "Know-Nothingism," particularly in the lower Shore counties, where for several years it dominated politics and took over some segments of the press.

The Know-Nothing movement grew out of an anti-Catholic and anti-foreign secret society called the Order of the Star-Spangled Banner. The society had an elaborate ritual and stern discipline. When members were asked about it, they were instructed to say, "I know nothing"—hence the name. The Know-Nothings believed the Vatican wanted to control the United States, that foreigners, especially Irish and Germans, brought dangerous, un-American ideas with them to America, and that radicals driven out of Europe after the unsuccessful revolutions of 1848 were plotting to seize the Republic.

They first gained strength in Baltimore, where their original aims were laudable reforms. They sought to break the power of the Democratic bosses who controlled the city through the Irish Catholic and German vote, and who cooped up drunks and loafers and voted them again and again. One of those so trapped, who died as a result, was an alcoholic poet and author named Edgar Allan Poe.

However, the Know-Nothings and their political wing, the American Party, resorted to methods at least as bad as the bosses they sought to oust. Members were required to swear they would vote for no one "unless he be an American-born citizen, in favor of Americans ruling America, nor if he be a Roman Catholic." They had to promise to obey all orders of the State Council, even if they personally disagreed. Candidates for office had to pledge that if elected they would "remove all Foreigners, Aliens or Roman Catholics" from any political jobs they controlled.

Baltimore Know-Nothing clubs rejoiced in such names as the Red-Necks, Rip-Raps, Black Snakes, Tigers, Gladiators, Ranters, and Blood Tubs. Many were called "plug uglies" because their favorite weapon was the carpenter's awl, which they used to punch holes in opposition voters and drive them away from the polls. The awls were attached to rubber bands fastened above the elbow, so that they vanished up the sleeve after being used. At a gigantic Baltimore rally in October, 1859, speakers stood under a huge awl three feet in length, while a blacksmith stood at a forge manufacturing awls for distribution. The Know-Nothings fought pitched battles in the city streets against old-line Democrats, and kept so many naturalized citizens and Catholics from voting that for a time they ruled Baltimore and most of Maryland. Their high point came in 1856 when Millard Fillmore, former president and the American Party candidate, carried Maryland—the only state he won—and Thomas Holliday Hicks of Dorchester County, the Know-Nothing candidate, was elected governor by a coalition of voters from Baltimore City and the Eastern Shore. Eight were killed and more than two hundred and fifty injured in election rioting that year.

The Know-Nothing program had great appeal to the native-born, almost entirely Protestant citizenry of the Eastern Shore. Politically their main strength was in former adherents of the Whig Party, which had disintegrated after the election of 1852, shattered by irreconcilable differences between proslavery Southerners and free soil Northerners. But their antiforeign, anti-Catholic doctrines attracted many Democrats as well.

In March, 1855, the *Cambridge Chronicle*, which had been a Whig paper, noted that the American Party candidate for town commissioner, William Kirby, had carried a recent election, seventy-six to five. From what he could learn, said editor B. G. Tubman, the party was "equally as strong in the country" outside Cambridge.

Although he denied membership in "any Know-Nothing society or lodge," Tubman gave the movement a strong endorsement. "We cannot but admire the object that they represent to have in view and recognize in their doctrines the first teachings and warnings of George Washington, our Country's father, to us and future generations of freeman. We sincerely hope this new party may effect much good—purify the political atmosphere and be of great benefit to our beloved country."

Shortly after that, on May 2, 1855, a new paper called the *American Eagle* was established as the official organ of the American Party of Dorchester. Tubman soon closed down the *Chronicle*, and within a year proprietor Reuben S. Tall was able to boast that the *Eagle* had "a larger circulation than any other paper ever published in the lower counties" of the Shore.

The *Cambridge Democrat*, as might be expected, thought very little of the Know-Nothings. It called the movement a "conspiracy of the clubs" to overthrow the state government, "in order that law and order may be trampled on all over the state, as for the last two years it had been in Baltimore." This object, the *Democrat* claimed in April, 1858, "is becoming day by day more apparent, well understood, and obnoxious."

There were some Know-Nothing papers on the upper Shore. The short-lived *Union Reformer* was established in Elkton in 1855 to promote the American Party, and after its demise the *Cecil Whig* flirted with Know-Nothingism for a time. But it was in the counties south of the Choptank that the movement achieved its strongest hold. "The Know-Nothing orators went through the country two years ago and preached flaming sermons," the *Worcester County Shield* reported in 1857, ". . . and the people responded favorably and elected an overwhelming majority of Know-Nothings to the legislature."

Know-Nothings on the Eastern Shore voted in 1856 for Millard Fillmore, shown in this cartoon as a peacemaker between North and South. He carried Maryland, but lost to Democrat James Buchanan. (Courtesy Library of Congress)

The *Shield*, a Democratic paper, asked scornfully why the Know-Nothings had not carried out their campaign promises. They "have had the control of Maryland for the last two years, and have done nothing to put down Catholics and foreigners and paupers and criminals. Petitions poured in on the last Maryland legislature, to have the nunneries inspected, but they absolutely refused . . . Alas, the chief fruits of Know-Nothingism are mobs and riots, murder and bloodshed."

Other splinter factions also sprang up as the Whig Party disintegrated. One was the Locofocos, a wing of the Democrats, whose name was said to have come from a self-igniting cigar which was popular at the time. Just what the Locofoco Party stood for was a puzzle to the *Cambridge Chronicle:*

> With the rapacious, it goes for Cuba, with the South for the repeal of all compacts favorable to the North—in New York it is clamorous for Free Soil, in South Carolina for unmitigated slavery—to commerce it promises free trade; to Pennsylvania and Louisiana protection to iron and sugar . . . With Young America on stilts, it strides over the land and over water, to annex the Pacific Ocean with all its cannibal islands—and sympathizes, no doubt, with the man in the moon.

But by far the most dangerous splinter group, from the viewpoint of the Eastern Shore, was an organization which had usurped the name of the old Jeffersonians, and called itself the Republican Party. On a platform opposing any extension of slavery, it was making rapid strides in the North. In 1856 its candidate for president, John C. Fremont, swept the Northeast and captured more than a million votes. To Eastern Shoremen it stood for what they hated and feared most: abolition of slavery and civil rights for blacks. Eastern Shoremen claimed this doctrine ran directly counter to God's will. Could any honest man, the *Worcester County Shield* asked in July, 1857, "be willing to unite with the fanatical Abolitionists who, with the insane proposal to elevate the negro race to a social and political equality with the white, are openly warring against a decree of infinite wisdom and the wise and wholesome institutions established by our patriotic forefathers? . . . God, the Infinite Ruler, has said, 'we must do unto others as we would that others should do unto us.'" Although there were differences of opinion on slavery, the *Shield* undoubtedly spoke for an overwhelming majority of Eastern Shore whites.

By 1860 the Know-Nothings' six-year reign of terror was at an end in Maryland. Their excesses had alienated even those who in the beginning had supported their program of ousting Catholics and the foreign-born from office. In Baltimore, a reform ticket won the mayoralty by nearly two to one, and the American Party, like the Whigs before it, simply fell apart. Hicks would be a lame duck govenor without any strong party organization behind him when, near the end of his term in 1861, he faced the fateful issues brought to a head by the onset of the Civil War.

In the election of 1860 the Eastern Shore, like all of Maryland, faced a far more fearful choice than that between Know-Nothings and Democrats. The nation was tearing itself apart over slavery. At issue was whether the American Union itself could or should be saved.

The *American Eagle*, established in Cambridge to support the Know-Nothing movement, soon boasted it had the largest circulation of any newspaper ever published on the lower Shore.

CHAPTER FOUR

Civil War
A SHORE DIVIDED

"CITIZENS OF MARYLAND!" said the *Cambridge Democrat* on October 24, 1860, "every sacred political tie which commands our veneration, binds us unalterably to the South, and with the South and her institutions are all our interests closely interwoven. Every blow inflicted on the South must be felt by Maryland, and if ever was a time when she should be united, it is now . . . Is it not your duty, then, as Southern men, to unite and vindicate the South by your support? . . . Mr. Breckinridge represents the principle you must prefer, and Lincoln the principle you must despise . . . Your vote for Mr. Bell is but evading the issue, disuniting the South, and weakening the bonds of union."

"The question to be decided on Tuesday next, is whether the Union shall be preserved," said the *Easton Gazette* on November 3. "A united South for Mr. Breckinridge will mean in the cotton states a united South for secession, for disunion, and for war with the North. Are the people of Maryland prepared for this? . . . If they are not, if they believe that secessionism at the South is no whit less reprehensible than sectionalism at the North, then let them vote for Bell and Everett, proclaiming thereby their detestation of both these heresies to freedom."

All up and down the Shore, newspapers were bombarding their readers with similar rhetoric as they lined up on opposite sides in the fateful presidential election which was soon to come. Of the four candidates, only the Deep South's John Breckinridge and the Constitutional Union Party's John Bell mattered on the Eastern Shore. Except as targets for abuse, Abraham Lincoln and Stephen A. Douglas could be ignored.

But how to choose? The newspapers spoke in clarion tones, but what they said was so conflicting that it was no wonder the Eastern Shore's voters were confused. They were united, as was the Shore's press, in dislike of Lincoln and all his new Republican Party seemed to stand for. But the issue they faced was not a clear-cut one: not Lincoln versus the South, or abolition versus slavery, or even one party against the other. What they

Left, John C. Breckinridge. (Courtesy Library of Congress)   *Right*, John Bell. (Courtesy Library of Congress)

must decide with their votes was how best the Union which their ancestors had helped put together with such pain and pride could be preserved. Breckinridge and the Deep South stood for preserving the Union only if it could be done on their terms. Bell, if he stood for anything at all, appeared to favor preserving both slavery and the Union on almost any terms.

It was a hard decision, the most difficult the voters had ever faced, or ever would. A vote for Breckinridge was clearly a vote against Lincoln and the abolitionists—but was it also a vote for secession and war, as the Unionist newspapers charged? A vote for Bell was a vote against war—but was it also a vote to divide the South, and thus help the abolitionists, as Breckinridge supporters claimed?

The Eastern Shore press, at least in the northern counties, was sharply divided on the issue. Probably nowhere else in America were the lines of local newspaper antagonism more clearly drawn. In the Southern states there was one predominant view, in the Northern states an opposite one. But Maryland, and especially the Eastern Shore, was in the middle, its people torn between love of country and support of slavery. In Elkton, Chestertown, Centreville, Denton, Easton, and Cambridge, each side had an editorial voice. The division fell along the following lines:

Cecil County: the *Whig* strongly pro-Union, the *Democrat* strongly pro-South.

Kent County: the *Kent News* pro-Union, the *Kent Conservator* pro-South.

Queen Anne's County: the *Centreville Times* (forerunner of the *Observer*) pro-Union, the *State Rights Advocate* (later the *Centreville State Rights*) pro-South.

Caroline County: the *American Union* pro-Union, the *Denton Journal* pro-South.

Talbot County: the *Easton Gazette* pro-Union, the *Easton Star* pro-South.

Dorchester County: the *American Eagle* (later the *Intelligencer*) pro-Union, the *Cambridge Democrat* pro-South.

In later years a belief would spring up that the Eastern Shore had been a hotbed of Rebel sympathizers when the war began. To an extent this was true; but the equal strength of Union support should not be overlooked. Its existence is demonstrated by the number of pro-Union newspapers and the fact that they included some of the most influential on the Shore. The *Cecil Whig* has been described as "probably the most radical journal in Maryland" during the war; the *Centreville Times* was Queen Anne's oldest paper; the *Kent News* so dominated its area that a new paper, the *Kent Conservator,* had to be organized to represent the Southern view; and the *Easton Gazette*, almost as radical as the *Whig*, was Talbot County's leading journal at the time.

South of the Nanticoke, there were no sharp distinctions. The lower counties, more closely aligned with Virginia, in general espoused the Southern cause, and this was reflected in the few newspapers which served them.

At the time of the 1860 election, there were only three papers on the Lower Shore: Princess Anne's *Somerset Union*, which was completely Southern in viewpoint despite its name; Salisbury's *Sentinel*, equally strong for the South; and Snow Hill's *Worcester County Shield*, which reluctantly and hesitantly supported the Union although its editor, H. Everett Smith, confessed he had great misgivings in doing so.

Writing in July, 1861, Smith graphically described the mental agonies he had gone through as he watched the nation split itself in two. The Union should be preserved, he thought; he had not in any way favored Southern secession. But neither did he have any sympathy "with the Abolition spirit, so improperly, but very strongly, intermixed with the necessary defensive action of the government." He hoped with all his heart that Maryland could remain neutral.

Although he favored the Union, "under which we still exist, and shall ever hope to," he recognized that many of his friends did not. He person-

In the Northern states, the 1860 presidential campaign was an "undecided political prize fight" between Lincoln and Douglas. But on the Eastern Shore these two did not count. The battle was between Breckinridge and Bell.

ally could never join the Union army, he declared, because "too many that are near and dear to us" were already fighting on the Rebel side. He had no desire to get in the way of their bullets, "or that they—though wrong, being yet sincere—run any risk from death missiles dispatched by us even in the righteous cause of the Union."

"And what a horrible state of things is this," he concluded sadly.

R. Reese Morgan, coeditor of the *Sentinel*, had no such qualms about possibly having to shoot his friends. Shortly after hostilities began, he

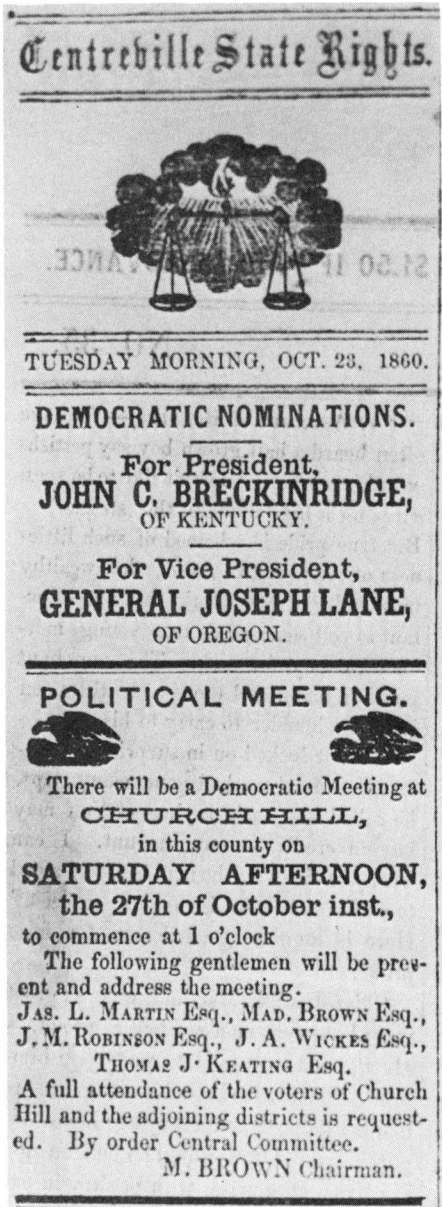

Editor Keating's political persuasion is quite apparent.

closed down the *Sentinel* and went south to join the Rebels, leaving Salisbury without a general circulation newspaper for the duration of the war.

Probably the most ardent Eastern Shore advocate of the Southern cause in the prewar period was Thomas J. Keating of Centreville. He founded the *State Rights Advocate* in 1857 with no other purpose in mind, and devoted its

SALISBURY SENTINEL.
Friday, August 10, 1860.

Salisbury Sentinel.
BY JNO. MORGAN & SON.
SALISBURY, MD,
FRIDAY, AUG. 11, 1860.

OFFICE DERANGED.

Owing to the deranged condition of our office, occasioned by the dreadful conflagration which has just laid our town in ruins, we are unable to issue but a portion of a sheet this week, and we are apprehensive that it will not be in our power to issue a full one the ensuing week. In consequence of the proximity of the fire to our office, we deemed it advisable to remove its contents, and in so doing our type was thrown completely into *pie*; and with our small force some considerable time will be required to rectify and distribute the same and crave the indulgence of our patrons.

☞ A meeting of the citizens of the town will be held at 8 o'clock this evening, at Bird's Hotel, for the purpose of making arrangements for investigating the origin of the late fire, and for the relief of the sufferers thereby.

MANY CITIZENS.
Friday, Aug. 10, 1860.

DREADFUL CONFLAGRATION!
SALISBURY IN RUINS.
PROPERTY DESTROYED TO THE AMOUNT OF NEARLY
$200,000,
SOME 60 HOUSES CONSUMED.

On Thursday morning last, between three and four o'clock, our citizens were aroused from their slumbers by the startling and alarming cry of fire!. It was some time subsequently to the first alarm ere the inhabitants generally were awakened, it being that period of time for sleep when persons generally slumber most soundly. In consequence, the fire had made considerable progress before much effort could be made for its extinguishment; but after assembling in full force, and putting forth the utmost exertions of which they were capable with the restricted facilities for its suppression at their command, the raging element speedily and rapidly extended from the building in which it originated to those adjacent, and from thence to others more remote, until nearly sixty tenements were consumed covering an area of some two and a half acres, and involving a loss in personal and real estate of some two hundred thousand dollars. By this dreadful calamity a large portion of the business part of our town is destroyed, and a number of our most worthy citizens deprived of shelter and support.

The desolation is complete, naught remaining but the denuded chimneys of the consumed buildings, except in one solitary instance, that of the Protestant Episcopal Church; its walls, which are brick, are still standing.

This dreadful fire originated in the building occupied in part by F. Newman, as a clothing store, and situated on Main Street about the center of the town.

From thence it completely devastated both sides of Main Street, extending from Mr. Oliver Tilghman's on the South side from Mr. Jno. White's to the corner of Boundry street and thence to Mr. C. F. Whitelock's dwelling. On the east of Boundry street, the buildings included between Col. Leonard's dwelling and Mr. J. Bird's Hotel were consumed. Also, on the street immediately north of Main several buildings, including the Protestant E. Church, were destroyed.

Three of our principal Dry Good Merchants were burned out, namely Wm. Birkhead whose probable loss is about $5000 —partially insured; Rider & Toadvine lost the most of their Goods, amounting to between 8 and 9000 dollars, insured about one half; S. C. Seabreaze, loss very considerable though insured to the amount of $5000. Mr. C. Whitelock lost almost the entire contents of his store, saving as we learn little or nothing whatever. The furniture generally was removed from the burnt buildings but much of it was injured in the removal, and we regret to learn that there is reason to suppose that much of that which was removed, as also the goods removed from the stores was subsequently stolen. Mr. P. Toadvine, and Dr. Wm. Rider were two of the largest property holders who sustained loss. Both were insured to a considerable amount, yet nothing near sufficient to cover their loss. Mr. Toadvine's it is computed will not be less than $12,000.

Below we give in detail the sufferers by his dreadful visitation.

Wm. S. Parsons,		Dwelling.
Jno. W. Morris,		do
C. F. Dashiells,	Store,	do
Jr. P. Rider,	Office,	
Pernell Toadvine,	do	do
Wm. Birkhead,	Store,	do
Amos Woodcock,	do	
F. Newman,	do	
S. C. Seabreaze,	do	do
Mrs. M. Owings,		do
Jno. Kaler,	do	do
Geo. Humphreys,	do	
Wesley Rider,		do
Mrs. Jane Collier,		do
Rev. J. Humbard,	do	do
C. Whitelock,	do	
Wm. Livingston,	do	
Jesse Dashiell,	do	
Levin Collier,	do	do
T. Parvin,	do	
Mrs. J. Wood,		do
I. H. W. Stanford,		do
B. Parker,		do
P. W. Bradley,		do
Dr. W. T. Smith,		do
Capt. Bush,	Hotel.	
Rufus Ennis,		do
H. J. Brewington,	Store	do
Mrs. Fish,		do
Dr. Wm. Rider,		do
Rider & Toadvine,	do	
Mrs. M. Mitchell,		do
Mrs. J. Maddux,		do
Isaac Nichols,		do
Mrs. S. White,		do
Wesley Williams,	Shop.	
H. T. Parsons,	Store.	
M. Taylor,		do
Jas. A. Venables,	do	
Mrs Evans,		do
Robt. Abdell,		do
David Vance,		do
Levin Houston,		do
Wm. Evans,		do
Mrs. Bopp,	do	do
Unoccupied,		4 do
Beside the Post Office and the Protestant E. Church.		

This calamity doubtless will excite the sympathy and condolence of the citizens of adjacent towns and cities, eliciting some substantial manifestation of their benevolence. Many of the sufferers have lost in the destruction of their property, their entire dependence, and without foreign aid it will be almost impossible for them to replace their lost possessions. The citizens of Salisbury whose property escaped the ravages of the devouring element, promptly extended their hospitality to the homeless sufferers, and all that they can do further for their relief will most certainly be done by them. But so large a portion of the community are sufferers, that it cannot be expected that much home assistance can be extended.

There is one feature at least in this calamity which imperiously demands sincere gratitude and thankfulness, and that is the wonderful preservation of human life. No life was lost and no one seriously injured, although those who were laboring to extinguish the fire and save property were surrounded by the devouring flames, and exposed to falling, burning fragments.

☞ Geo. Humphreys of F. has secured the small Store house adjoining Capt. Rotan's Store, where he is prepared to accomodate his friends and customer, as usual with Boots, Shoes, and Gaiters.

COMMISSIONERS SALE.

By virtue of an order of the Circuit Court for Somerset County, sitting in Equity, the undersigned Commissioners will sell at public auction at Bush's Hotel, in the town of Salisbury, on Saturday, the 18 day of August next, at 2 o'clock P. M., all that

HOUSE AND LOT

in Somerset County, near the town of Salisbury, of which Mary Davis died, seized. This Lot lies on the East side of the County road leading to Spring Hill, and on the North side of the road leading from said County road to Bailey's or Humphreys Mill.

Terms of sale: One hundred dollars in cash on the day of sale, the remainder to be secured by the bond of the purchaser to the State of Maryland conditional for the payment of the purchase money and two years with interest, day of sale.

WILLIAM S. PARSONS,
WILLIAM WALLER,
HANDY FOOKS,
PERRY W. BRADLEY,
PERNELL TOADVINE,
Commissioners.
July 28, '60—ts.

NOTICE.

We hereby caution and forwarn all persons whomsoever from trespassing on our lands with dog or gun, or in any way whatever, under the penalties of the laws in such cases made and provided.
G. W. PARSONS,
M. A. PARSONS.
July 28, '60—ly.

The *Salisbury Sentinel* of August 10, 1860, reported the "dreadful conflagration" which had left the town in ruins. Soon after, the editor closed the paper and went south to join the Rebels.

Centreville's *State Rights Advocate*, edited by Thomas J. Keating, was the most forthright pro-South paper on the Eastern Shore.

columns largely to proslavery propaganda, often to the exclusion of other news. In the *Advocate* and its nominal successor, the *Centreville State Rights*, Keating published nothing which would give comfort to his enemies, and used material couched in the most virulent terms if it favored slavery or promoted Southern solidarity. Even the short stories he printed as entertainment bore pointed titles: "Another Yankee Trick" was the tale of how an evil-minded Northerner tried to sweet-talk a lovely Maryland belle, and how her boyfriend outwitted him.

Typical of the Keating approach was his prominent display, in the issue of March 13, 1860, of the text of a speech delivered in the Maryland House of Delegates by a proslavery representative, Colonel C. W. Jacobs. It began:

> Free-negroism is an excrescence, a blight, a mildew, a fungus—hanging on [and] corrupting the social and moral elements of our people in Maryland. It has already to a great extent contaminated the slave population and rendered them comparatively worthless.

Jacobs went on to present a halcyon view of slave life before the "fungus" of freedom infected Maryland blacks. "Our slaves were happy and content . . . Their labor [was] always reasonable, and never required in bad weather or unreasonable hours." Slave children did no work at all before they were ten or twelve years old. Slaves who became ill were nursed "by our wives and daughters" and attended by the family physician. "And when death comes we bury them decently in the old graveyard, where the family lies, and bedew their graves with the tear of heartfelt affection."

Such idyllic pictures of Maryland slavery appeared often in Eastern Shore newspapers before the war. Editors told readers what they wanted to believe:

Ownership of *Uncle Tom's Cabin*, from which this illustration was taken, was a penitentiary offense in antebellum Maryland. (Courtesy Library of Congress)

that slavery was a beneficent institution, and that slaves were happy in their bondage—or had been before life was complicated by emancipation and other Northern-devised contaminations.

There was no legal way such propaganda could be countered. Under Maryland's harsh censorship laws it was a crime punishable by ten to twenty years in prison to prepare or circulate printed matter having a tendency to stir up discontent among blacks. The laws were intended primarily to halt the flow of Northern abolitionist literature into Maryland, but they also applied to local newspapers. No Eastern Shore editor, even if he wanted to, could dare to publish any material critical of slavery without running the risk of going to prison.

The censorship applied even to individual ownership of books. In 1857 the *Cambridge Democrat* reported the trial of a free black, Sam Green, who was charged with having in his possession a copy of Harriet Beecher Stowe's famous antislavery novel, *Uncle Tom's Cabin*. Green was found guilty and sentenced to ten years in prison; he actually served five of them before it was revealed the book was not his, but had been planted by the "party of gentlemen" who had raided his house looking for evidence that he had been helping blacks escape via the Underground Railroad. The *Democrat's* only complaint was that he was not also convicted for possessing a map of Canada and some other papers "having a tendency to create discontent, etc., among the people of color in the State." Despite "the mass of evidence given, to show the prisoner's guilt," and the fact that "nine-tenths of the community in which he lived, believed that he had a hand in the running away of slaves," the judge ruled that the law did not apply to these other documents.

"We trust, that at the next meeting of the Legislature there will be such amendments as to make the law on this subject, perfectly clear and comprehensible," said the *Democrat*. "Slavery must be protected or it must be abolished."

Keating's advocacy was so strong that late in 1860 his paper was named by the *Baltimore American* as one of only two all-out "disunion papers" in Maryland, the other being the *Patapsco Enterprise*. All other Maryland publications at least hedged their positions, according to the *American*. Keating accepted the designation gladly, provided it did not mean "that we advocate secession as expedient—for we have not done that—but because we number it among the rights of the states." Within a few weeks, however, after South Carolina seceded and other states lined up to join her, he called on Maryland to join the Confederacy.

In the 1860 presidential contest Maryland neither spoke out in "tones of thunder" for Breckinridge, as Keating had urged, nor gave a "clarion call for Bell and peace," as had been demanded by the pro-Union press. The vote was almost evenly divided. Breckinridge carried the state by only 762 votes out of nearly 90,000 cast; and Bell, Lincoln, and Douglas, the "Union" candidates, received a clear majority among them. Most Marylanders, it was evident, still hoped a compromise could be reached which would avoid the horrors of war. They wanted the Union; they wanted slavery; and they wanted peace.

Lincoln's election was a bitter pill for the Eastern Shore to swallow. Nevertheless, the antisecessionist *American Union* of Denton managed to

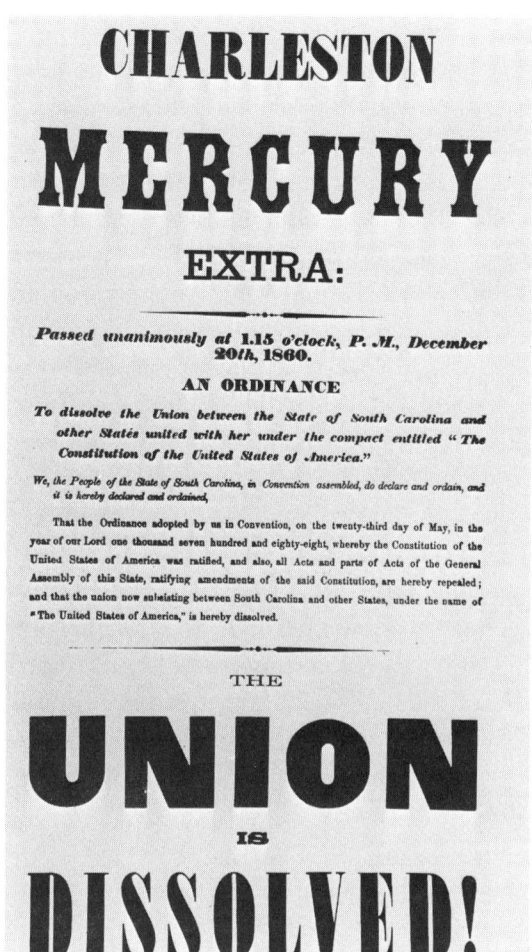

South Carolina's Ordinance of Secession was first announced in an "extra" of the *Charleston Mercury*. (Courtesy esy Library of Congress)

greet even this fateful development with a certain optimism. Its editor, J. H. Emerson, had not supported Lincoln, who received only twelve recorded votes in Caroline County. But in the *Union* of November 13, 1860, Emerson described the new president as "one of the most conservative men of the Republican ranks," a native of Kentucky who had never shown any disposition to "destroy Southern institutions" such as slavery.

Emerson roundly condemned Southern "extremists" for their violent reaction to Lincoln's victory. "Their course reminds us . . . of the VIPER, which on being teased, works its self into a rage, and in very spite will turn and thrust his fangs into his very own person. They seem to have lost all common sense . . . and in their political frenzy and distempered brain, imagine the whole Northern people, and even the people of border States, to be their most hostile enemies."

Even the *Kent Conservator*, hastily created in the fall of 1860 by J. Leeds Barroll to give the Southern cause a voice in opposition to the pro-Union *Kent News*, did not think Lincoln's election in itself was sufficient cause for secession. "The Union has given us seventy years of peace among ourselves" the *Conservator* said, and it should be preserved if at all possible.

Other Eastern Shore papers echoed this view, although few agreed with Emerson that Lincoln was a "conservative." Most considered his victory a calamity to be exceeded only by the greater calamity which secession might bring. As the *Cecil Democrat* put it in its issue of November 29, "We stand between Northern Nullification and Southern Secession, and say—THE UNION MUST BE PRESERVED . . . We will say, to the fanatics of the North, 'Down busy devils, down.' To the South we will say: 'Stay your hand, snatch not one star from the glorious galaxy of States.'" Editor H. Vanderford, Jr., insisted that the fact he had supported Breckinridge did not make him a "disunion" man. He still thought some sort of compromise could be worked out.

But that did not happen. The cotton states organized the Confederacy; Lincoln prepared to bring them back into the Union by force; and the question became: what should Maryland do about it? The *Kent Conservator* enthusiastically endorsed the idea of a convention to be held in Baltimore by the "friends of Southern rights." Editor Barroll reported in glowing terms in the *Conservator* of February 9, 1861, that a meeting held at the Kent County courthouse to choose delegates had been "a great success."

> It was a grand and lucid demonstration of the principles and doctrines of our republican form of government. It was an outpouring of the patriotism, virtue and the intelligence of men of all classes and professions, who are willing to discard party predilections and come up to the rescue of their state and country from the perils of war, desolation, and death.

The *Kent News* had charged that holding a convention at that critical point would mean "secession, and civil war in our borders." Barroll jibed: "Why, Mr. News, or you who write for the News, do you believe that the chairman of this meeting [Judge Ezekiel F. Chambers] would be the organ of a movement for secession, and the inauguration of 'civil war in our own borders?' The chairman is a citizen of age, experience, wisdom, patriotism, and in these times of sacrifice, he has more negroes than he is willing to yield to the Black Republicans . . . He is not a man to give his negroes and his life to appease the offended, blood thirsty Demons of Abolitionism."

In Talbot County, where an election was held on the convention, the idea was rejected by the voters by a substantial margin; but the pro-Rebel *Easton Star* jeered that "none were happy about the result except Quakers and darkeys."

The convention was held in Baltimore, although without official sanction. It adopted resolutions declaring its love for the Union, its love for the Constitution, its solidarity with the Southern states, and its opposition to "forcible coercion" by the federal government. It said Maryland should consider secession only as a last resort. That was as far as the movement ever got.

Even when hostilities began with the attack on Fort Sumter, the dream of Maryland neutrality remained strong. The *Kent News,* while it condemned South Carolina for having "commenced a war against the Union" and said she would be responsible "for all the evils to follow," described Maryland's position in these words:

> We of Maryland can wash our hands of all responsibility, for we have had no part or lot in the matter—neither do we desire being involved or drawn into it, in any way whatsoever . . . The Abolitionists and the Disunionists have alone brought on this unhappy state of things, and let them bear the burdens, and do the fighting.

Other Shore papers, however, made no secret of their sympathy with the South. The *Somerset Union* of May 21 urged a big turnout at a meeting of citizens "who are opposed to the war policy of Abraham Lincoln, and in favor of the recognition of the independence of the southern Confederacy." The same issue carried a letter from a Somerset County boy, William W. Croughan, telling how good life was in the Confederate Army and urging others to come to Virginia and join him.

It gave page one display to another letter, this one from a Virginia lady who defiantly told a northern friend there was no hope of restoring the Union:

> Never again, until you can make the South run with rivers of blood! Until you make our cities heaps of ashes, and the public buildings the abodes of bats and owls, until you have wasted our fair land, and turned it a thousand years back into the darkest ages, can you ever regain it. Nor even then . . . There is no more hope now of a reconstruction than there is of all going back to the British Crown.

To counteract this sort of propaganda, Unionists revived the old *Somerset Herald,* the county's first paper, which had gone out of business several years earlier. Starting in June, it poured out an equally strong stream of propaganda for the federal government. At the top of page one was the Union motto, *E Pluribus Unum.* Beneath it the paper carried a woodcut of an American flag atop a half globe, and the words of the "Star-Spangled Banner"—not then America's national anthem but a patriotic favorite. The *Herald* said editorially: "We believe that the great mass of the people of the loyal states are in favor of crushing out the rebellion by every available means." And it carried advertisements urging Somerset County youths to volunteer for the Union army as members of the Home Guards being organized into the First Eastern Shore

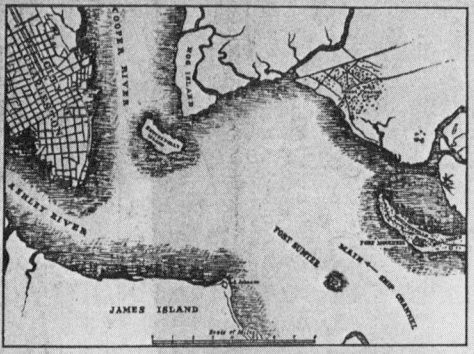

The firing on Fort Sumter, as reported in the *New York Herald* and the *Easton Star*.

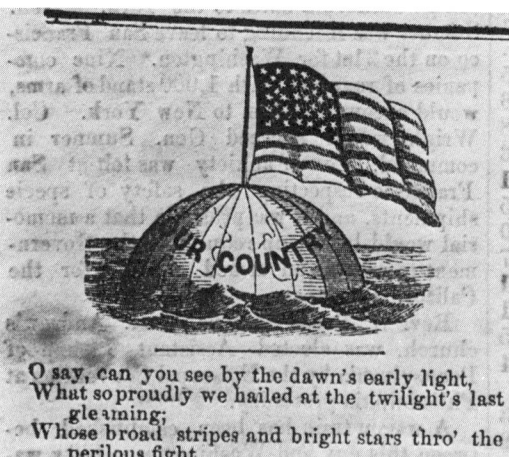

Top, despite its name, the *Somerset Union* was an all-out pro-Southern paper. *Above and right*, the *Somerset Herald* featured woodcuts showing its support for the Union, the Flag, and the Constitution.

Regiment. These included a statement from the secretary of war pledging that the guards would be "stationed on the Eastern Shore of Maryland" and used "only for home protection." The *Union* responded by giving top display to articles from Richmond papers telling of "brilliant" Rebel victories, with hundreds of Yankees killed and many captured.

This openly slanted coverage on both sides extended to every county. Such papers as the *Cecil Democrat,* the *Easton Star,* and the *Cambridge Democrat* picked up their war news directly from Southern papers smuggled through the Union blockade. Union papers got theirs by clipping the New York dailies or the *Baltimore American.* When the Confederates under General Evans whipped the Northerners at Ball's Bluff near Leesburg, Virginia, in October, 1861, the *Somerset Union* borrowed even its headline, "Our Late Brilliant Victory," from the *Richmond Dispatch,* and gloated that "we" (meaning the South) had killed, wounded, and drowned at least six hundred of the enemy, and taken six hundred prisoners and six pieces of artillery. On the other hand, when federal forces, after a dismal start, finally won a modest victory by capturing Fort Henry in Tennessee, the *Easton Gazette* proclaimed it on page one under the headline: "The Stars and Stripes Again Waving in Tennessee," and brashly predicted the war would soon be over. "Secesh is now on its last 'pins' and ere long it will be known only by name and the amount of evil it has caused," wrote editor William H. Councell. "It is emblematic of sin, misery and outrage."

Recalling the flying of the Stars and Bars on Easton's main streets, the *Gazette* added, "Even our quiet little town was at one time disgraced by the 'accursed thing,' though it sprang up like a reed and was *cut down* like grass."

Most Eastern Shore editors, in the tradition of their predecessors, carried their bias beyond the editorial sections, or even the headlines, into the news itself. No attempt was made to be objective, honest, or fair; facts were twisted to suit the writer's views; and outrageous opinions were inserted wholesale into what purported to be coverage of local events connected with the conflict. The doctrine of simply reporting the facts and letting readers make up their own minds, if it had made any headway elsewhere in American journalism, certainly had not yet touched the Eastern Shore.

Probably no Maryland incident during the entire war aroused more public excitement than the arrest and beating of Judge Richard Bennett Carmichael in his Easton courtroom in May, 1862; and none demonstrated more clearly the extremes of bias to which Eastern Shore newspapers were capable of going under the pressures of war.

The facts in the case were relatively simple. Judge Carmichael's prosecessionist rulings from the bench had convinced federal authorities that he was a menace to the Union cause, and they ordered his arrest on a treason charge. On

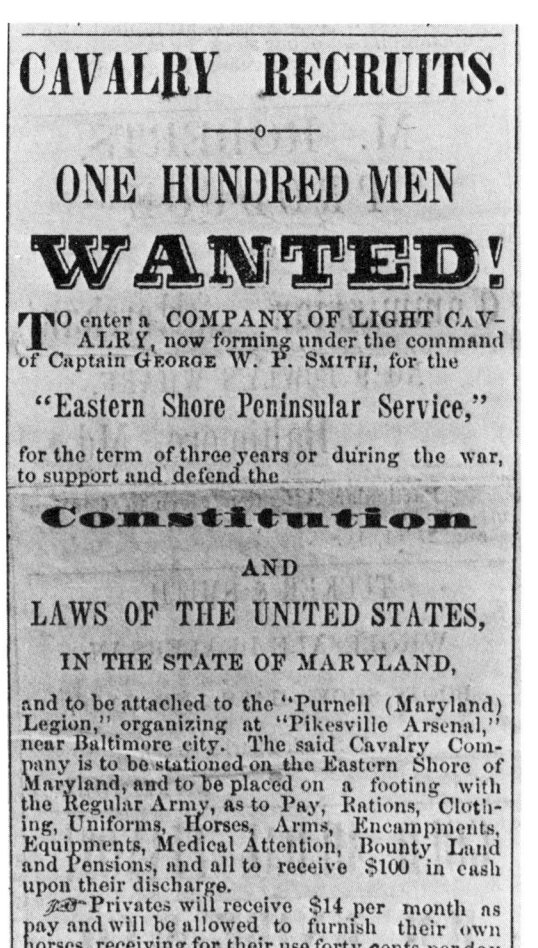 

Pro-Union papers featured ads seeking Home Guards as Union volunteers. Although promised they would be stationed on the Eastern Shore, many wound up fighting at Gettysburg.

May 27, federal marshals entered the room at the Talbot County courthouse where, as a judge of the Seventh Maryland Circuit, he was conducting a trial. When they attempted to take him into custody, he resisted, was beaten with their gun butts, and knocked bleeding to the floor. Later he and three other men were taken by steamer to Baltimore and locked up at Fort McHenry. Eventually the charge was dropped and he was released without a trial.

The rights and wrongs of this sensational incident are not what concern us here; it is the way in which these facts were reported by the two Easton papers, the pro-Union *Gazette* and the prosecessionist *Star*, which is more significant from a journalistic point of view.

The *Star*'s lead article, published June 3 under a headline reading, "Arrest of the Honorable Richard B. Carmichael," made no attempt to tell readers what had happened. Instead, it began:

> Tuesday, the 27th day of May, 1862, will long be remembered as a memorable day in Easton. It was one of those terrible days, like the 19th of April, 1861 [when Federal troops had clashed with a pro-Southern mob in Baltimore], which will afford a theme for the historian centuries hence, if the providence of God shall spare the world that long. We have never seen anything like it, not even in the histories of the civil wars of the Netherlands under the bloodthirsty Alva . . . It was reserved for the free and Christian United States Government, upon the soil of Maryland, to enact a tragedy to surpass in atrocity the most infamous deeds recorded in History.

An uninformed reader might be forgiven for concluding from that phrasing that hundreds of innocent civilians had been slaughtered in Easton streets, or perhaps beheaded as had been the custom in the cruel Duke of Toledo's day. But no: a couple of columns later it developed that the judge had suffered bruises and minor head wounds, bad enough in themselves but hardly amounting to an atrocity comparable to the beheading of eighteen thousand Dutchmen.

The *Gazette*, which had had first crack at the story, had started its account on May 31 with more facts and less hyperbole; but midway down the column it too had shifted without warning from reporting to editorializing:

> This lamentable occurrence, which has caused great excitement in our community, may be termed an appropriate denouement to the fell spirit of treason which for the last twelve months has swayed a great mass of our people as if they were under the influence of some demonical spell. It appears as if the Secession party of this county has labored by every available means to bring us into actual collision with the government, and to subvert the very foundation of society. Their schemes for the past year have been in utter defiance of law, and of the peace and welfare of our citizens. They have regarded neither the will of the people of the State or the government of the United States, but have openly defied both . . . Talbot County . . . has become a byeword and a laughing stock to the rest of the State . . . precisely as if the county had passed an ordinance of secession and was already incorporated in the Southern Confederacy.

As to what had gone on, that same uninformed reader might have wondered if the two papers were reporting on the same occurrence. Although both claimed to get their versions from eyewitnesses, there was wide disparity.

According to the *Gazette*, when Marshal James S. McPhail notified Judge Carmichael of his arrest, the judge snapped back: "I deny your authority." According to the *Star*, he merely asked by what authority the marshal was acting, and then requested to see the official papers confirming it.

According to the *Star*, the judge ordered McPhail "to take off his hat, which he did instantly." According to the *Gazette*, McPhail simply raised his hat "politely as if making a salutation and then replaced it on his head."

According to the *Star*, Special Officer John L. Bishop "commenced to swear and grow boisterous," and when the court crier, at Judge Carmichael's direction, went to the window and called out for the sheriff, Bishop choked and assaulted him. According to the *Gazette*, Bishop was not swearing and boisterous at any time. However, the *Gazette* did not deny that he had choked the crier, Will H. Sheppard.

According to the *Gazette*, the judge then kicked the marshal. According to the *Star*, this was impossible; there wasn't room between the bench and the wall for him to swing his leg.

Next, said the *Gazette*, "the Deputy Marshal [McPhail] again turned to the Judge, and perceiving that resistance would be offered, directed Officer Bishop to arrest him, who accordingly took hold of him, when a scuffle occurred, in which the Judge was several times struck over the head, and several other persons, who were near, were severely injured. The Judge was secured, and the courtroom speedily cleared."

The *Star*'s version was much more lurid. "Bishop seized the Judge, and he and McPhail . . . and two others . . . commenced to choke him and beat him over the head with revolvers. He was dragged from his seat and beat and kicked in various parts of his body in the most brutal manner. He defended himself the best he could with his naked hands against their assaults, but what resistance could an unarmed man offer to [four] armed men who seemed bent on taking his life? . . . The conduct of the Marshal and his deputies was atrocious in the extreme."

And so it went. The point here is not to reargue the case of Judge Carmichael, but to demonstrate the extent to which biased and emotional reporting by two of the Eastern Shore's most prestigious newspapers added fuel to the already blazing passions of war.

In any case, Judge Carmichael's arrest was only the beginning of the federal crackdown on dissidents. Even the press was not immune; the Union was at war for its very life, and Constitutional guarantees such as freedom of speech and the press could not be let to stand in the way of a Union victory.

Among the first Eastern Shore editors to feel the scourge of Union censorship was Albert G. Gullett, editor and publisher of the *Denton Journal* of Caroline County. Exactly what Gullett wrote that stirred the wrath of federal officials is not clear, since no issues of the *Journal* from that period are known to have survived. However, it is clear that he was far from being alone in expressing pro-Southern views in Caroline County, where Rebel sentiment was strong.

The *Kent News* of August 23, 1862, reported that a federal marshal backed up by several policemen, a squad of cavalry, and a company of infantry had sailed from Baltimore to Denton aboard the steamer *Balloon* the previous Sunday night, and on Monday (August 18) had arrested twelve persons on charges of "disloyalty and treasonable practices." Editor Gullett's name headed the list. Interestingly, four of the others were physicians, indicating the prominence of the dissident leadership.

The men were taken to Fort McHenry and at least some, including Gullett, were moved on to Fort Delaware. Gullett and several—but not all—other Caroline Countians had a hearing in Baltimore September 10 before Major General Wool, and were released upon their pledge henceforth "to support the constitution of the United States" and "not to take up arms against the government thereof."

Presumably Gullett kept his pledge. At least, there is no indication in the scanty record that he was again arrested or that publication of the *Journal* was interfered with. But much too little is known about the affair to reach any firm conclusions.

By the spring of 1863, federal officials were ready to go even further in silencing "treasonous" editors and others. They adopted the view that those who admired the Confederacy were welcome to go there, and if they hesitated, Union troops would escort them into Virginia and tell them: "Don't come back."

Their first Eastern Shore target for outright exile apparently was J. Leeds Barroll, the "disloyal" editor of the *Kent Conservator*. On April 18, 1863, the *Chestertown Transcript*, another pro-Southern paper founded in 1862, reported tersely:

> Yesterday morning, about 9 o'clock, Brig. General Lockwood, accompanied by General Rogers of the Eastern Shore company of Home Guards, arrived here in a government steamer. A squad of the soldiers immediately proceeded to the office of the *Kent Conservator*, and arrested the editor, J. Leeds Barroll, Esq., after which his office was searched, we learn. Mr. Barroll was allowed one hour to make arrangements for his departure, at the lapse of which time the party steamed off.

Barroll's "crime," it developed, had been to reprint an article from the *St. Mary's Beacon* which was extremely critical of similar arrests of numerous persons in Baltimore. The *Beacon*'s editor, a Mr. Downes, was also being held aboard the steamer.

A week later the *Transcript* quoted the *Baltimore Daily Gazette* as saying that the two editors had been "sent beyond the lines on Sunday evening [April 19]." The *Kent News* also reported Barroll's exile, adding this comment:

☞ Yesterday morning, about 9 o'clock, Gen'l. Lockwood, with a company of Col. Rogers' Eastern Shore Regiment of Home Guards, arrived here in a Government steamer. A squad of the soldiers immediately proceeded to the office of the *Kent Conservator* and arrested the editor, J. Leeds Barroll, Esq., after which his office was searched we learn. Mr. Barroll was allowed one hour to make preparations for his departure, at the lapse of which time the party steamed off. The arrest, we are informed, was caused by the publication of an article reviewing some of the recent arrests in Baltimore city, from the *St. Mary's Beacon*, the editor of which paper was also on board the steamer.

We are not informed of the destination of the prisoners.

Announcement in the *Chestertown Transcript*, April 18, of the arrest of *Kent Conservator* editor J. Leeds Barroll.

Our friend will have a hard road to travel in Dixie. Not being the owner of twenty negroes, he will not be exempt from the conscription laws in the Confederacy; and all Marylanders in the South have to go into the army. We presume, ere this, he has been assigned a place in the ranks.

We regret the imprudent publication by Mr. Barroll of the treasonable article which caused his arrest; but we are informed he remarked at the time that he expected to be arrested for publishing it. If men will be so foolhardy as to commit acts which they know to be forbidden by the national authorities, they must bide the consequences.

Beyond these few facts, nothing has been learned about Barroll's exile. The *Kent Conservator* evidently died when he was banished; but where he went, whether he was in fact drafted into the Confederate forces, and whether he ever returned to Chestertown all are unknown to this writer.

Next to feel the wrath of federal authorities was H. Everett Smith of the *Worcester County Shield*, whose reluctant support of the Union had changed into outright favoritism toward the South. He was arrested and taken to Baltimore on a charge of publishing "disloyal articles," and was ordered to be sent South, but was finally permitted to return to Snow Hill on his promise not to print any more offending material. By August he was back in the editor's chair and still complaining about Lincoln administration policies; but this time he was careful to quote a New York newspaper rather than to comment on his own. His target was the use of black troops in the Union army, which Lincoln had authorized earlier that year, and an alleged war department letter saying that the blacks were "destined to wield the sword of just retribution." Smith quoted the *New York Journal* as saying this was no way to restore the Union. "It would prompt to a war of races, in which the blacks of the South shall be arrayed against their masters, thirsting for revenge and wielding the sword of just retribution . . . In what respect infuriated negroes are better than savages no one can say. Yet we have a letter here from one high in the confidence of the government, giving encouragement to the prosecution of a war in which negroes shall be urged on by the fiendish desire of revenge."

Evidently that was considered something less than outright disloyalty. Smith was not again bothered by the federals.

In May came the turn of Tom Robson, the fire-breathing secessionist editor of the *Easton Star*. Robson had been a thorn in the side of federal officials, national as well as local, ever since the start of the war. In January, 1862, he was arrested after publishing an article ridiculing Union troops stationed at Camp Kirby, outside Easton, as "Caroline County sand diggers" and "Lincoln's pet lambs." Major William Kirby, in charge of the camp, forced him to sign a parole promising not to publish any more such "personal" remarks.

But Robson added a rider saying "nothing herein contained shall be considered to debar me of my editorial privilege of commenting upon the actions of wrong doers, be they in the army or otherwise," and went right on lambasting the Union and its supporters. His handling of the Judge Carmichael affair angered federal authorities all the way to Washington, and his continued jibes irked the troops. On the evening of November 25, 1862, after having a few illegal drinks at the Union Hotel in Easton, a group of them went to the *Star* office next door, dumped the type on the floor, smashed furniture, and damaged the press. The opposition *Gazette* said piously that it served Robson right because of the "disloyal sentiments the *Star* was habitually uttering," but pro-South friends in Easton collected a fund of six hundred dollars to help Robson pay for the damage.

When Robson published a locally written poem, "Noble Ashby," lamenting the death of Confederate General Turner Ashby, the federals decided they had had enough. Reportedly on a direct order from President Lincoln, Robson was arrested on the evening of May 8, 1863, given fifteen minutes to say goodby to his family, and placed on board the steamer *Balloon* for transportation to Fort McHenry.

From Baltimore, Union troops escorted him southward through federal lines and into the Shenandoah valley. There, according to a contemporary

The *Easton Star*'s bold advocacy of the Southern cause brought about the arrest and exile of editor Thomas K. Robson. Examples shown here are the satirical poem at left attacking William Price, author of a strong treason bill in the Maryland legislature, and Robson's publication of the full text of Jefferson Davis's inaugural address as President of the Confederacy.

The Battle of Gettysburg, as depicted in a contemporary drawing. At Culp's Hill on the morning of July 3, 1863, Eastern Shore men from the Union and Rebel armies met face to face in some of the fiercest fighting of the war. (Courtesy Library of Congress)

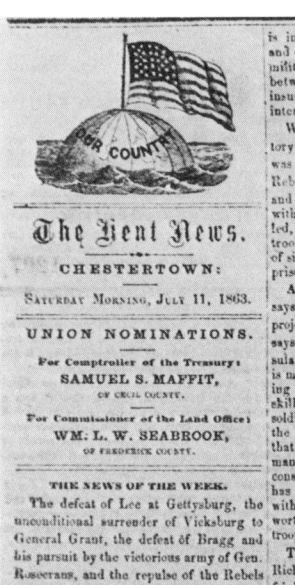

Gettysburg as reported in the pro-Union *Kent News*.

account, "they left him seated, cooling his heels on his trunk in the middle of a bare, winding road, dust-filled and desolate." Soon he was picked up by a Confederate troop detail and, after explaining who he was, eventually was released as a civilian. He took a job as a government clerk in Richmond, but was conscripted for military service by the very government whose interests he had promoted so faithfully on the Eastern Shore. Drafted into the Senior Reserve for the defense of Richmond, Robson got out of it by proving to the satisfaction of the authorities that he was "an exile entitled to asylum in a friendly nation."

With the *Star* silenced for the duration, a new Democratic paper, the *Easton Journal*, was created in August, 1863, to fill the gap. Editor Arthur Brown carped at the Lincoln administration and supported his 1864 presidential opponent, General George B. McClellan, but was careful to avoid any comment even hinting at treason.

The *Easton Gazette* couldn't resist crowing over the downfall of its bitter rival, the *Star*. "There is no paper this side of Charleston that has been more severe upon the cause of the Union," editor Councell wrote. He also charged that Robson's friends deserted him when he was arrested. "They pretended that he had been advised and counseled to pursue a different course. What bosh! What meanness, what skulking, what cowardice, for them to throw the whole blame [on the man] who has allowed himself to be used for their convenience."

Robson was not the only Eastern Shore editor to be harassed by Union soldiers. In Centreville Thomas Keating incurred the anger of some Home Guards, chiefly from Caroline County, by remarks which appeared in his *Centreville State Rights* after the troops occupied the Queen Anne's County courthouse in March, 1863. Just what was said is not clear, since no issue of the paper for that period has survived. Writing in the 1880s, historian Frederic Emory quoted Keating as commenting, "as far as we know they have all behaved very well since they have been in our midst," but that hardly seems likely to have upset the Carolinians. At any rate, they decided they had been insulted, and according to Emory, "repaired to the office of the *State Rights* to demand an apology." Keating refused, "whereupon the soldiers scarred the type and broke the press and other apparatus." Another account says they scattered the loose type along Lawyer's Row, the street on which the newspaper office was located.

When Captain Andrew Stafford learned of the affair, he ordered the soldiers to pick up the type, and said he would order a court martial. He also offered to assist Keating in repairing his machinery but, says Emory, "subsequently refused, guaranteeing, however, that he should not again be molested."

Early in December, 1863, fire completely destroyed Keating's office. Tradition says the fire was set "by pro-Union men from Kent County," but a letter written by Keating to his father-in-law reveals that he, at least, did not believe the rumors that it had been incendiary in origin.

"I cannot believe that," Keating wrote. "I am satisfied no one has any such enmity toward me." He accepted the alternative explanation, that the fire had started in an ash barrel belonging to a neighbor which was up against a wooden wall of Keating's combined law office and newspaper plant. Skeptics had expressed doubt that so hot a fire could have started in such a casual manner. The letter, dated December 7, 1863, was for many years in the possession of a descendant, the late Miss L. Parker Keating of Centreville.

After the fire, Keating did not resume publication of his paper, and the Eastern Shore opposition to Lincoln lost one of its ablest and most lucid exponents. Writing in 1887, Emory, who was himself a Southern sympathizer, characterized Keating's editorship as "fearless and able," and said his "vigorous assertion of constitutional principles . . . entitles him to the respect and gratitude of all who deprecate the use of force and illegal methods in stifling the popular voice." Presumably Emory was referring to the fire.

By the summer of 1863 even the Unionist papers on the Shore were increasingly critical of federal actions. The continued presence of Union troops was a constant irritant, and the public had been shocked by the arrest and brutal beating of Judge Carmichael; but the issue which most alienated the Eastern Shore press was the North's growing insistence on abolishing slavery. As the war changed from a struggle to save the Union to a crusade against slavery, Eastern Shoremen grew more and more torn between loyalty and dissent. Their attitude was well expressed by Congressman John W. Crisfield of Princess Anne in a speech to the House of Representatives which several papers published in full.

Crisfield was proud of Maryland's loyalty to the Union, and was "not enamored of slavery" but defended it against the "evil passions" of Yankee radicals. Negroes must be kept in servitude as long as they remained in Maryland, or "degradation, poverty, and ultimate extinction" would be their fate. He was the owner of slaves, Crisfield told the House:

> They are the descendants in a great degree of the woman who nursed me. They . . . look upon me as their protector. I am in truth their only friend. Am I to turn them off as outcasts on the world? I have been my whole life engaged in their protection. I have an affection for them, and have a duty to perform for them . . . They have labored for me, it is true, but they have in turn received from me quite as much as they have given me.

Crisfield said he did not seek to perpetuate slavery but favored gradual emancipation and colonization for Maryland blacks.

Some pro-Union editorialists agreed with him. They blamed the South itself for the fact that slavery was being destroyed faster than they thought practical. As early as February, 1862, the *Cambridge Herald* pointed out that while Southern leaders claimed they were fighting for the sacred institution of slavery, the war's effect was bringing about emancipation in Missouri, Kentucky, and western Virginia. "Under the United States government, slavery was as sacred as the law of marriage or the right of suffrage," the *Herald* said. "Now hundreds of square miles of the best slave territory has passed into a system of freedom . . . Jefferson Davis is truly the great emancipator." Echoing this theme, the *American Union* of Denton declared that "slavery, because of this Rebellion, has received a mortal stab from those professing to be its best friends." The *Kent News* complained the secessionists were responsible for "all the evils we are now laboring under . . . high taxes, depreciation of property, and abolition of slavery. They have done more injury to the institution of slavery in the past twelve months than the crazy fanatics of the North could have done in one hundred years to come."

Not all the news, however, was of war, high taxes, and abolitionism. In May, 1863, Eastern Shore papers took time out from their bickering to report on the great prize fight "for the American championship" which took place at Charlestown on the North East River in Cecil County May 5. Among the twenty-five hundred spectators, according to the *Kent News*, were "all the principal shoulder-hitters, bullies, blacklegs, and thieves, who infest Baltimore, New York, Philadephia, Boston, and Cincinnati."

As the *News* indicated, it was a classic matchup of brawn versus skill. Mike McCoole of St. Louis, the western champion, was "an immensely powerful young fellow, deficient in fistic science." Joe Coburn of New York, hero of the East, was noted for his "skill, gameness, quickness and great experience in the tactics of the ring." Although McCoole had a twenty-pound weight advantage, Coburn was the betting favorite at one hundred dollars to eighty dollars. According to the *Cecil Democrat*, the stake was two thousand dollars a side.

Because prize fighting was illegal in most states, the location was kept a secret until the last minute. The two men and their entourages met in New York, then got on trains and rode to Charlestown, just across the Maryland line, where the ring was set up near the tracks of the Baltimore & Philadelphia railroad.

"Sixty seven rounds were fought," the *Democrat* reported, "Coburn being declared the victor. He was able to walk away with his friends, but his antagonist was carried away in a cart." At week's end McCoole was still confined to bed in a Cecil County hotel, but was said to be recovering. Coburn and friends were long gone, two thousand dollars richer.

They weren't the only ones to profit. "A number of pocket books changed owners on the occasion, the light fingered gentry being out in great force," the *Democrat* said.

Down in Salisbury, there was a contest of quite another kind. This was between the youthful Union soldiers stationed at Camp Wallace just outside town and the saucy young women who sympathized with the Rebel cause and would not give them the time of day. The battle lines were drawn in a curious publication called the *Sharpshooter*, established as a camp newspaper in March of 1864.

The *Sharpshooter* was a small, four-page weekly which carried no advertising and sold for three cents a copy, or ten cents a month. Ostensibly its purpose was to report on Camp Wallace doings, but in fact its anonymous editor seems to have been obsessed with the perfidy of "the female rebel," a species discussed in detail in the issue of May 14, 1864. Judging from the paper, these appear to have been in abundant supply in Salisbury at the time.

In its lead editorial, the *Sharpshooter* scolded female Rebels unmercifully. "Such women are under the domination of fancy and feeling . . . They enquire not for causes; they regard not consequences! They feel, therefore reason is ignored, and logic is defied! . . . They feel, therefore the rebellion is right, and peace, honor, truth, virtue must perish . . . It is with them, all sentimental feeling, all sentimental folly."

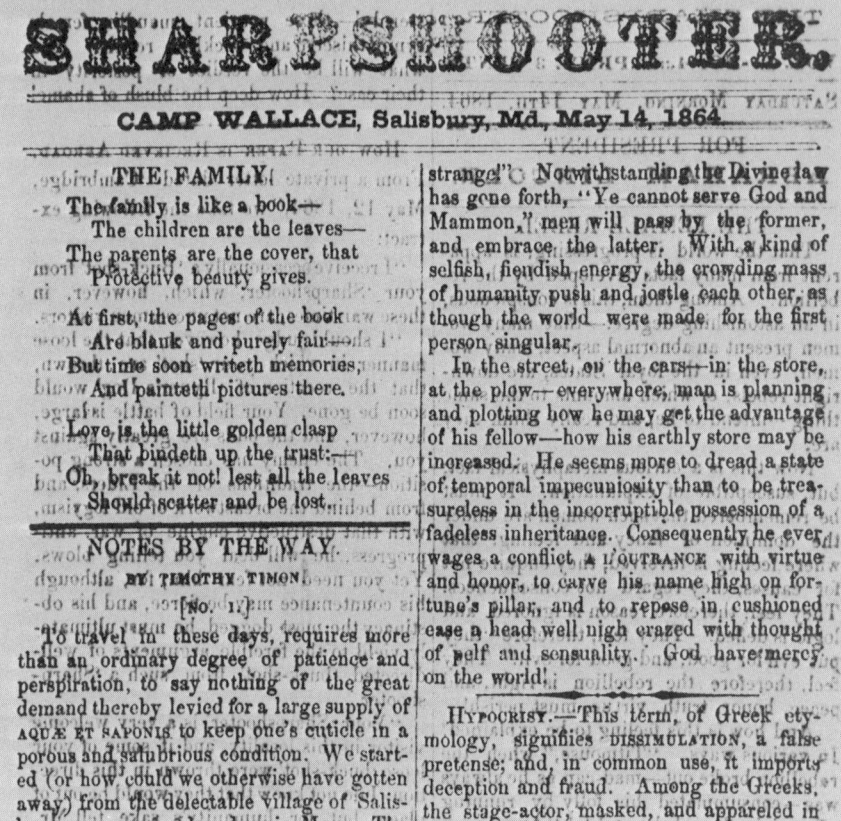

The *Sharpshooter*, a camp paper published for Union troops, was Salisbury's only wartime newspaper. The edition of May 14, 1864, is the only extant issue known. (Courtesy Dr. Laurence G. Claggett)

Several separate news items carried out the same theme. Salisbury ladies had been observed stepping aside as they passed the United States Marshal's office so as to avoid walking under the Star-Spangled Banner. "Let them be warned," the *Sharpshooter* cried. Also lamented was the fact that some ladies, not themselves disloyal, let their conduct be dictated by females "of the rebel persuasion." They should know by now, the paper said, "that there is not a disloyal woman in Maryland that is to be trusted." Another item reported that a Salisbury "lady(?)" had considered herself grossly insulted because a gentleman condemned the rebellion in her presence. She was beneath contempt, in the opinion of the *Sharpshooter*; she deserved nothing less than banishment to the South, being guilty of "the very worst form of dishonor and treason."

> INSULTED.— We heard that a lady (?) of Salisbury felt grossly insulted, and became highly indignant, the other day, because a gentleman, in her presence, spoke in terms of condemnation against the Great Rebellion. A person, (man or woman,) who would feel insulted for such a cause, while living under the protection of this benign Government, and enjoying its blessings and privileges, is utterly unworthy of ANY consideration, much less such as would compromit the honor of a loyal man. Such a traitor deserves, at least, banishment beyond the leniency and protection of the lines of the Union Army. And an individual who could be muzzled by such spurious etiquette, is a deluded victim of the very worst form of dishonor and treason.

> "Coming events cast their shadows before."
>
> ☞ Why is it, that some of the loyal ladies of Salisbury allow other females, of the "rebel persuasion," to dictate to them "rules of etiquette?" Have they not yet learned that there is not a disloyal woman in Maryland that is to be trusted?

> SALT ENOUGH TO SAVE IT.—Thank God, there are enough noble women and men left in Salisbury, who are uncompromisingly loyal to humanity and their country, to save it from the hand of the Destroying Angel.

> ☞ A young lady in Salisbury says 'she thinks the Sharpshooter is detestable.' No doubt of it. It contains too many truths to be a favorite with Rebels.

Items from the *Sharpshooter* show its editor's peeve about pro-Rebel Salisbury girls.

Such an excess of indignation gives rise to the suspicion that the *Sharpshooter*'s young soldier-editor was speaking from experience. But whether or not he had personally been cold-shouldered by Salisbury girls loyal to the South, he did not waste all his ammunition on them. In the same issue was a potshot at the town commissioners, who according to the paper were empowered to pass ordinances removing nuisances. "We suggest that the first Ordinance they pass, shall be one removing themselves.—Nothing they could do would be more conducive to the prosperity of [the] town." Slaveholders, of whom there were many in the area, were condemned as "that monied, but brainless aristocracy, which seeks to raise itself upon the ruins of virtue and honor."

"Let everything that hath a voice praise the Lord for the late victories of the Union army," was a sentiment expressed on page one with which a good many

Salisbury citizens did not agree. If the May 14 issue of the *Sharpshooter*—the only extant edition known—is a fair sample, improved community relations were not among the objectives for which the paper was designed.

Easton had a similar problem with "disloyal ladies" who refused to walk under the Union flag. There the provost marshal for the Army district, Thomas A. Wollaston, was also proprietor of the Union Hotel at Goldsborough and Washington streets. He hung a flag above his door but, according to Dr. Samuel A. Harrison, "the ladies of disloyal sentiment avoided the side of the street on which it hung, and so scornfully refused to walk under it." These included most of the women of Easton, "even those who had loyal husbands and brothers," Dr. Harrison said.

The *Easton Gazette* reported on November 29, 1862, that Wollaston had replaced his flag with a new and much larger one, suspended from a rope which stretched clear across Goldsborough Street to the Easton bank opposite the hotel.

"We hope those of the fair sex who have hitherto taken to the middle of the street to avoid walking under it—or to make a display of their ankles—will now be able to wend their way without molestation or hindrance," the pro-Union *Gazette* jibed.

(According to Dr. Harrison, a newspaper called the *Sharpshooter* was also published at Camp Kirby, the Union encampment outside Easton; but no copies of this paper have been found.)

On a more serious aspect of the home front, the Federal campaign to recruit Eastern Shore slaves which followed Lincoln's 1863 decision to use black troops in the field drew bitter protests even from the "loyal" press. Slaves were supposed to be taken into the army only with their masters' consent; but the *Kent News* charged that hundreds were being "abducted," leaving farmers with no one to work their fields. "The large number of slaves taken from our county has most seriously obstructed agricultural operations, and further depletion of labor would be hurtful in the extreme," the *News* commented on October 10, 1863. "We already hear of persons who will be compelled on this account to discontinue farming after the present year."

Worse yet, in the eyes of proslavery loyalists, was the growing demand for emancipation of all Maryland blacks. This was bad news for Eastern Shore Unionists. The *American Union* claimed it was being deliberately fostered by "Rebels and sympathizers with treason" in order to divide the Unionists politically and weaken their power. Calling them "political skunks who preach treason and are whining about emancipation," the Denton paper said "they will continue to stink in the nostrils of all truly loyal citizens." The *Kent News* thought those raising the question were "busybodies" from outside Maryland

and "the non-slaveholders of Baltimore city" who "seem determined to press this subject upon the attention of the people of the State, directly against the wishes of the great body of Union men in the countries."

Whatever the source, the question did succeed in dividing the Unionists into radical and conservative factions in the fall elections of 1863. The radicals, representing majority Northern opinion, wanted to press for abolition of slavery with all possible speed; the conservatives, representing majority Eastern Shore opinion, wanted to move slowly, if at all. However, the result, at least in Kent County, was an episode which had nothing to do with slavery, but with a crude and almost ludicrous election-stealing scheme.

On November 7, 1863, a hasty and incomplete edition of the *Kent News* appeared. Its two inside pages were blank and the usual short stories and feature articles were missing from its front page. On page four was a message from coeditors William B. Usilton and James H. Plummer:

> APOLOGY.—It is hardly necessary for us to apologize for the appearance of our paper today, as our readers very generally are aware that we were arrested on Tuesday last, on some frivolous pretext, and sent off to Baltimore in company with other "prisoners."

Behind this announcement was a dramatic series of events which had kept Chestertown in turmoil all week. As pieced together from the *News* and other sources, here is what had happened.

Back in October the local leader of the radical Unionists, John Frazier, Jr., had concocted a bold scheme for winning the election and, not incidentally, getting himself elected clerk of court, the most lucrative office in county government. It was classic in its simplicity: why not simply arrest all the conservative Union leaders and hold them until after election day? That would not only prevent them from last-minute campaigning but would frighten off conservative voters and, he thought, guarantee the election for him.

Through an intermediary, Frazier suggested the arrests to Colonel Don Piatt, chief of staff to Major General Robert C. Schenck, Union commander in Baltimore. Frazier's pitch was that Kent County was in a state of near insurrection, and that the conservatives themselves were planning to arrest several radical leaders for violating the Maryland slave code by "abducting" Negroes for the army. Colonel Piatt bought the story, and ordered Lieutenant Colonel Charles Carroll Tevis of the Third Maryland Cavalry to make any necessary arrests in the course of his duties as "peace-keeper" at the election.

Tevis sailed into Chestertown Monday morning, November 2, at the head of about two hundred cavalrymen and infantry. Some of the troops later told the *News* they had been warned to expect armed resistance and were astonished "at finding the utmost peace and order prevailing in our community."

Tevis reported at once to the Kent County provost marshal, who by no coincidence happened to be John Frazier, Jr. Frazier fed him some tales about the strong opposition in Kent, reportedly including the claim that "Kent Countians were as disloyal as any in the Rebel states." There was talk, Frazier said, that "disaffected persons" would attempt to seize the polls on Wednesday, election day.

Taking all this at face value, Tevis set in motion what amounted to a military takeover. On Monday afternnon Union troops occupied the jail, freed a number of black prisoners, and arrested jailer D. A. Benjamin. Mrs. Benjamin tried to flee, but "was insultingly driven back with oaths," according to the *News*. In a raid on the courthouse, guns belonging to the Reed Rifles, a local militia group, were seized. Homes of prominent citizens were visited, and all weapons confiscated. Then began the political arrests: J. K. Hines, Frazier's opponent for clerk; James B. Ricaud, candidate for the state senate; several election judges; and other leading conservatives.

On Tuesday afternoon Frazier showed up at the *Kent News* office accompanied by a file of soldiers. He "commanded" the two editors to print fifty copies of an order signed by Tevis, who instructed "every truly loyal citizen to [give] full and ardent support to the whole Government ticket . . . None other is recognized by the Federal authority as loyal or worthy of the support of any one who desires the peace and restoration of this Union." Needless to say, the government ticket was the one Frazier was running on.

Usilton and Plummer were then arrested on the charge of having published a letter urging resistance to the abduction of Negroes by federal recruiters. They were marched to the wharf and put aboard the steamer *Nellie Pentz*, where they found the other "caged birds" huddled in a saloon cabin. As the *Pentz* sailed down the Chester for Baltimore, she passed a steamer bringing local Union soldiers home to vote. The captain of this vessel told the *News* he recognized those on board, and knowing "their decided Union sentiments . . . supposed the Government, in consideration of former valuable services, was honoring us with a trip of pleasure."

In Baltimore they were taken to headquarters, where Colonel Piatt expressed shock at the number and prominence of the men arrested. When Ricaud read a copy of Tevis's order, Piatt said it was a direct violation of orders by President Lincoln and General Schenck against interference in local elections. Tevis had "strangely misinterpreted" his orders, Piatt said; he was "a very good soldier and not much of a politician." The Kent Countians were free to go. Transport was hastily rounded up, and by dawn on election day, all were back in Chestertown.

As their story spread, Kent Countians poured out to the polls to make sure Frazier's scheme would not succeed. The whole government ticket was de-

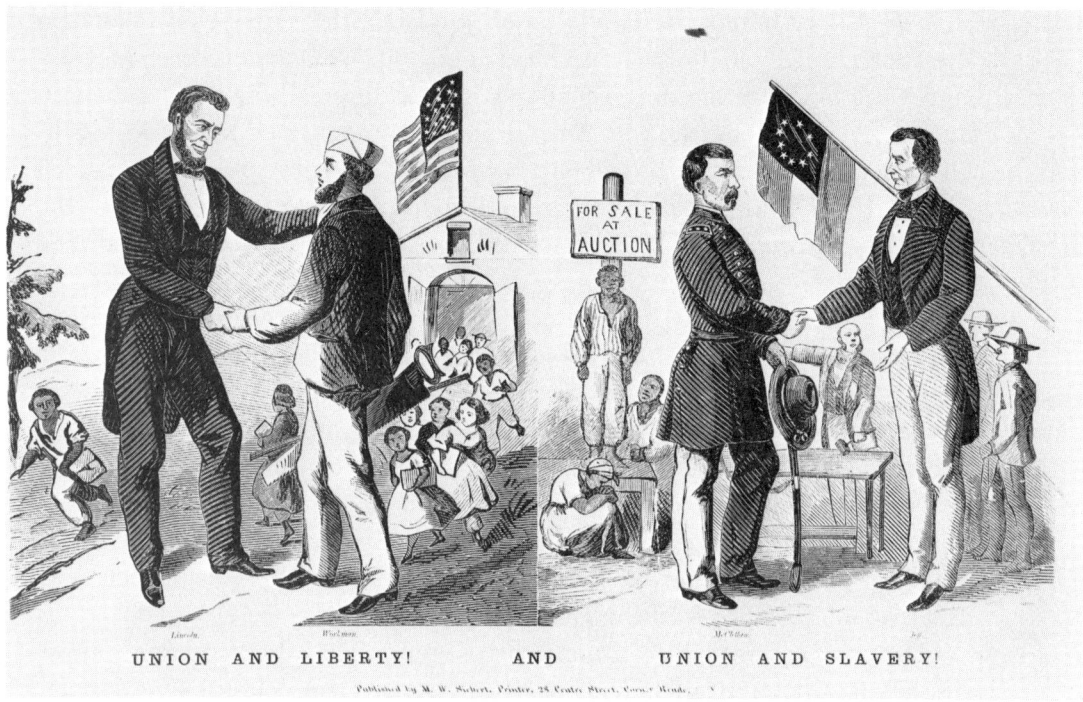

Lincoln's reelection campaign against General George McClellan in 1864, as viewed by a national cartoonist. The Eastern Shore favored McClellan, but was much more concerned about a proposed new Constitution freeing Maryland slaves. (Courtesy Library of Congress)

feated, and Frazier lost to Hines by a margin of nearly ten to one. On top of that, both Frazier and Tevis were placed under arrest on orders from General Schenck's headquarters.

The *News* called editorially for a "full and fair investigation" of the incident. "We shall get it, we are sure," the two editors said. "We have confidence in the patriotism and integrity of the President and General Schenck, and to them we will not look in vain."

But their confidence was misplaced. Five days later Tevis was restored to duty with only an official reprimand. Frazier was allowed to keep his post as provost marshal pending a final decision on his case which became enmeshed in a long political argument and never was announced.

By the time of the 1864 elections, Maryland emancipation had become the burning issue of the day. Two separate votes were held. On October 12 balloting was conducted on a "radical" new Maryland constitution which would abolish slavery immediately; and on November 8 the voters chose between President Lincoln and his Copperhead opponent, Democrat George McClellan. Antiadministration newspapers charged widespread fraud, especially in the voting on the constitution. The *Cecil Democrat* claimed that proconstitution election judges had thrown out many "legal votes" by applying the "Cecil County Catechism," a tough series of questions designed to weed out all who had ever even expressed sympathy with the Southern cause or "rejoiced" at a Union defeat.

In Caroline, the only Eastern Shore county where a majority for the new constitution was claimed, the *Denton Journal* denounced the election as "a farce . . . conducted with the most outrageous unfairness." In the Denton district, said the *Journal*, "no one was permitted to vote who was suspected by the judges to be hostile to the adoption of the new constitution. Some of our best citizens were turned down even after their 'loyalty' had been vouched for by the leading spirits of the so-called Union party. It was the purpose of the judges in the election here to have a majority in favor of the constitution at all hazards, and they accomplished their purpose."

The *Journal* also charged that "the contemptible Administration pimps" who acted as election judges had not given an honest vote count. In one district, it said, the tally showed only forty-seven votes against the constitution although eighty-nine men on the poll books certified they had cast negative ballots, and five others were known to have voted the same way.

Proconstitution papers, on the other hand, said that many disloyal persons had perjured themselves by taking the required oath of loyalty to the government on grounds it was not binding, and election judges permitted them to vote because they "lacked the firmness" to reject challenged ballots.

The Eastern Shore as a whole voted against the constitution and emancipation of slaves by more than two to one. But this margin was more than cancelled by the vote of Baltimore city, where the announced vote was 9,779 for, 2,053 against. Statewide balloting showed a majority against the constitution. However, absentee voting by soldiers in Union army camps gave it a razor-thin victory margin of 375 votes out of nearly 60,000. It took effect immediately; all slavery in Maryland was declared abolished as of November 1, 1864.

In the presidential election, there again were charges of fraud. The *Chestertown Transcript* said that in Talbot County, which Lincoln carried, "a large portion of the people were deprived of their elective franchise." Many of them were told that they were not loyal, said the *Transcript*, although only a few weeks before, when the constitution was at stake, "they had been returned as legal and qualified voters." The *Transcript* made no such charge about Kent County; there McClellan had swamped Lincoln, 1,269 to 412.

Then came the fearful drumroll of events which ended the war.

On February 17, 1865, the Confederates gave up Charleston, South Carolina, where it had all begun.

On April 3, Richmond fell.

On April 9, General Lee surrendered at Appomattox Court House.

On April 14, Lincoln was shot; and on April 15, he died.

The swift tide of news was simply too much for the Eastern Shore press, with its weekly rather than daily deadlines, to absorb. By the time an editor commented on one event, another and more cataclysmic one had occurred.

A sampling of comment on Lincoln's assassination, however, shows that even the most bitterly antiadministration Eastern Shore editors were shocked

Lincoln's death, shown here in a contemporary drawing, horrified even his bitterest opponents on the Eastern Shore. (Courtesy Library of Congress)

SURRAT.   BOOTH.   HAROLD.

War Department, Washington, April 20, 1865,

 **$100,000 REWARD!**

THE MURDERER

Of our late beloved President, Abraham Lincoln,

IS STILL AT LARGE.

$50,000 REWARD

Will be paid by this Department for his apprehension, in addition to any reward offered by Municipal Authorities or State Executives.

$25,000 REWARD

Will be paid for the apprehension of JOHN H. SURRATT, one of Booth's Accomplices.

$25,000 REWARD

Will be paid for the apprehension of David C. Harold, another of Booth's accomplices.

and appalled. The *Cecil Democrat*, for example, had opposed the war, had criticized Lincoln's every act, and had supported both Breckinridge and McClellan against him. But editor Vanderford had been pleased with recent evidence of the President's moderate attitude toward the defeated South, especially his "malice toward none, charity for all" speech at his second inauguration March 4. Now all that was destroyed in an instant by an assassin's act of "madness." In its issue of April 22, the *Democrat* called the assassination "that most horrible of all crimes." Of Lincoln it said: "The seal of good intent was fixed upon his acts, and the red right hand of his murderer has secured them from possible miscarriage. Never, never, if he had lived for ages . . . could his coronet have held a brighter jewel than the tribute a grateful people with one accord ascribe to him . . . Moral courage—that sublimest of all human attributes—illuminated his latest words. His beam cannot expire."

The *Chestertown Transcript* had been engaged in bitter criticism of Lincoln's reconstruction policies. In an editorial published April 15, the day he died but before the news reached the Eastern Shore, it called them "miserable political shuffling without one ray of hope for a speedy peace or a return to constitutional liberty." However, by April 22 it had changed its mind, praising his "individual leniency, and his exercise of executive clemency" toward Confederate leaders. "The whole body of the Southern people," it said, "had more real cause to regret that he should have been thus taken . . . than his political friends. The country truly mourns, and not without cause."

The *Maryland Citizen* of Centreville put it more simply. "The people never knew how much they loved Abraham Lincoln until he was struck down," the *Citizen* said.

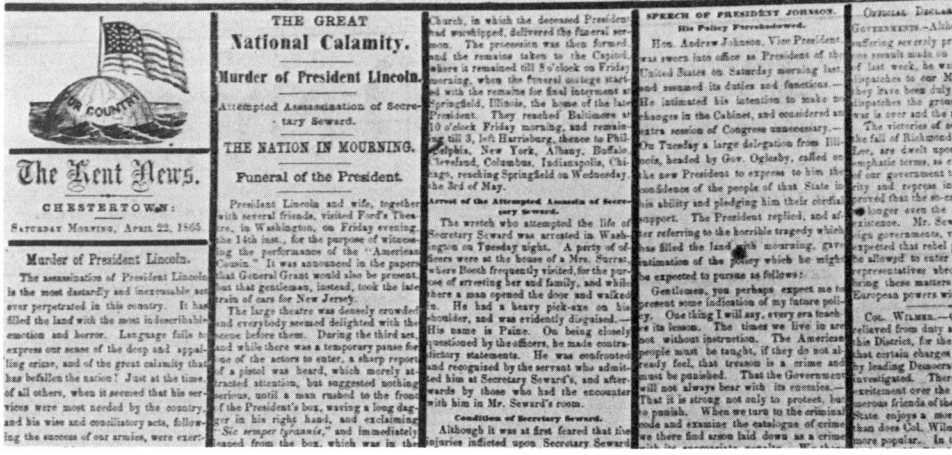

"The Great National Calamity" as reported in the *Kent News*.

CHAPTER FIVE

The Long Siesta
1865 TO 1923

AFTER the thunderous climax which ended the Civil War, the Eastern Shore press—like the Eastern Shore itself—was happy to return to the more mundane problems of day-to-day living.

New issues faced the Shore, but for the most part they presented problems with which an editor could grapple without the soul-wrenching agonies of choosing war or peace, union or disunion, slavery or freedom. The railroads for which everyone had hungered so long were coming at last, and through the late 1860s the papers kept readers informed of progress with weekly bulletins. The Eastern Shore line, which had been a dream since 1835, bisected the peninsula by way of Delaware and the southern Shore counties, ending up in 1866 at the rough and raw waterfront village of Somer's Cove or Annamessex, soon to be renamed Crisfield for the company's president, John W. Crisfield. West of it, the Maryland and Delaware crept southward past Goldsborough, Greensborough, and Hillsborough, to reach Easton in 1869 and its southern terminus at Oxford two years later.

As of 1865, only fifteen newspapers, out of the scores created in the enthusiasm of the 1820s and 1830s, had survived the rigors of agricultural depression, political bitterness, and wartime shortages and inflation. All were in county seat towns: the *Whig* and *Democrat* in Elkton; the *Kent News* and *Transcript* in Chestertown; the *Observer* and *Maryland Citizen* in Centreville; the *American Union* and *Denton Journal* in Denton; the *Gazette* and *Journal* in Easton (although the *Star*, temporarily suspended, would soon be back in business); the *Democrat, Herald,* and *Intelligencer* in Cambridge; the *Somerset Herald* in Princess Anne; and the *Worcester County Shield* in Snow Hill. For the most part they reflected the new face of American politics; nine (or ten, counting the *Easton Star*) were Democratic, and six, in varying degrees, leaned Republican.

Wherever they touched, the railroads created new towns and transformed others; and with them came a new wave of newspapers, founded less on political partisanship than on the optimistic belief that railroads inevitably meant prosperity and progress. Within the next four decades an astonishing eighty-two new newspapers in twenty-nine different Eastern Shore communities would come into being. Nearly everyone who could set a stick of type—and some who couldn't—would try his hand. Doctors, lawyers, ministers, storekeepers, druggists would become part-time publishers; and if many of them got burned, a few succeeded.

Salisbury had been a sleepy village until the Eastern Shore Railroad reached it. It burgeoned swiftly into a thriving town, especially after it was made the seat of the newly created Wicomico County in 1867. Within a dozen years five newspapers sprang up where none had been before: the *Salisbury Advertiser* (1867), the *Eastern Shoreman* and the *New Era* (1868), the *Bachelor* (1870), and the Salisbury *Times* (1879). The *Wicomico News*, *Wicomico Record*, and *Peninsula Patron* all followed in the 1880s.

Both Crisfield's first papers, the *Index* and the *Leader*, were established in 1872, the year the town was renamed and incorporated, and about the time the railroad finally reached the waterfront. In Worcester County, where only Snow Hill had maintained prewar newspapers, the *Berlin Times* (1872), the *Newtown Record* (late 1865), and *Newtown Gazette* (about 1869) all blossomed with the advent of rail transportation. The latter two were merged into the *Record and Gazette* even before Newtown, in 1878, became Pocomoke City. Rail lines also created the climate for the *Maryland Courier* in Federalsburg (1872), the *Greensborough Free Press* (1881), the *Hurlock Advance* (1898), and Ridgely's *Caroline Sun* (1902).

With or without the stimulus of railroads, newspapers popped up in all sorts of unlikely places, often to vanish just as suddenly. At one point or another during the post-Civil War era Church Hill, Crumpton, Sharptown, Queenstown, Rising Sun, Chesapeake City, Port Deposit, North East, Perryville, Trappe, Oxford, and St. Michaels all boasted weekly or monthly publications. Preston in Caroline County had at least five, though not at the same time. Even Gluckheim, a now-vanished post office in eastern Dorchester, provided the dateline for a paper. The *Ruralist*, a monthly farm journal, was distributed from there although printed in Federalsburg.

For the major centers, it was a period of prolific if not exactly intense competition. In 1884, seven newspapers were being published at the same time in Cecil County—the *Cecil Democrat*, *Cecil Whig*, *Cecil County News*, and *Elkton Appeal*, all in Elkton, and the *Cecil Call* of Port Deposit, the *Rising Sun Journal*, and the *North East Star* elsewhere in the county. Talbot County had seven about the same time: the *Gazette*, *Democrat*, *Ledger*, and *Star* in Easton, along with the *Talbot Times* in Trappe, the *Comet* in St. Michaels, and the *Oxford Enterprise*.

Founded in 1872, the *Crisfield Leader* was one of the lower Shore's outstanding papers for many years.

The competition, however, was more apparent than real. Editors, following age-old Eastern Shore tradition, derided each other's product in print, sometimes in rough and even offensive language. But this was mostly a matter of politics, not be taken literally or personally, as it once had been. Lorie C. Quinn of the *Crisfield Times*, a Democratic paper, and William R. Reese of the Republican *Crisfield Leader* blasted each other regularly in their respective editorial columns, but in private life were neighbors and close friends. Wilson M. Tylor, publisher of the highly successful and strongly Republican *Easton Gazette*, temporarily bought both the *Easton Star* and *Easton Democrat* in 1896 to keep them from going under, and then not only arranged their merger but permitted the new owners to print the combined *Star-Democrat* in his own shop until they could round up enough capital to buy new equipment. It appears he hated the idea of not having a Democratic paper to rail against.

Tylor's gesture was symbolic of the relaxed state of Eastern Shore journalism as a whole during the post-Civil War era. There was none of the aggressive battling for circulation and advertising dollars which was revolutionizing the press in mainstream America. The rise of yellow journalism, with its sensational headlines, emphasis on sex and crime, and vaunted exposés of graft and corruption in high places, created not so much as a ripple among Shore newspapers. And with good reason; the business of putting out a small town weekly had almost nothing in common with the publishing of a New York daily except that both used printer's ink and paper.

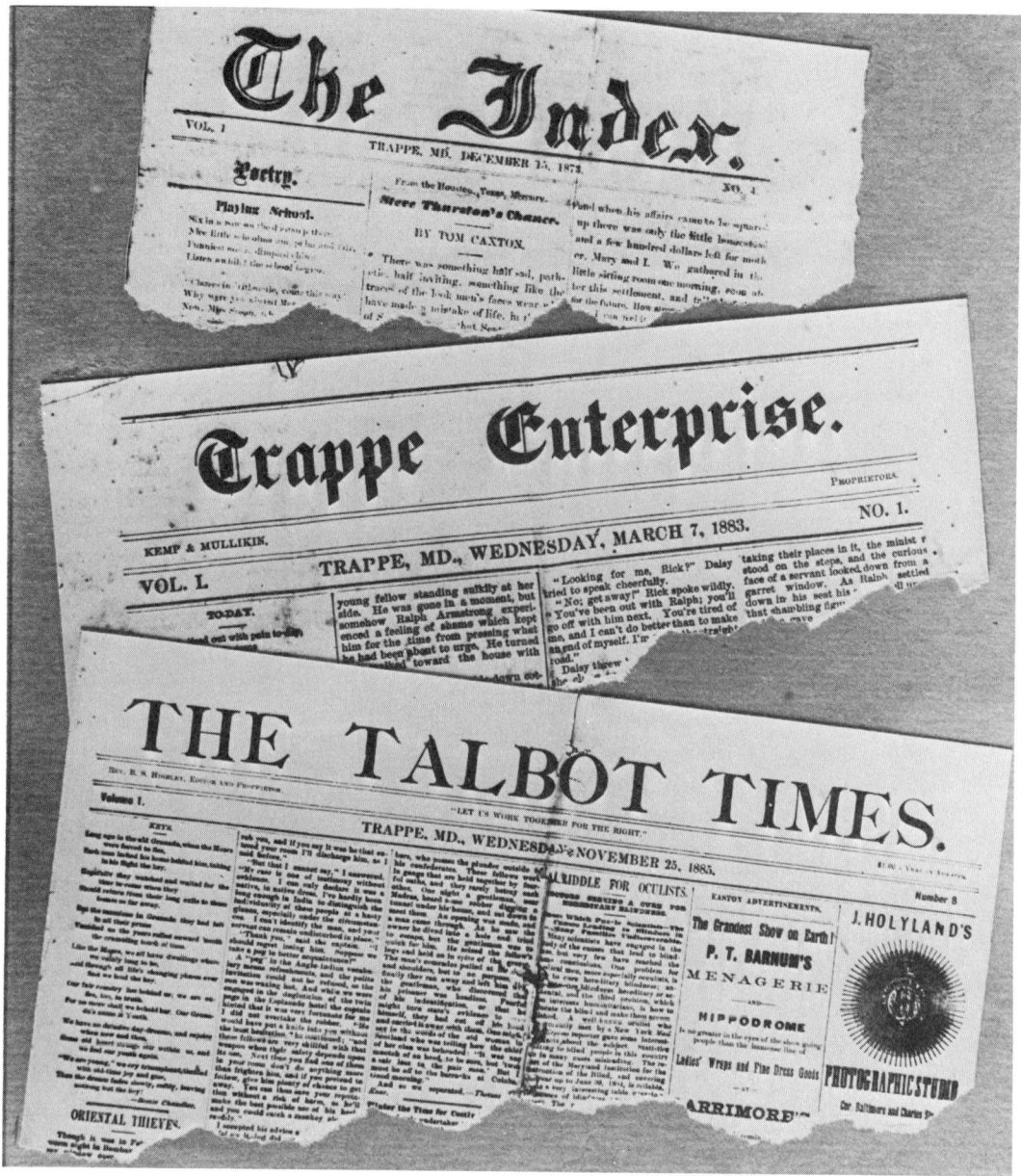

Trappe, with a population of about 600, had three different newspapers between 1873 and 1902. (Courtesy Laird Wise)

The New York publishers who created the new journalism epitomized by Hearst and Pulitzer were in the business of selling newspapers. News was their merchandise; and to be saleable it had to be exciting, dramatic, appealing to the baser human emotions. Conflict, disaster, the unique, and the grotesque sold papers; "good" news did not. The aphorism that "when a man bites a dog, that's news," became a ruling dictum, to the everlasting discredit of American journalism.

None of this applied to journalism on the Eastern Shore. The publishers of county weeklies were not epecially interested in building circulation; and even if they had been, there were no great masses of potential buyers to which to sell papers. They accepted whatever advertising happened to walk through the door, but they didn't go looking for it with aggressive sales tactics. As late as 1940 Samuel E. Shannahan, long-time editor and general manager of the *Easton Star-Democrat*, boasted that he had never solicited an advertisement in his life, and this despite the fact that during most of his career the *Star-Democrat* had had active competition from at least two other local papers.

In any case, even a successful county weekly was not an economic unit in itself, but an adjunct of a printing company in which the main profits came from legal advertising and job work. The newspaper was in effect a form of advertising for the printing firm which published it. Its circulation came from that portion of the public which agreed with its politics, and hopefully there would be enough of them to keep it in business. Although exact cost-accounting breakdowns were unknown, few if any newspapers during this period were moneymakers in themselves. They were, in almost all cases, part of a package which at best provided a comfortable living for one or two families and low-paid employment for a few others.

So while the big city dailies titillated readers with stories about the sad fate of school girls decoyed into houses of ill fame, and with scare headlines on such sensations as "Fiendish Parents!" and "Alive in a Coffin," the Eastern Shore weeklies showed little change from their appearance in the first half of the century. Eastern Shore editors saw no reason to emulate their metropolitan counterparts. Exposés might be fashionable in New York City, which as everybody knew was a den of sin anyhow, but what was there to expose about a region which in the opinion of most residents closely resembled the Garden of Eden? How could one lay bare the "evils" of worker exploitation by greedy capitalists when there were almost no factories and even fewer capitalists?

Political corruption was even less likely as a source of news sensations. When S. Ellwood Patchett launched a new paper called the *Independent* in Easton in 1885 with a dramatic story about the "gambling hells" which allegedly existed with official connivance, he was greeted with hoots of laughter. The whole town already knew there were poker games in the back rooms of certain stores, just as it was possible to get "medicinal spirits" from certain druggists even though Easton had officially gone dry in 1874. Such things did not constitute corruption; they provided a service.

THE ADVOCATE,
A Weekly Religious and Literary Journal,
Published at CHESTERTOWN.

Methodist in its religious sentiments and Republican in its political, but liberal towards all.
Circulates all over Maryland and Delaware, and largely in Pennsylvania, New Jersey, Virginia and West Virginia.
Its present circulation is something over 600, with a steadily increasing subscription list. Subscription price, $1.25 a year, in advance.

T. BURTON, Publisher and Editor.
N. W. AYER & SON, Advertising Agents, Philadelphia.

G. E. LAMBERT,

MANUFACTURER OF
Carriages, Express Wagons, &c.
CHESTERTOWN.

LOUIS K. STAM,
DEALER IN
FURNITURE,
PAINTS, OILS, GLASS, PUTTY,
Kalsomine, Wall Paper, Window Curtains, &c.
CHESTERTOWN.

C. W. C. JOHNSON,
Justice of the Peace,
CHESTERTOWN.

JAMES A. SHAW,
DEALER IN
GROCERIES,
BOOTS & SHOES,
AND
FURNITURE,
Chestertown.

J. A. PERKINS,
DEALER IN
GROCERIES,
NOTIONS,
Tobacco, General Merchandise, &c.
CHESTERTOWN.

WHEATLEY BROS.
DEALERS IN
GROCERIES,
Provisions, Tobacco & Cigars,
CHESTERTOWN.

The Salisbury Advertiser
—AND—
EASTERN SHOREMAN, (Consolidated.)

This paper has the largest circulation of any newspaper in the State (except the city of Baltimore). It goes to every State in the Union and most civilized countries, and is one of the best advertising mediums. Terms moderate, considering circulation.

Published every Saturday Morning by L. MALONE, at
SALISBURY.

THOS. HUMPHREYS,
Attorney at Law,
SALISBURY.
Practices in the Courts of Wicomico, Somerset, Worcester and Dorchester Counties.

THOS. F. J. RIDER,
Attorney and Counselor at Law
SALISBURY.
Practices in the Courts of Wicomico, Somerset, Worcester and Dorchester Counties.
Attorney for Merchants and Manufacturers' Mercantile and Collection Agency. Baltimore and Philadelphia references given when required.

HUMPHREYS & TILGHMAN,
SALISBURY,
Manufacturers, Wholesale & Retail Dealers and Shippers of all kinds of
YELLOW PINE LUMBER
Dressed Flooring, Building Lumber, Box Boards,
SHINGLES, LATHS, PEACH CRATES IN SHOOKS, &c.
ALSO GENERAL MERCHANDISE.   Orders by mail promptly attended to.

J. M. DASHIELL,
Justice of the Peace,
SALISBURY.

Life.   Fire.   Marine.
F. C. TODD,
GENERAL INSURANCE AGENT,
—AND—
Collector of Claims,
MAIN STREET,
SALISBURY.

EASTON LEDGER,
Published every Thursday at Easton,
JULIUS A. JOHNSON, - - Editor.

Has a large circulation in one of the richest counties of the State and is a valuable medium for advertising.

Terms of Subscription:
$2.00 per Year. - - $1.50 if Paid in Advance.

E. L. ZIMMERS,
WAGONS, CARTS.
HORSE SHOEING A SPECIALTY.
EASTON.

WM. J. HOLLAND,
ST. MICHAEL'S,
Runs the Stage daily from St. Michael's to Easton at 11.30 A. M. Returning leaves Easton daily 3 P. M. ROUND TRIP ONE DOLLAR.

Eastern Shore newspapers tooted their own horns in a Maryland directory of the 1880s.

Advertising page from the *American Union* of Denton.

Comic strips, half-tone photographs, feature-laden Sunday editions, cabled foreign reports, press association news, and such examples of "journalistic enterprise" as Stanley's highly publicized search for Livingston, all made their debuts in the New York press of the 1880s and 1890s, but no such things appeared in Eastern Shore newspapers until half a century later.

In fact, about the only journalistic innovation on the Shore was that, some time around 1890, a few of the more progressive editors began, cautiously and in moderation, to print a little local news on page one. This was indeed a daring change; throughout Eastern Shore journalism's first century, the front page had been devoted to political essays, short stories, and advertising, while whatever coverage there was of local events was relegated to page two or three, under the editorial masthead.

Just who deserves credit for this bold breakthrough is uncertain. James C. Mullikin, in his *Story of the Easton Star-Democrat*, gave the laurels to Wilson Tylor of the *Easton Gazzette*, whom he described as a "paragon of editors." Long before competing papers tried it, according to Mullikin, Tylor "had ruthlessly removed the advertisements, the boiler-plate reading matter, and the fiction from the front page and was using that page for a brave show of local news." Papers such as the *Cecil Whig*, the *Kent News*, and the *Salisbury*

By 1916, local news had become dominant on page one.

Advertiser may have changed their format at about the same time; certainly the "new look" was in vogue by the time the Shore's first daily, the *Cambridge Banner*, came along in 1897.

Such "enterprise" as existed among Shore newsmen sometimes backfired. In 1874 a youthful coeditor of the *St. Michaels Comet*, faced with the problem of preparing an enticing ad for a piece of Royal Oak property which had little to recommend it, had a brainstorm. He inserted a purely fictitious statement:

> According to unpublished statistics the health centre of the United States is a circle with Royal Oak as the centre and a radius of four miles.

The statistics were indeed unpublished, because he had just invented them; and the "radius of four miles" had been devised for the purpose of taking in St. Michaels but leaving its rival, Easton, out of the "health centre" area.

The advertisement was published in the *Comet* without attracting any comment, and both the young writer and his senior partner, the Reverend Mr. William M. Poisal, thought that would be the end of it. But the story would not die. A metropolitan paper picked up the item and published it as fact, and other major dailies followed suit.

For the next twenty-five years, the statement that Royal Oak was the healthiest place in America was published and republished, expanded and embellished. The four-mile radius became ten miles, letting in Easton, and once was shrunk to a "circumference of four miles," which made it a very small area. The statistics were variously credited to the 1890 Census, the United States Bureau of Vital Statistics, and the National Health Bureau. According to *Land of Legendary Lore*, an 1898 book about Talbot County by Prentiss Ingraham, "some years ago the United States Government sent out officers for statistics of healthfulness of the entire country, and, with Royal Oak, four miles from Oxford, as the centre, the ten miles around as the circle, statistics showed that this part of Talbot County held the palm." A collection of a hundred clippings was compiled giving the "facts" about Royal Oak's unique distinction as they had appeared in newspaper editorials, magazines, books, real estate catalogs, and advertising leaflets in cities ranging all the way to Chicago, San Francisco, Los Angeles, and Manila in the Philippines.

Eventually the one-time coeditor could stand it no longer. Identifying himself only as the Reverend Mr. Poisal's "wicked partner," he confessed responsibility for the hoax in an article published in the *Baltimore Sun* August 19, 1899. After quoting some of the more outlandish versions of the story, he admitted: "There is not a word of truth in it, and never was. The story is a fable, a pure invention. No such statement was ever made in a census report, or by the 'United States Bureau of Vital Statistics,' or by the 'National Health

Bureau,' or by 'officers sent out for statistics of healthfulness' . . . Mr. Poisal's wicked partner which was, having long since repented of his sins, thinks the fable should be exploded."

In physical appearance, as in content, Eastern Shore papers continued to resemble James Cowan's 1790 *Maryland Herald* rather more than they did the metropolitan dailies of 1890. They had expanded in size since Cowan's day, and some had gone to eight or more pages; but many were still printed on the Gutenberg-style hand presses which had served their forebears. When Lorie Quinn founded the *Crisfield Times*, he used "an old Washington hand press, which in expert hands could print possibly 60 to 75 papers an hour." On this he produced his weekly press run of 300 or so copies. More prosperous papers, however, did acquire power presses; the *Easton Gazette* advertised its "steam print" for job work as early as 1879.

Banner headlines were unknown, not as a matter of taste but for a simple mechanical reason. The flat forms used on the presses required column rules to hold a single column. Stereotyping, which utilized mats and cast metal plates to save wear and tear on type, eliminated the need for column rules; but although it was introduced in New York as early as 1854, it was not practical on the small Shore papers. Also too expensive, for most of the period, was the linotype, developed in the 1880s by Ottmar Mergenthaler, a Baltimore inventor. It could cast a full line at a time by using molten lead and a keyboard; but editor-printers on the Shore continued for many years to set type laboriously by hand. Cost problems also barred much use of photographs. Half-tone zinc engravings, which enabled city dailies to print photos with shades of gray as well as black and white, required a costly engraving department with acid baths for etching the zinc. As late as the 1950s, even such a comparatively up-to-date paper as the *Easton Star-Democrat* had to send its photographs to Philadelphia, where zinc engravings were made and sent back, hopefully in time for the next week's edition. "It made for some hairy deadlines," admits Norman Harrington, former *Star-Democrat* editor and general manager.

Advertising illustrations had been used ever since Cowan introduced wood cuts into *Maryland Herald* advertisements for sailing packets, real estate offerings, booteries, and the like in the 1790s. But they were crude and simple, more symbols than pictures. Identical woodcuts were employed to picture competing steamboats, rival hotels, and other enterprises. For years on end the symbol of an escaped slave was a woodcut of a black with his belongings in a cloth on a stick slung over his shoulder; females were identified by a bandanna headcloth.

In the post-Civil War era the quality of advertising illustrations improved as zinc engravings, etched on plates directly from artists' drawings and produced in metropolitan plants, began to appear in Eastern Shore papers. National advertisers provided "boilerplate," whole advertisements and even entire sections including poetry and essays along with advertising. This was prepared elsewhere and furnished ready for printing to the small town editor. But local advertising remained mostly a matter of varied type sizes, boldface headlines, exclamation points, and "plugs" slipped into the paper in the guise of news items.

Despite all their shortcomings, it would be a mistake to presume that Eastern Shore newspapers were behind the times in relation to their communities. They faithfully reflected the society of which they were a part, just as yellow journalism with all its strident excitement reflected changing social conditions in mainstream America. If Eastern Shore journalism seemed rooted in the past, so was the Eastern Shore itself. In the long, drowsy interval between the end of the Civil War and World War I, its population decreased and its economy stagnated. The tide of history had swept westward and northward, leaving it stranded; in a nation which was rapidly becoming industrialized, it remained entirely rural both in economics and viewpoint.

But it was a restful stagnation. Eastern Shore people wore their isolation and poverty as comfortably as an old shoe. They were, as an old-timer has put it, "too happy to realize we were poor." And there were advantages to being out of the thick of things. No great wave of European immigrants poured in to create problems of assimilation; no industrial giants arose to pollute the air and water; no social cataclysms threatened revolution and ruin. Economic booms and panics made little difference to people who had little to lose in the first place. Shore residents did not want newspapers which would stir things up and remind them of what they were missing. When they were not enjoying the simple pleasures of fishing, hunting, eating, and gossiping, they were looking to the past, imagining a blissful Southern-oriented time which never had been, when life was a merry round of parties on the great plantations, with happy "darkies" singing, dancing, and doing the work, before the wicked Northerners swept it all away by destroying slavery.

There was one exploited class—the blacks—and one slum area in every community, usually called "darktown." But this was not a matter of editorial concern even to the Republican papers which solicited black votes at election time. By common practice the blacks who comprised nearly a third of the Eastern Shore's population were ignored in the newspapers except as servants, criminals, or objects of crude humor.

Of more seeming importance was the "Yankee invasion" of the Eastern Shore, which began even before the end of the Civil War (and, of course, is still going on, although the invaders now threaten to outnumber the natives). As early as November, 1864, newspapers in the southern counties were reporting that "scarcely a steamer or stage arrives, that does not bring land buyers" from the North and from the Western Shore of Maryland, and that "in many instances farms have already changed hands." The "Yankees" were operating on the theory that former slaveholders, deprived of their labor by emancipation, would have to sell their land at depressed prices. The continued influx produced sharp editorial debate along predictable party lines in the 1870s. Republican papers echoed *Easton Gazette* editor William H. Councell, who charged that die-hard Southern sympathizers were snubbing the newcomers, calling them "carpet-baggers" and greeting them with cold suspicion. "Let us suppress . . . those baneful sectional prejudices," Councell admonished his readers. Democrats cheered *Easton Star* editor Thomas K. Robson, who shot back that "no such prejudice or hostility exists. A Northern man or woman settling here will be . . . treated as kindly by our people as they would be by any people in any part of the country." Robson admitted, however, the Eastern Shore ladies were "remiss in making social calls on strangers."

More esoteric issues fascinated some editors. One of the most curious of all post-Civil War Shore papers was the *Bachelor*, founded in Salisbury in 1870 with two bachelor editors, Charles F. Holland and George W. M. Cooper. Although they put out a full sized weekly, their chief aim in life seems to have been to ridicule the institution of marriage, and this they carried out with gusto. Under the slogan, "Free and Fearless," they featured such articles on page one as "Remarkable Courtships—Pops the Question at Sight," and "Ancient Customs—Marriage—Birth—Death." This offering, in the issue of August 13, 1873, started with the comment that "there are few who do not at some period of their lives dream of marriage, of its joys—rarely of its trials," and proceeded to delineate some of the more exotic marriage customs of ancient Europe, such as the whipping of bridegrooms as part of the ceremony. Inside the paper was a gossip column lampooning Salisbury social life.

The *Bachelor* lasted only four years, being absorbed by the *Salisbury Advertiser* in 1874—reportedly because one of the "free and fearless" editors decided to get married after all.

Most Shore papers campaigned sporadically for civic improvements; but in the comfortable somnolence of Eastern Shore life, getting the town fathers to do anything about anything was not an easy chore. The *Kent News* took up the cudgels for better street lighting, complaining in its issue of November 24, 1888, that "Chestertown is miserably supplied with light. Probably we are behind any town our size on the peninsula . . . About 65 miserable kerosene 'flickers'—that have little more force than tallow dips—do duty as street lights, and our dwellings and business houses are suffering still the danger and inconvenience of coal oil."

An agent of the Edison Company had been trying to persuade Chestertownians to put up an electric light plant, and, said the *News*, "we are talking now about the matter. What will be the practical outcome remains to be seen."

Unhappily, it turned out that not enough town business leaders could be found who were willing to invest five hundred dollars apiece to finance the company unless they could be guaranteed it would show a profit. The *News* referred scornfully to the "crokers and fault-finders" who demanded ten percent on their money before they would do anything to help the town; but it was nearly eleven years before the paper was able at last to announce, on January 14, 1899, that "the Electric Light Company are ready to begin work on the streets of Chestertown just as soon as the town commissioners sign the contract."

Even though most of the Shore went "dry" in the 1870s under local option laws, prohibition and control of illicit liquor sales remained an issue of great concern on the Methodist-dominated peninsula. One problem was that, while sales might be barred in a dry community, there was nothing to prevent residents who were so minded from going to Baltimore and bringing back all the whiskey they pleased; and in fact many Eastern Shoremen did so. Local druggists also featured "medicinal spirits" in their newspaper ads, although just how sick a customer had to be to qualify for a dosage varied from town to town. "Moonshine" still flourished in the rural areas; and in such waterfront towns as Crisfield, bootlegging and speakeasies were a problem long before they became a familiar part of the national scene.

In this ambivalent climate, crusading against liquor was almost a civic duty for the Eastern Shore press. Nearly every editor vigorously supported temperance for public consumption, no matter what his personal tastes might be. Some papers were actually taken over by prohibition forces and operated as propaganda organs for their cause. The *Record and Gazette* of Pocomoke City was partly owned by a syndicate of prohibitionists headed by Lawrence Hastings of Snow Hill, and in the 1880s served as the official publication of the Prohibition Party of the Eastern Shore. The *Federalsburg Courier* also was published as a prohibitionist paper when it was owned by the Heffron brothers between 1885 and 1890.

Not all the efforts of the earnest temperance crusaders met with success. A notable exception was Crisfield, a haven for watermen and sailors where drunken brawls were common. The *Salisbury Advertiser* of August 16, 1873, reported on the sad outcome of an expedition by a trainload of Methodist women from Salisbury who had gone to Crisfield with the intention of converting the ungodly and wiping out the evils of liquor. As condensed by John R. Wennersten in "The Almighty Oyster" (*Maryland Historical Magazine*, Spring, 1979), the results were not quite as expected:

Editorial office of the *Kent News*, Chestertown, about 1890. *Left to right*, William B. Usilton, Sr., editor and publisher; William B. Usilton, Jr., later editor; and an unidentified visitor. (Courtesy William B. Usilton III)

The women were dressed in their best finery and paraded through the streets to the delight of the watermen. Later the town thronged to the twenty-five revival tents that the ladies had established a short distance from the town at Nelson's Woods. Unfortunately a fierce rain and electrical storm disrupted the proceedings before Crisfield's lost souls could be rescued. To many Crisfield Methodists it seemed that even nature was leagued against the Holy Writ and the public peace.

The town commissioners voted Crisfield dry on December 8, 1875, but that did not end the problem. Thirty-four years later, editor Lorie Quinn of the *Crisfield Times* reached the reluctant conclusion that "Crisfield would be far better off if open licensed saloons were permitted."

Writing in the issue of August 14, 1909, Quinn estimated that fifty or more "speakeasies," and "walking barrooms"—the term for bootleggers who carried their booze with them as they strolled the streets—were operating in Crisfield.

"It seems that anyone who desires 'Town Booze,' can get it in any quantities and at any time . . . The condition is one of the worst and most disgraceful that has ever existed in any city in the state . . . Much of this liquor is manufactured in Crisfield, and is said to contain snuff, ginger, fine cut tobacco, wood alcohol and a small amount of cheap whiskey." It sold for fifty cents a pint, and Quinn estimated ten to twenty barrels were disposed of on Saturday nights in the waterfront section of town.

Like most Eastern Shoremen, Quinn blamed the problem on "strangers," the standard scapegoats for anything that went wrong. He recommended that all "stranger vagrants should be rounded up" and run out of town if they couldn't show some good reason for being in the area. That would "remove at least a portion of the blot that has fallen on this peaceful, law-abiding community."

As usual, nothing much was done beyond a few raids by local law officers. When Carrie Nation, the famous "saloon smasher and grand reformer in general," paid an unannounced visit to Crisfield a year later, the *Times* reported with some amusement that "all the speakeasies closed up business" as soon as word spread she had arrived. The whole town waited to see where she would start wielding the axe which was her trademark. But Mrs. Nation disappointed them; she announced that she had simply come to give a lecture at the Lyric Theater, and that was all she did.

Two weeks later the *Times* was able to report that Mrs. Nation had put on a better show for the residents of Parksley on the Virginia Eastern Shore. After her lecture there, "she went to a local pool room and billiard parlor with the cry 'This is the hole,' [and] started in to smash things in general. She caused considerable disturbance, causing the men to fight among themselves . . . Mrs. Nation was finally taken bodily out of the place by the proprietor."

Especially in the smaller communities, the story of a newspaper was often a desperate and unsuccessful struggle to survive. Typical was the case of the *Chesapeake Chesapike* of memorable name, established in 1876 in Chesapeake City. Just why its founder, Harry Moss, wanted a newspaper named "for a fighting fish of the Bay" remains a mystery; but in any case he gave up and sold out to Dr. D. H. B. Bower after only two years. Dr. Bower, less romantically inclined, changed the name to the *Chesapeake Record*, and a year later moved the whole operation to North East, where he published the paper as the *North East Record* until he too gave up in 1882.

Another Cecil County paper with problems was the *Rising Sun Commercial*, a short-lived journal sponsored by a local merchandising firm. Soon after it began publication in 1878, it carried an announcement: "This copy of the *Rising Sun Commercial* is printed in the office of the *Oxford Press*, where it will be printed hereafter. The proprietor of the printing office here flatly refuses to print the *Commercial* any longer." The *Press* was published in Oxford, Pennsylvania. However, the experiment did not work out; the last known issue of the *Commercial* is dated October 11, 1879.

Eastern Shore journalistic history is studded with records of such hopeful beginnings and quick demises: the *Crumpton Gazette*, later the *Crumptonian*, which went through four editor-publishers between its birth in 1865 and its death in 1869; the *Times* of Pocomoke City, started in the 1880s by a young lawyer, J. Lloyd Wilkinson, but wiped out forever by the great fire of November 22, 1888, which reduced most of Pocomoke City's business district to ruins; the *Index* of Trappe, which lasted just a year and never had a circulation of more than a hundred; Salisbury's *Bachelor, Eastern Shoreman,* and *Wicomico Record*, all quickly absorbed by the *Salisbury Advertiser*; and, in more modern times, the *Eastern Shore Journal*, which survived for just six weeks after its brave beginning in Easton in January, 1976. The list could go on and on.

But there were also success stories. In Queenstown two brothers, H. M. and M. W. Aker, tried their hand at putting out a newspaper purely as an experiment in January, 1882. Their first efforts were amateurish in the extreme; but they persisted, attracted some financing, and gradually acquired skill. The *Queenstown News* lived on as a family enterprise until its last editor, Michael Aker, had to close it down in 1956. Neither it nor the print shop in which it was produced ever made much money—Mike Aker is said to have slept in a bunk over the press in his later years—but it served a small Eastern Shore community well for more than seventy years.

Another paper which started on a shoestring was the *Wicomico News*. In 1887 Marion V. Brewington was working at the *Salisbury Advertiser* as an apprentice printer for seven dollars a week. He asked for a raise, but was turned down. Angered, he persuaded his bother, Harry L. Brewington, to join him in buying the year-old *Wicomico News* on borrowed funds. They didn't get much for their money except an ancient Washington hand press and a miscellany of used type; they served as compositors, pressmen, editors, and publishers themselves. But over the thirty-one years the *News* turned into a very profitable enterprise, and the Brewingtons became Democratic political leaders and substantial men of affairs.

The endemic race prejudice which too often has marred the Eastern Shore's self-image as a land of peace and plenty showed up in its newspapers from time to time. Only a few instances need be cited: they serve to demonstrate the emotionalism which underlay white attitudes toward race throughout the period, and to some extent still do.

Back from his exile after the end of the Civil War, Tom Robson revived the *Easton Star* in September, 1865, on the strength of an official order from

THE QUEENSTOWN NEWS

VOL I. QUEENSTOWN, MARYLAND, FEBRUARY 4 1882 NO 5

Guiteau,s Mail.

Mr Scoville at length came upon one upon which he bestowed more than a mere passing notice. "I have heard from these parties before," said Mr Scoville, a grim smile flitting over his careworn face. "This is from a firm in Philadelphia, who have a process of arresting decay in meats, fruit or vegetables by subjecting them to a certain continuous, even temperature in a refrigerating chest. They propose to take Guiteau's body as soon as he is hung, subject it to this process in a chest with glass sides exposing it to view and then exhidit it in this country and in Europe, giving the relatives of the refrigerated corpse one-half of the net proceeds. I don't know but that is a better offer than the one I have just received from St. Louis of $5,000 outright for the body. I wish you would say that after to-day no further notice will be taken of any letters addressed to Guiteau. I shall take his mail every day and dump it unopen into the Potomac river. It will aid materially in filling up the Potomac flat, but beyond that is of no earthly use.

A Woman Worth Having

Mrs Charles Vincent, Portchester, N Y. One night lately, while her husbend was out, and nobody should of been in but herself and a servant girl she went into the hall and saw three men coming down stairs with big bundles. She snatched the bundle from the first man, flung it into the corner, throttled the robber threw him heavily on the floor. She then pushed the second over the first. He fell, and she tramped on him got his bundle and threw it into the parlor. The third burglar knocked her down, but she rallied and got his bundle away from him. Then all three of the men got frightened and ran, and she kicked the last one going out the door, and the terrified servant girl stood back in the hall and looked on in apt admiration. In the bundles were two sealskin sacques, a seal dolman, a camel's hair shawl, several dresses and things worth in all $1.200

A Few years ago efforts were made to acclimatize English sparrows in Southern Australia, Now a premium of a cent apeice is paid for their destruction, and their eggs bring 3-4 of a cent apeice.

In Congress are eight Irishmen, four Scotchmen, five Englishmen and three German.

"I observe that Gambetta has resigned," remarks Mr. Roscoe Conkling and, after adjusting his necktie, adds: 'He had an illustrious precedent."

Earliest known issue of *The Queenstown News*, dated February 4, 1882. The lead story was about Charles Guiteau, murderer of President Garfield. (Courtesy the Reverend Edward Carley)

Office of the *Free Press*, Greensboro, about 1900. In foreground is John Dukes Plummer, son of founder Risdon Plummer. The combined office and composing room was over J. W. Porter's snack bar. (Courtesy Robert H. Taylor)

President Johnson revoking its suspension. He continued as editor until his death September 20, 1888, as "unreconstructed" and as opinionated as ever, although his militancy shifted from the Confederacy to race.

The *Star* bluntly labeled the Republicans, who supported black voting rights, as the "Nigger Party" in headlines as well as in body type. The Democrats were the "White Man's Party." In the 1870 Congressional election, when blacks voted for the first time under protection of the Fifteenth Amendment, Robson harangued voters with the fear that a Republican victory would mean "the negro will very soon be able to poke his nose into anywhere a white man can put his." He said the issue was a simple one of "white supremacy or black domination." A predominantly black meeting in Easton was headlined "The Nigger Fandango" and the Republican candidate, Henry Torbert, was said to have "frothed and fumed on the stump, and told stories to amuse the negroes."

Republicans somewhat defensively replied that fears of black domination in Maryland were ridiculous. The *American Union* of Denton pointed out that there were only thirty-five thousand black voters in Maryland compared with one hundred thousand whites, and that the blacks were demanding no offices. "If the Republican Party should triumph, would not white men still be at the helm of the ship of state? Are not Republicans white in complexion?" the *Union* asked.

However, Robson's racist campaign succeeded, and when the Democrats won, the *Star* crowed in its headlines: "the Nigger Party routed . . . the Cause of White Man Vindicated . . . the White People of the Whole Country Waking Up to the Dangers of Negro Domination."

About the same time, Chestertown passed an ordinance designed to keep blacks from voting by requiring that only owners of local real estate could take part in town elections. A black resident got around this by giving each of about forty blacks a foot or so of real estate, thus making them eligible. The *Kent News* denounced this as "a fraud" and a "contemptible evasion of law." However, the *Freedmen's Journal*, another Chestertown newspaper which was sympathetic to the blacks, later revealed that ninety-seven whites who lived outside town had taken part in a similar scheme, each becoming owner of a square foot of land on Mill Street. One of them was *Kent News* editor James H. Plummer.

"Which was a fraud and which was honest?" the Easton *Gazette* asked in reporting this. To "ordinary people" the two actions might seem remarkably alike, but "to Kent County the difference between them is evident. One is mean, low-lived and fraudulent, because it was done by a 'nigger,' the other a munificent and liberal action because it was done by a white man."

A far more ominous foreshadowing of things to come was reported by the *Marylander* of Princess Anne in June, 1897. This was a lynching made unusual by the fact that the black victim, William Andrews, had already been convicted on a rape charge and sentenced to hang when he was seized by a mob and lynched.

The *Marylander* reported the incident in full detail in its issue of June 15. Andrews, charged with "ravishing" a white woman at Marion on May 5, had been held in Baltimore for safekeeping until time for his trial June 9. A crowd of four hundred to five hundred men gathered outside the courthouse at Princess Anne while his case was heard. The trial itself was little more than "shotgun justice"; he was brought into court, arraigned, and a jury chosen which began hearing evidence at once. He had pleaded not guilty, but this was stricken when his attorney said Andrews had confessed his guilt in a conversation held just before he was brought from the jail. A plea of guilty was then entered, and Judge Henry Page instructed the jury to bring in a verdict in accordance. They did, unanimously, and Andrews was sentenced to hang.

Staff of the *Easton Gazette* in the 1880s. Second from right is believed to be Wilson M. Tylor, *Gazette* editor for twenty-seven years.

Judge Page went outside and explained to the mob that Andrews had been duly found guilty and sentenced to hang "on such day as the Governor should name, which should be a soon one." For a time it appeared that the crowd might let sheriff's deputies take the condemned man back to jail. But suddenly, said the *Marylander*, "men began to hit him with canes, umbrellas, clubs, pieces of plank and anything that could be found. The officers fought like demons to protect him, but . . . it would have taken a regiment with fixed bayonets to have saved him from that crowd." After being beaten into unconsciousness, he was hanged from a walnut tree, ironically on Church Street.

Shortly afterward, a jury of inquest rendered its verdict: "We find that on the 9th day of June, 1897, at Princess Anne in Somerset County, certain people, to the jurors unknown, feloniously, voluntarily, and with malice aforethought, did . . . tie a rope around the neck of said William Andrews and hang him to a tree."

At one time the *Easton Gazette* office was in the structure built by Thomas Perrin Smith about 1812 to house the *Republican Star*. The building now is headquarters for the Chesapeake Bay Yacht Club.

That was the end of that. If there was any further investigation, it got nowhere. In several respects—the fact that Andrews had been taken to Baltimore, the cursory trial, the mob vengeance, the failure to investigate, even the mention of "a regiment with fixed bayonets"—it foretold events which would rock the Eastern Shore and all of Maryland in 1931 and 1933.

To many nineteenth-century Eastern Shoremen, violence was a way of life. That was especially true of the rough watermen who dredged and tonged for oysters in the waters of Pocomoke and Tangier sounds. For more than half a century there was literal warfare, with numerous casualties and many boats sunk, over the seemingly limitless oyster beds of the Chesapeake—a warfare which ended only when the supply of oysters began to run out.

The struggle dates from early in the nineteenth century. "Pirate boats" from New York waters, coming down to raid the lush Chesapeake beds, met armed resistance from the local watermen, and Virginians were warned to stay in their part of the bay both by gunfire and by Maryland laws against poaching by "foreign" oystermen. The earliest reference this writer has found in a Shore newspaper indicates the Virginians were dredging far north of their legal territory in the 1840s. The *Centreville Times* reported that a sheriff's posse had

Easton Ledger staff and press about 1895.

come down the Chester River "in pursuit of several foreign vessels which were oystering with dredges in violation of the law." Five vessels, it said, were seen between Hell Creek and Love Point on Kent Island. Four of them were captured with about one thousand bushels of oysters aboard. The boats were to be sold "for the benefit of the State" of Maryland. The crews, presumably from south of the Potomac, were released after paying fines.

The wars were fought on three separate fronts: "drudgers" against tongers; Marylanders against Virginians; and, on occasion, all the oystermen against the marine police who manned the patrol boats. By law the dredgers were barred from the shallow waters on which the tongers depended for a living, and Marylanders and Virginians from oystering in each other's territory. In practice, these rules gave rise to bitter and protracted disputes in which pitched battles were fought and killings were not uncommon.

Interstate warfare heated up during the Civil War, when the development of packing houses and canneries in Baltimore created a vast new market for oysters. The day book of a wartime storekeeper later published by the *Crisfield Times* bore this notation for October 1, 1863, "Oyster war in the sound—two boats sank." The Maryland-Virginia boundary line beneath Chesapeake Bay was so vague that no one knew who had a legal right to what, and in any case Virginia and Maryland were officially at war. The rugged watermen from Tangier Island on the Virginia side and Smith Island in Maryland were less interested in the great issues of the Rebellion than in their oyster rights, and they settled things on an *ad hoc* basis with guns and even cannon.

Once the Civil War ended, efforts were made to achieve peace in the oyster war. The *Salisbury Advertiser* reported in June, 1872, that commissioners from the two states were meeting at Crisfield in an effort to settle the dispute, and again in February, 1877, that a demarcation line had been agreed on which gave Virginia the largest share of the disputed waters, including more than 23,000 acres of prime oyster beds. The embittered Smith Islanders ignored the "line of '77," and continued their raids across it for the next twenty years under the guns of Tangier Islanders and Virginia patrol boats. The fighting petered out only when the heavy dredging and lack of any program for reproducing young oysters depleted the beds in the early 1900s.

Contemporary comments on the warfare from Eastern Shore newspapers are scarce because nearly all pre-1908 issues of papers from Crisfield, which was most concerned, have been lost. But the national press gave it colorful coverage. The *New York Times* reported in March, 1894, on a battle in which the Virginia oyster police schooner *Tangier* had pursued Maryland oystermen back to Smith Island. There it met a fierce hail of bullets from twenty-five Marylanders with repeating rifles firing round after round from hastily thrown-up breastworks. The *Tangier* beat a hasty retreat to port at Onancock, Virginia. According to Hulbert Footner's *Rivers of the Eastern Shore,* Virginia and Maryland watermen in 1895 were engaged in a pitched battle on Woman's Island when a Virginia patrol boat hove in view. The rivals quit fighting each other and joined forces to drive off the hated minions of the law. The Virginia officers then sought help from a Maryland patrol boat, and between them they "licked the combined oystermen."

At the same time "oyster pirates" from both states caused constant trouble by raiding the shallow beds of the tongers, chiefly at night, and dredging up oysters illegally. Tongers constructed crude shanties on stilts at selected bars where armed guards kept watch for the raiders. The *Marylander and Herald* of Princess Anne told of the capture, in September, 1912, of one of the famous Somerset County pirates, Ernest Cox. After a fierce exchange of gunfire, he was seized by local tongers at the Connel oyster bar on the Manokin River. The *Crisfield Times* of January 18, 1908, carried the story of the capture of William Stant, "said to be the most daring oyster pirate in Virginia." Stant had often boasted that he would not be arrested alive, the *Times* said, but was surprised by the steamer *Commodore Maury*, flagship of the Virginia oyster navy, aboard which were top officials of the State Board of Fisheries. He at first showed fight, and then "cut away the dredge and tried to escape. The searchlight of the Maury was kept on him and after a short chase he was captured."

Long after the Maryland-Virginia warfare ended with the depletion of the oyster beds, the interstate bitterness continued. As recently as 1949, the *Crisfield Times* printed an angry report on the fatal shooting of a Crisfield watermen, Earl Lee Nelson, by a Virginia police officer who had detected Nelson crabbing in Virginia waters. Calling it "a most atrocious crime," the *Times* quoted witnesses as saying, "here was murder, violent, uncalled for, done without any excuse whatever." A murder warrant was issued in Maryland for the officer, David Acree, but Virginia authorities refused to turn him over for trial. Instead, a Virginia grand jury exonerated him, ruling the shooting was accidental. That brought another blast from the *Times*.

Another aspect of the boom period of oyster dredging was the brutal treatment given crews by oyster boat captains. In many cases these were drunks or derelicts shanghaied from the low dives along the Baltimore docks, or foreigners lured aboard by promises of good pay and working conditions. Once on the boats they were half starved, beaten, worked continuously, and given no medical treatment. Horror stories were common. As one example, the *Crisfield Times* in the 1890s told the story of a Baltimore youth, eighteen-year-old Isaac Spreet, who had been kidnapped in downtown Baltimore by two men who at first offered him forty dollars a month as a cabin boy and then, when he refused the offer, seized him and took him aboard the oyster boat *Lightning*. There he was beaten often and in fourteen days received but one piece of bread, plus what he could steal. His father, a prominent Baltimore businessman, reported him missing, and police finally rescued him after receiving a tip that a boy had been seen being forced aboard the *Lightning*.

Another case, reported in the *Marylander and Herald* January 30, 1917, was that of William McPherson, who had been promised fourteen dollars a month wages by skipper Noah Holland of the bugeye *Ariel* but was treated as a slave. McPherson lost nine fingers and nine toes to frostbite. He eventually was awarded a judgment of one thousand five hundred dollars in damages against Holland.

Throughout the "long siesta" period, Eastern Shore editors alternately lamented the Shore's lack of progress and boasted of its virtues. In August, 1881, the *Record and Gazette* of Pocomoke City insisted that "it is no longer a disgrace to be called an Eastern Shoreman," but granted that the Shore needed "more population and capital to develop our lands, consume our products, and multiply our business enterprises." In May, 1908, by contrast, the *Crisfield Times* described Crisfield as "the pride of the Eastern Shore, noted for its delicious seafood, its beautiful women, fine bathing, hustling business enterprises, and many other things which are naturally a source of local pride." It noted that the town also was the home of "probably the oldest inhabitant on the Shore," 104-year-old Mariah Parks.

If there was one quality which characterized outstanding Eastern Shore editors, it was not their crusading zeal or aggressive journalism, but their sense of identification with their home communities. They were boosters for their towns, their counties, and the Eastern Shore against the entire "outside world," which was everything beyond the borders of the narrow peninsula on which they lived. That went even for the Delaware counties, which were regarded as mere step-children of the shore, and for the rest of Maryland—especially the big and bullying city of Baltimore. And they were more than mere boosters; most were community leaders, town officers, members of countless civic commissions and boards.

Samuel E. Shannahan, who was editor of the *Easton Star-Democrat* from 1910 until he dropped dead at his desk December 7, 1942, was in this respect the small town editor personified. Born in Easton December 19, 1873, he spent all his life in the town he served. He learned his trade the old-fashioned way, as an apprentice and later a journeyman printer in the *Gazette* shop under Wilson Tylor, a scholarly and successful editor. Shannahan's family had been on the Eastern Shore for generations; his father, John H. K. Shannahan II, was a well driller in demand throughout the area; his brother, John H. K. Shannahan III, was a writer on Eastern Shore lore whose *Steamboat'n' Days* is a classic in its field.

Shannahan and his associate, Clement E. Bray, *were* the *Star-Democrat* as far as its public face was concerned. Both trained printers, they did the inside work of producing the paper; and between them they covered every newsworthy event in Talbot County from the day Bray joined the paper in 1917 to the day Shannahan died.

As an editor, Shannahan was utterly chauvinistic—and proud of it—as far as the interests of Talbot County and the Eastern Shore were concerned. He gave his county saturation coverage, and did not waste a line on events beyond the limits of the Shore. When he started as editor, the *Star-Democrat*'s front page carried advertising on four of its six columns, with a two-column "hole" in the middle for news. Shannahan moved the ads inside, and devoted the entire front page to local news. On inside pages, along with additional coverage of events in Easton and Talbot County, he featured lengthy articles on the county's history and traditions. Some of these he wrote himself; others were penned by John W. D. Jump, the Easton Publishing Company's long-time secretary, and by

Samuel E. Shannahan.

Wilson Tylor, who had retired as *Gazette* editor in 1912. Shannahan's goal was to have everything in his paper locally oriented and locally produced, and he succeeded so well that in 1937 the Maryland Press Association chose the *Star-Democrat* as the best weekly newspaper in the state.

    A list of Shannahan's civic activities gives reason to wonder how he found time for the prolific writing which filled the paper's pages every week. He was secretary of the Protestant Episcopal Diocese of Easton from 1910 on; treasurer of Trinity Cathedral; chairman of the Board of State Aid and Charities for twelve years; president of the Easton Rotary Club; treasurer of the Easton Emergency Hospital (now Memorial Hospital), and of the Talbot County Free Library; an organizer and later president of the Maryland Press Association;

Left, Baltimore department stores bid for Eastern Shore business with large display ads. Some even promised free steamboat fare to attract customers across the Bay. *Right*, Automobiles were a rare novelty when this story was published in the *Easton Gazette* September 7, 1901.

member of the Board of Visitors and Governors of Washington College; member of the board of the Children's Aid Society; a director of the Claiborne-Annapolis Ferry Company, and of the Farmers & Merchants Bank of Easton.

All this public activity served a dual purpose: as a reporter, he did not have to cover meetings because he was there anyhow in an official capacity; and as editor, he could be sure that projects in which he was interested received proper publicity. This may have violated the journalistic tenet that the press should play an "adversary" role in dealing with official affairs; but if there was an element of conflict of interest in Shannahan's double posture, it was usually in a good cause.

The strength of his contributions was well expressed by an editorial pub-

Star-Democrat printing shop about 1930. At left is editor Samuel E. Shannahan.

lished in the *Baltimore Sun* the day after he was found slumped in death at his desk by a fellow employee:

> There is hardly a resident of Talbot County whom he did not know, hardly a point on its endless and beautiful water front which he could not describe clearly, hardly one of its ancient homes with whose rich history and traditions he was unfamiliar. Of his capacious memory, and of his devotion to the men and the monuments of Talbot County, *The Sun* has had many happy reminders over a long term of years. He was a stout-hearted advocate of the Eastern Shore's viewpoint on all issues, with so many friends on the Western Shore that his death yesterday causes great regret on both sides of the bay.

Another in the same mold was Lorie C. Quinn, founder of the *Crisfield Times* and its editor and publisher for more than sixty years. Born in Newtown, later Pocomoke City, in 1864, he learned printing and editing there on the *Record and Gazette*, and then established his own newspaper, the *Eastern Shoreman*. Two years later he moved the entire plant to the new town of Crisfield, and launched the *Times* as a Democratic paper to oppose the Republican-oriented *Crisfield Leader*.

In his *History of Crisfield*, Woodrow T. Wilson says of Quinn's early struggles as a Democratic editor in a Republican town:

> If vegetables, chickens, oysters and fish and crabs could be traded for a subscription to the *Times*, the trade was made, for there was a growing family to feed . . .

There were weeks when the money to buy the paper on which to print the *Times* was not to be had so the edition could be on the streets Saturday morning, but somehow, if this happened, it appeared on Monday. At times the press broke down, a typesetter went on a "spree" and didn't show up for work, the office was cold and the ink didn't work freely, a form was pied . . . but it was all in the day's work.

Advertising by local merchants, with few exceptions, was nil . . . Certainly the prospects for wealth from a new newspaper in Crisfield in the early '90s could not be considered golden.

Crisfield at that time was one of the roughest communities in Maryland, a town built on oyster shells, a hangout for sailors and watermen, just emerging as a railroad, seafood, and shipping center. In an anniversary edition published in 1954, the *Times* said of it: "Everything the old west ever had, Crisfield had in its young days, saloons, bawdy houses, anything to satisfy a sailor's needs . . . Women seldom were on the streets after dark without an escort. Stabbings, shootings, fist fights were daily and nightly occurrences."

But the town was growing, and Quinn's *Times* grew with it. Like Sam Shannahan in Easton, he made himself an integral part of the community. The *Times* led the fight for street improvements, better sanitation, better schools and public buildings, and for law and order; if Quinn never did quite succeed in eradicating sin in Crisfield, he at least established a statewide reputation for crisp, convincing editorials. He was a member of the Board of Town Commissioners and, after Crisfield was incorporated as a city in 1910, served as its second mayor. He was a representative in the legislature from 1908 to 1912, and for many years a member of the City Council. It was said he knew more about civic affairs than anybody else in Crisfield. As a businessman, he built and developed the "Brooklyn" section of downtown Crisfield, and established a successful dehydrating business for crab scrap.

His wife, Katie, was as active as he was. In the couple's younger days she wrote most of the personal items and some of the news stories in the *Times*, as well as considerable poetry. She was in large measure responsible for the establishment of Crisfield's first hospital and library. All of Quinn's five sons were trained in printing at the *Times* shop; and two of them, Lorie, Jr., and Egbert, later served as editors. But until his death July 15, 1953, the elder Quinn retained his title as senior editor.

Dr. Edward J. Clarke, editor and publisher of the *Worcester Democrat* from 1922 to 1953, came from quite a different background from Shannahan or Quinn. Where they were practical printers, he was a scholar and educator. A graduate of St. John's College in Annapolis, where he got his master's degree, he became a teacher at Washington College in 1887 and remained there more than thirty years. From 1889 to 1918, he was head of the Department of English

Lorie C. Quinn.

and for part of that time also taught history. From 1918 to 1922, when he returned to his native Worcester County to take over the *Democrat*, he was superintendent of Kent County schools. As an editor, despite his scholarly attainments, he was noted for his folksiness; he conducted a weekly column, "Chirps," which was widely read for its "homey" philosophy and opinions.

Even in an era when family-owned, hometown-oriented newspapers were the rule, the Usiltons of Kent County created a remarkable record. For more than a century, they published the *Kent News*, now the *Kent County News*. William Barger Usilton was one of Chestertown's pioneer editors, a loyal though sometimes unhappy Unionist in the Civil War and a strong booster for Kent County afterward; William Barger Usilton, Jr., was associated with the *News* in every capacity from errand boy to editor; Frederick Usilton was editor in his time; and William Barger Usilton III was editor and editor emeritus until his death in 1982, although the Usilton family no longer owned the paper.

Wilson M. Tylor, owner-editor of the *Easton Gazette* for many years, left an indelible stamp on the town he graced as newspaper publisher. A Quaker and a former teacher, he was quiet and reticent in manner, but dressed with formal Victorian elegance. He was a scholar, a poet, a lover of great literature—in brief, the direct opposite of the slangy, hard-driving, hard-drinking newspaperman who would become the stereotype of the profession in the 1920s. Nevertheless Tylor's *Gazette* took on the tough issues of the day—politics, race relations, economics, community needs—without flinching. His editorials were models of reasoned argument; under his leadership the *Gazette* was probably the best edited and most successful paper on the Shore, even though it was staunchly Republican in an era of Democratic ascendancy.

Born near Denton June 2, 1856, Tylor became a teacher in the Caroline County schools at eighteen, and director of the Friends School in Easton before his twenty-first birthday. He later served as principal of Marshall Seminary in upstate New York before returning to the Eastern Shore and buying the *Gazette* July 25, 1885. From then on newspapering and the welfare of Easton were his life. Even after he sold the *Gazette* in 1912, he continued to write historical and scholarly articles for the *Star-Democrat*. His role in saving that paper from extinction by buying and merging the *Easton Star* and the *Democrat* in 1896 has already been noted; in addition both Sam Shannahan and Clement E. Bray, coproprietors of the *Star-Democrat*, had learned their trade as printer's devils under him at the *Gazette*. One of Tylor's contributions in later life was an annual New Year's poem reviewing in rhyme the chief events in Talbot County during the previous year—not great literature but no less popular for that. He returned as *Gazette* editor in the 1920s in an unsuccessful effort to revive the newspaper's waning prestige. But it was too late; the *Gazette* expired November 1, 1929, after 112 years. Tylor died August 7, 1941, at the age of 85, as distinguished a journalist as the Eastern Shore has known.

Preoccupation with local affairs typified the small, short-lived weeklies even more than the larger and more successful ones. The only known issue of the *Sharptown Herald*, dated March 7, 1903, sheds no light on the great issues of the day, or even on what the editor's politics might have been. But it provides a splendid run-down on a recent fox hunt of the Sharptown Sporting Club. On Monday (March 2) its members had proceeded to Owl Swamp. There "a fox was soon put on the run and chased continuously for seven hours." On Tuesday, with seventeen hounds, they returned to the swamp again and "in a short time a reynard was again on the run and moved up as far northeast as Portsville, and southwest as far as Riverton. The chase was about ten hours." Wildlife lovers will be glad to know that during the entire season, not a single fox had been captured or killed; all had been "allowed to return to the den and rest for another chase."

The *Peninsula Ledger* of Pocomoke City carried a lead editorial July 4, 1896, on the successful season just completed by the Pocomoke Round Table Society, a literary club. Opined the *Ledger:* "In towns of this size it is no easy matter to keep up interest in a society or club which is purely literary. The

Left, Dr. Edward J. Clarke. *Right*, Wilson M. Tylor as a young man.

experiment has often been tried, and the trials have usually ended in apathy, discord, failure and disgust. To this rule the Round Table Society has proved a marked exception . . . Long live the Round Table!"

Its successor paper, the *Ledger-Enterprise*, took an even stronger stand in 1905 against fences in the town. Under the caption "The Fences Must Go!" it argued that fences around town dwellings no longer were needed now that Pocomoke City had passed a law prohibiting cattle and swine from roaming at large, and trampling lawns, flower beds, and shrubbery. Taking fences away "would make our streets appear broader, our lawns larger." Carried away by his crusade, the editorial writer went on:

> "The fences must go!" is the cry of our civilization. Let us heed it. Let us act upon it. Let us gracefully yield to the appeal. Pocomoke cannot afford to lag behind her sister cities, which are stirring to add to the comfort, and the convenience and the advanced and refined taste of their citizens.

The *Cambridge Era*, founded in the late 1870s, had two mortal enemies—Democrats and booze. Its first publisher, James E. Reese, described its policy as "Republican in politics . . . independence in everything, neutral in nothing." The paper delighted in calling the Democrats such names as "Old Hunkers," "Potato Bugs," and "Court-house Barnacles." "They propose to rule to the crack of doom, but the people of Dorchester have ruled otherwise," it declared.

On the liquor question, the *Era*'s issue of March 23, 1878, expressed pleasure that Cambridge now had a temperance society with more than five hundred members. "Whiskey may not be responsible for half the vices and crimes attributed to it by the average temperance lecturer, but any man is better off without than with it," the *Era* said. "Cold, sparkling water is the most invigorating beverage after all."

An editor's politics were not always as fixed and immovable as they seemed. When Lorie Quinn was editor of the *Eastern Shoreman* in Pocomoke City, he was a Republican to the hilt. He crowed over the "divided Democracy" in Somerset County, and urged his party to nominate "tried and true Republicans, that can be relied on in all emergencies to stand firm." But when he went to Crisfield a year or so later to found the *Times*, he made it a Democratic Party organ from the beginning. The reason wasn't that Quinn was fickle; it was that his politics were secondary to his intense desire to have a newspaper of his own. In Pocomoke there already was a Democratic paper, so he had to favor the Republicans. In Crisfield the opposition was Republican, so he became a Democrat—and stayed that way for more than sixty years. By his day the once fierce ideological differences between the two parties had largely vanished; the Republicans had become almost as conservative as the Democrats.

A similar political flipflop by the *Salisbury Courier* was more embarrassing than anything else to editor Alan J. Benjamin. He conducted the *Courier*, starting in 1899, as an aggressive Republican newspaper in opposition to the Democratic *Wicomico News*. When he left for his honeymoon in 1904, he turned the editorship over to Dr. Sidney Bell; but when Benjamin got back he found that Dr. Bell had converted the hidebound Republican sheet into a Democratic one. If the *Bachelor* had still been around, it might have pointed a moral: never go on a honeymoon.

So rolled by decade after decade of isolation and narrow self-concern for the Eastern Shore and its newspapers. Nevertheless, even as they ignored the outside world, change was imperceptibly in the air. It was the *Kent News* which, although unknowingly, first foretold the development which, more than any other single thing, eventually would bring an end to the Eastern Shore's long slumber.

Reporting on plans for the dedication of a new park and fountain on Chestertown's central square in August, 1899, the *News* mentioned that a novel contraption called a "horseless carriage" or "automobile" would be featured at the ceremony. The steam-powered vehicle, built in Baltimore, was said to be the first of its kind ever seen on the Eastern Shore south of Cecil County.

The *News* went on to give an enthusiastic account of how the fad for automobiles of all sorts—steam, electric, and even gasoline—was sweeping America. A hundred electric cabs were in operation in New York; Chicago had a motor ambulance; at least two cities were using self-propelled fire engines; and the number of privately owned vehicles numbered "well into the hundreds." "A trip of 720 miles, from Cleveland to New York, over all kinds of country roads, has actually been made in a gasoline carriage," the *News* reported in wonder.

"All the arguments," the article continued, "[are] in favor of the automobile and against the horse. It is ready without having to be hitched up. It can be more easily stored, no stable being necessary. No coachman is required. It is safer, can be guided with greater accuracy and turned in less space. It doesn't have to be hitched when left standing." However, automobiles were expensive. Readers were warned that "a good electric carriage for family use cannot be obtained for much less than $2,000."

On Tuesday, August 15, the steamer made a "speed run" from Tolchester to Chestertown, covering the twelve miles in record time—an hour and five minutes. The *News* of August 19 carried a detailed account of this memorable trip as told by John S. Vandergrift, one of the operators.

"At the start we were followed by a crowd of men and boys who kept up with us until we climbed the hill, when we rapidly left them. Our steam gauge showed 60 pounds, but soon ran up as high as 162 pounds. Occupants of teams eyed us with staring countenances as we flitted by them . . . Farmers rushed to their road gates to see us go by while workmen in the fields looked with astonishment upon us." At one point the vehicle was moving so fast that the wind blew out the fire under the boiler. But the crew got it going again, and "we entered Chestertown amid the hurrahs of crowds of people who lined the streets from College Avenue to Water Street."

It would be a while before the horseless carriage took hold on the Eastern Shore. Roads were bad and money scarce; and anyhow most Eastern Shore folks were not really in that much of a hurry. But by the 1920s, the automobile age was in full swing, and its arrival signaled the end of an era.

More than any other factor, Henry Ford's "tin lizzie," which could be had in any color you wanted as long as it was black, changed the face of the Eastern Shore forever. Cheap auto transportation freed the farmers from dependence on marketing centers within an easy drive of a horse-drawn wagon or buggy, and so doomed the prosperity of the smaller towns and villages. Auto travel also ended the dominance of the great bay steamboats, and eventually the railroads.

The auto age was in full swing by 1920. This scene shows Easton's public square on Saturday afternoon. Cars were parked with rears to the curb because most had to be started by hand cranking.

Then came in quick succession radio, the Great Depression, World War II, television, and the Bay Bridge. The world poured in on the Eastern Shore in an irresistible torrent; and the long siesta was over, for the Eastern Shore press as well as for the way of life it had faithfully mirrored.

CHAPTER SIX

Modern Times
CONFLICT AND SURVIVAL

THE modern era has not been kind to print journalism on the Maryland Eastern Shore. The local press has been beset by controversy, accused of shoddiness and bigotry, crippled financially by its electronic rivals in radio and television. Its family proprietors, rooted in hometown traditions, have been replaced by outside corporate owners. Its numbers have dwindled to their lowest ebb since the early flowering of the 1820s, and the outlook is that in years to come still fewer county weeklies will manage to survive.

All this was far in the future when the period we have arbitrarily defined as "modern times" began. As convenient a date as any to mark the start of the era is December 3, 1923, when the first issue of a new daily journalistic venture called the *Evening Times* appeared in Salisbury.

Historically speaking, the nation and even the sleepy Eastern Shore were in the midst of profound and rapid change. Flappers, jazz, bootleg booze, gang warfare, and political corruption were beginning to point the way to the problems and complexities of today's world. In Washington, Calvin Coolidge had just replaced Warren G. Harding in the White House; in Germany, Adolf Hitler was writing *Mein Kampf* in Landsberg prison; in Italy, Mussolini was consolidating his Fascist grip on Rome. The automobile age was in full swing; as the Cambridge *Daily Banner* noted on December 1, eleven thousand Americans were killed in traffic accidents that year.

Journalistically speaking, the arrival of the *Evening Times* marked a new departure for the Eastern Shore. It and its successors, the *Daily Times* and *Sunday Times*, would become the Shore's largest and most modern newspapers, as they still are.

The older *Daily Banner*, founded in 1897, gave its sister daily's birth only a backhanded salute. On December 1 it carried its page one slogan, "Only Daily on the Peninsula," for the last time. On December 3 this was replaced by "Over 25 Years Old," without any explanation for the change. The two papers were not really competitive, since their circulation and advertising territories scarcely overlapped, but the *Daily Banner* did not welcome a rival for its title of "leading" Shore newspaper.

Salisbury *Times* newsroom in the 1920s. In foreground is Charles J. Truitt, then a youthful editor.

The group of Salisbury businessmen who launched the *Times* chose as their news editor twenty-three-year-old Charles J. Truitt, who had started as a reporter at six dollars a week for the weekly *Wicomico Countian*. Four years later he and his cousin, Alfred Truitt, bought the *Times*. For the next sixty years, as editor, publisher, local historian, head of Salisbury radio and TV stations, and adviser to younger news people, Charlie Truitt was deeply involved in Wicomico County journalism.

As he neared his eighty-first birthday, Truitt recalled in a 1981 interview some of the struggles and achievements of those early days. The *Times* was an eight-page paper, printed on a flatbed "web" press, which meant that paper was fed to the forms in a web running from rolls suspended in the press room. It was a complicated and not always trustworthy arrangement.

"If the temperature wasn't just right, or the wind made a draft in the press room, the web would break and we'd have to stop everything and glue it back together by hand," Truitt said. "Sometimes it would hold us up for a couple hours."

The *Times* received the daily output of national and international news from the Associated Press wire service, but the AP setup in the 1920s was no more modern than the web press. The news came in by telegraph wire and key, just as messages did in the railroad telegraph stations. An operator sat in the *Times* office all day, reading the dots and dashes and typing out the stories as they came through. Then Truitt selected the items he wanted to use.

"We got our AP news from the *Philadelphia Bulletin*," Truitt recalled. "There wasn't any Baltimore AP bureau then. And on weekends we had to get AP coverage by way of Pittsburgh, because the *Bulletin* was published only on weekday afternoons."

At that time there were no radio or TV networks to flash instant election returns, so the *Times* arranged a primitive information service. On election nights city officials roped off a block of Main Street in front of the newspaper office. As soon as the ballots were counted, totals were telephoned to the *Times*. There the results were inscribed on glass slides and projected from the second floor of the building to a brick exterior wall of Collier's drug store across the street. As crude as this may seem today, when TV pundits announce election results long before the polls close, it was very popular. Crowds overflowed the entire block to get their first news of how the voting was going in Wicomico County and throughout Maryland.

Truitt stayed with the *Times* for seventeen years before moving into the field of radio as vice president and general manager of the newly established station WBOC in 1940. Later he helped organize WBOC-TV, the Shore's first television station, WBOC-FM, and WBOC-CATV, its first cable outlet.

Among the weeklies, "modern times" in the 1920s and 1930s brought little change from their format and viewpoint of half a century earlier. They remained home owned, home edited, and home oriented. Local names were what made news. The *Chestertown Enterprise* boasted on August 2, 1939, that its current edition contained the names of 928 people who "made news last week in Kent County." Typical items told of a man who "had the misfortune to break his little finger while at work," and another, who had been in the hospital with sinus trouble and now was "looking better but still has a pain in his head."

World War II was just five weeks off on July 27, 1939, but the crisis wasn't mentioned in the *Democratic Messenger* of Snow Hill. Instead the *Messenger* gave prominent display to a challenge issued to Worcester County tobacco chewers by Bill "Dink" Timmons of Hungrytown, who "claims to be the

The Salisbury *Times*' first building, on Main Street.

champion long distance tobacco spitting king of these here parts." According to the *Messenger* Timmons had won the title in a spitting match at Libertyville "when a Timmons stream—propelled from a steady between-the-fingers stance—splashed 18 feet 2 inches away from the line."

Such localization was deliberate. As the editor of the *Chestertown Enterprise* explained, "It is the general idea of those of us who are making a life and living in the country newspaper field that we should stick pretty closely to local subjects, delving into the national and international only when it has a direct bearing on lives of the people whom we serve." For example, baseball star Jimmy Foxx was news because he was from Queen Anne's County; Joe DiMaggio might be a better hitter, but he was not news because he was from San Francisco.

Frank Goodwin, who studied Eastern Shore newspapers of the 1930s as part of a doctoral thesis on the Shore's social organization later published by the University of Pennsylvania, compared the front page of an issue of the *Dorchester News*, then published in Hurlock, with the front page of the same day's *New York Times*. He found that the *News* mentioned two hundred eleven names, the *Times* only twenty-four. The *News* reported that there had been six club and church meetings since the last edition and there would be seven more before the next edition. It gave details of three deaths, a christening, an engagement, an accident, results of a benefit sale, the governor's congratulations to a newly named federal judge, and the announcement of a law to outlaw pinball machines, and told where farmers could sign up for the 1939 Agricultural Conservation Program. The *Times* devoted its front page to a British and French guarantee that had been extended to Rumania and Greece, a threatened coal strike, actions of Congress, the appointment of a new ambassador to Spain, and the plans of a group of financiers to stabilize securities if war should come.

"Strangers viewing the front page of this county weekly for the first time are apt to say that it contains little, if any, news," Goodwin declared. But they would be wrong. To persons living in the Hurlock vicinity, the fact that a local boy had been bitten by a dog or that Mrs. Joe Jones was visiting friends in Wilmington was more interesting than who, if anybody, was going to be ambassador to Spain.

The era of outside ownership was only faintly foreshadowed in Goodwin's study. Of twenty-two county weeklies whose editors took part in the survey, twenty-one were locally owned in 1935, the start of the survey period. Two were sold to outsiders during the next five years but, as Goodwin pointed out, the predominance of local ownership remained strong.

This was equally true of the editors. Eighteen of the twenty-two papers were edited by their owners; fifteen of the editors had been born in the county in which their paper was published and three in an adjoining county; sixteen represented at least the third successive generation born in the same area. Three-quarters had gone to high school in the county. Outside influences were minimal. Only half were college graduates, and only six had had any newspaper experience elsewhere before becoming editors.

The editors were church members, nineteen to three. They were joiners; all but one belonged to at least one club, and five belonged to nine or more. They were boosters; most were active in service organizations. They admired businessmen; fifty-five percent picked bankers, fertilizer dealers, insurance salesmen, or those in similar occupations as their county's outstanding leaders. They were, of course, all white, all of British, Scottish, or Irish ancestry, almost all Protestants. It goes without saying that they were all males. In short, they were of the type which in the 1930s were called Babbitts, and in the 1960s would be called WASPs, neither term carrying a favorable connotation among the intelligentsia.

But they were exactly the sort of men most likely to find contentment and a sense of fulfilment editing a small newspaper in the 1930s on the Eastern Shore of Maryland. And they were well tailored to their communities.

"County weeklies are published for home folks and . . . by home folks," Goodwin concluded. "Hired editors are rare . . . and professional training in journalism is rare." As a result, he felt that Eastern Shore newspapers were "a force for maintaining the *status quo* rather than a factor introducing innovations and change . . . There is little in the weekly to cause sleepless nights . . . or to foster in the readers feelings of helplessness, hopelessness, or frustration."

This was reflected in complacent press comment on the state of things on the Eastern Shore. The *Dorchester News* (August 4, 1939) was pleased to note that two new neon signs had been put up on Main Street in Hurlock, an indication "that business people are wide awake to the needs of attracting patrons to our town." The *Chestertown Enterprise* in 1940 gave examples of why Kent County was "such a desirable place to live"—the thrice-weekly collection of garbage in Chestertown, and the efficient system of warning people when the water was going to be shut off by sending a fire truck up and down the streets with a clanging bell.

However, the *Enterprise* feared that other forms of "progress" might destroy the cherished serenity of the isolated Eastern Shore. Its editor warned that a bridge across Chesapeake Bay, then under discussion, could bring the "trash of East Baltimore" to "overrun the Shore" every weekend. Nor were improved highways and better automobiles an unmixed blessing. Reporting that a clothing store robbery in June, 1938, had the earmarks of a gang job, the *Enterprise* added ominously: "This section has felt free from organized crime due to its geographic location . . . However good roads and fast motor vehicles have gradually removed this security."

The rival *Chestertown Transcript* pooh-poohed the notion that gangsters were moving in. "Kent County is fortunate in being free of the crime rackets that exist in the more thickly populated areas" (meaning Baltimore), it said. "If some system can be worked out whereby the punishment for minor offenses . . . would be dreaded by the offenders the criminal work of officials would be practically eliminated."

The *Transcript*'s issue of April 20, 1940, well expressed the Eastern Shore's self-satisfaction as World War II threatened to engulf the world: "Judge Thomas J. Keating in charging the Grand Jury . . . stated that both the Court and Jury can feel very thankful that there are places existing during these days of world turmoil where people can live in peace and quiet . . . It is a true reason why this county is such a desirable place to live. Gangsters have made no inroads here."

If either paper was aware of what good use the dreaded gangsters had made of the Eastern Shore's isolation during the Prohibition years, when boatloads of illicit liquor by the thousands were brought ashore at dark, deserted landings and hauled by truck to the northeastern metropolitan centers, they made no mention of it. Such things were somebody else's problem as long as the trucks weren't unloaded in Kent County or elsewhere on the Shore.

Most Eastern Shore newspapers, in fact, had opposed the end of Prohibition in 1933, an echo of their many years of supporting teetotalism. Fred Usilton, editor of the *Kent News*, was an example. He applauded those who opposed repeal in a local vote on the issue as "an army of eight hundred people who are interested in the best welfare of our citizens." But *Worcester Democrat* editor Edward J. Clarke chided Usilton for bad reporting in failing to mention that fifteen hundred other Kent Countians had voted *for* repeal. In his weekly column, "Chirps from the Democrat's Pen," Clarke said repeal was surely coming and would be a good thing. Many of the "old evils of the saloon days," he thought, could be prevented under new laws.

The Great Depression of the 1930s was seldom mentioned in the county weeklies, but it took a substantial toll among them. Under the pressures of economic hard times, eleven Eastern Shore papers closed down or were forced to consolidate in order to survive. Perhaps by sheer coincidence, the demise of the *Easton Gazette*, one of the shore's strongest papers for more than a hundred years, coincided almost exactly with the collapse of the stock market in 1929. "Black Tuesday," when market losses totaled fifteen billion dollars, was October 29; the *Gazette* was published for the last time November 1.

The *American Union* of Denton, which ended its seventy-two-year career as the *Caroline Independent*, went under in 1932, the Depression's worst year. So did the *Federalsburg Courier*, founded in 1872, and the *Berlin-Ocean City News*. The *Perryville News* was consolidated with the *North East Advertiser*, a move which enabled the combined papers to survive until the 1950s. The *Cecil County News* folded in 1937; the *Wicomico News* in 1938; the *Eastern Shore Republican* in 1939.

The *Centreville Record* also was a Depression victim but was given a dramatic reprieve. It suspended publication April 14, 1932. Early the next year a New York advertising man, Owen B. Winters, bought the defunct paper and revived it as the *Queen Anne's Record*, with a declaration that the fifty-eight-year-old paper was "too young to die." In the inaugural issue, February 23, 1933, Winters explained his reasons.

> Here, asleep and futile, awaiting the touch of practiced fingers, were all the symbols of communication, type, the whole eloquent vocabulary of the English language. Here were words for telling the news, words for righting wrongs, words for selling goods. Then the mute press, patiently waiting, the sooty files, an unbroken chronicle of nearly sixty years. After such service in a community a newspaper becomes a living breathing thing. The *Record* should carry on.

Winters introduced big city journalistic techniques to the placid Eastern Shore. The *Record*, says one account, "quickly established itself as a virile, even crusading newspaper. It was breezy and written in interesting fashion, with numerous features and a 'tailored' layout. A number of its innovations were adopted by other papers, and it has been said that the *Queen Anne's Record* did more to improve Shore newspapers in its brief existence than any other paper had done before."

But some of the new ideas did not set well with the conservative folk of Queen Anne's County. A gossip column done in the style of Walter Winchell might be all right for New York, but it was a bit too brash for Centreville, Maryland. Who was expecting a "blessed event," and who had been seen where with whom, somehow didn't seem the proper fare for a county weekly. It was better to stick to the tried and true news, such as covered dish suppers, church socials, and visits with friends in Sudlersville.

After less than four years, the *Record*'s experimental "new journalism" came to an end. In November, 1936, it was merged with the *Centreville Observer* to form the *Queen Anne's Record-Observer*. A few of the innovations were continued; but for the most part the *Record-Observer* reverted to the old ways. Since then it has been a solid, substantial county weekly, but "virile" and "breezy" are not exactly the words associated with its style.

A few brave souls bucked the economic trends and tried to start new papers despite the hard times. Most quickly failed. A revival of the old *Centreville Times*, launched in August, 1932, lasted only until November, 1934. The *Talbot County Record*, intended as a sister paper to the *Queen Anne's Record*, produced only a few issues in the summer of 1935.

One which did not fail, however, was the *Preston News*, now the *News & Farmer*, published in the little Caroline County town of Preston but circulated in seven Eastern Shore counties through a tie-in with local chapters of the American Farm Bureau Federation.

Max Chambers.

Its founder and longtime owner, Max Chambers, brought out the first issue September 16, 1937, and somehow managed to keep it going through depressions, wars, droughts, floods, and numerous name changes until he retired on his eightieth birthday, July 1, 1980. Since then it has continued under Scott Warehime, a native of Carroll County on the Western Shore but now a resident of Caroline.

Chambers was perhaps the last of the old school of Eastern Shore owner-editors. A native of Salisbury, North Carolina, he worked in Baltimore before receiving an A.B. degree from Washington College in Chestertown and settling in Caroline County as a teacher. In addition to the *News & Farmer*, he published the *Vegetable Growers Messenger* and the *Maryland Poultry Digest*, had connections with other farm publications, and served as public relations counsel for the Maryland Farm Bureau and various government agencies.

Like his fellow publishers of the first half of the twentieth century, Chambers was not a crusader but a joiner and booster. A listing of his activities issued at a recognition dinner for "Mr. Max" in August, 1980, is impressive: district director of the National Youth Administration and assistant to the director of the National Bureau of Training in World War II; Maryland Commissioner for the New York World's Fair; chairman of the Preston Planning and Zoning Committee; founder and executive secretary of the Maryland Fishing Fair Association; founder and president of the Caroline Historical Society; member of the Maryland Bicentennial Executive Committee and chairman of the Caroline County Bicentennial Committee; a director of the Del-Mar-Va Council, Inc., Boy Scouts of America, and holder of the Silver Beaver Award. He is a Mason, a Shriner, a Lion, a Methodist, a Farm Bureau member, and a charter member of the Caroline Country Club. He has also operated a tomato canning factory.

A high point of his career came when he discovered, after years of patient research, that Charles Dickinsen, who had been killed by Andrew Jackson in a celebrated duel, had not been buried in Tennessee as supposed but had secretly been brought back to Caroline County and interred at his home estate, Wiltshire Manor. Through use of a modern metal detector, Chambers located the casket and had it removed to a more accessible site and marked by a stone slab and historical marker.

Typically, the news was reported in the *News & Farmer* in small, single-column headlines. Only once in his forty-three-year career as editor did Chambers deviate from his policy of using no headlines larger than eighteen-point type. That was on August 16, 1945, when—a day later than the metropolitan dailies—the paper announced in the largest type Chambers could find:

THE WAR IS OVER

JAPS SURRENDER

Other highlights have been Chambers' friendship with President Truman, whom he met during the war, and citations from two Maryland governors—as a Distinguished Citizen of the Maryland Free State from Governor McKeldin and for outstanding service to the agriculture and seafood industries from Governor Tawes.

In his earlier years Chambers established "goals" for Caroline County and listed them on the *News* editorial page. When they were fulfilled, they were shifted into the "goals achieved" column. A spot check indicates the slow and stately pace of Eastern Shore progress: of twenty-three goals set for 1938, twenty were still on the list in 1940. A parkway at the Lutheran church, a brick pump house, and electric power for the village of Choptank had been achieved; but road improvements, new industries, elimination of open privies, and a host of other goals were still in the future.

If the Eastern Shore's weeklies still reflected in the 1930s the easy ways of earlier times, it was the Shore's two dailies—and principally the Salisbury *Times*—which were suddenly thrust into the cold glare of national publicity for the way in which they treated the 1931 lynching of a black man in Salisbury. The *Times* and the *Daily Banner* were denounced in the metropolitan press as "pathetic sheets" which had "no courage and no decency." Eventually the entire Eastern Shore became embroiled in a war of scornful name calling which was largely fought in the newspapers.

The storm developed in a series of events so interlocked in cause and effect that none can be judged without considering the others. Nor can the role of the newspapers be understood apart from that of the public for which they spoke. It was an ugly period in Eastern Shore history, and ugly things were done and said. As always, the press reflected attitudes and moral standards, right or wrong, that were peculiar to the Eastern Shore.

First event in the series came October 12, 1931, when a Worcester County farmer, Green K. Davis, his wife, and two daughters were murdered in their home near Taylorville. Evidence led investigators to an Ocean City tenement house. There Yuel Lee, a sixty-year-old black farm hand who had recently been fired by Davis, was arrested and charged with the slayings.

From the beginning, Lee's guilt was prejudged by the lower Shore press and public. Headlines left no room for doubt that he was the killer; angry local opinion demanded a swift trial and execution. But the International Labor Defense League of New York City, charging that Lee could not get a fair trial with local counsel, sent Bernard Ades, a Baltimore attorney, to represent him. Ades managed to get numerous delays, and to make the case something of a *cause célèbre* in the "liberal" segment of the metropolitan press. This was bitterly resented by Eastern Shore journalists and much of the public.

"Everything Bernard Ades said got in the papers and made headlines," says Truitt, to whom the memories of that period are still vivid after half a century. "The answers to his statements never got printed. Some of the stories that appeared in the *Sunpapers* of Baltimore and the Philadelphia *Record, Ledger,* and *Inquirer* were not only sensational but they were untrue, bore no relation to the facts." As local correspondent for the Associated Press as well as managing editor of the *Times*, Truitt says he was shocked by such deliberate fabrications.

As one example, a city newspaper said Ades had been attacked by a mob in Snow Hill as he went to the courthouse to file a motion for a change of venue. This was picked up by the wire services and widely published. "Nothing of the sort happened," Truitt said later. "I was there as a reporter for the *Times*. There was no attack. There weren't more than three or four people around. Absolutely, that was the most ridiculous thing I've ever seen newspapers do."

On the lower Shore, Ades was regarded as a Communist agent, working to arouse black resentment against the whites. When he succeeded in getting a change of venue to Cambridge and later to Towson, that made the white majority angrier than ever.

Such was the state of things when, on December 4, 1931, Daniel J. Elliott, a

Salisbury lumber dealer, was shot dead while talking on the telephone in his office. Matthew Williams, a black employee, was arrested for the shooting. At first he was reported to have killed himself, and the *Times*, again presuming his guilt, carried a banner headline in its evening edition: "Negro Slays D. J. Elliott and Self." Late that afternoon it was learned he was not dead but had been taken to Peninsula General Hospital for treatment of a gunshot wound. According to George Corddry, Salisbury historian, a bulletin was posted in the window of the *Times* office correcting the original story and revealing Williams' whereabouts.

That evening a group of men went to the hospital, got Williams, and took him to the courthouse square. There they hanged him from a tree in full view of numerous witnesses, including Truitt. Later the body was dragged through Salisbury streets behind a car, suspended from a utility pole, and set on fire.

As managing editor of the *Times*, Truitt faced an agonizing decision. How should he handle the story the next day? He filed a factual account with the Associated Press, but, deciding that the newspaper's first obligation was to cool down Salisbury's emotionally explosive atmosphere, omitted almost all details of the lynching in the *Times* of December 5.

Although it had been giving banner-line play to the Yuel Lee case, the *Times* used only a one-column head on the Williams story. This did not say Williams had been lynched but instead stated that a coroner's jury would "investigate slayer's death." Except for a lead paragraph reporting the hanging and a comment that "the opinion prevails that many of those participating . . . came from other sections of the peninsula," the brief article was devoted entirely to plans for an investigation. Once more it took for granted that Williams had killed Elliott.

In a page one box, the *Times* management stated:

> This paper is today omitting the details of the demonstration here last night . . . for the very obvious reason that almost every reader of the paper has had an opportunity to learn of them first hand from eyewitnesses. The facts which formed the background for the demonstration and the direct causes are also well known, and a repetition of them would be superfluous. The slaying of Mr. Elliott was deplorable, as was also the mob scene.

Readers were warned to "pay little heed to the overdrawn pictures that will be painted by metropolitan newspapers whose only purpose is . . . to increase their own circulations." The *Times*, on the other hand, was "a part of the Eastern Shore, and always tries to serve the best interests of the peninsula . . . When violence is done, it behooves every one of us to cooperate in speeding up a return to absolutely normal and harmonious conditions."

Page one of the Salisbury *Times*, December 5, 1931.

Fifty years later, Truitt still thought the decision was the right one. "Unless you've been through a thing like that, you can't comprehend what it's like," he said, shortly before his death in 1982. "The whole Shore was emotional about the thing. The Yuel Lee case had been batted around so much in the courts that people were very angry. When you see people ready to do anything, follow any suggestion that's made to them, you know you'd better be careful or you'll upset the whole community."

At the time, however, the omissions brought down a storm of criticism. In the *Evening Sun*, Henry L. Mencken, famous columnist and editor of *American Mercury* magazine, poured his special brand of vitriol on the Eastern Shore in general and Eastern Shore newspapers in particular. Entitling his column "The Eastern Shore Kultur," Mencken singled out the *Times* and the *Daily Banner* of Cambridge as prime examples. The *Banner* had deplored the lynching "formally, but only formally; the rest of its comment was devoted to hysterical ravings against Baltimore and disingenuous attempts to distort and conceal the facts." As for the *Times*:

> [It] went to the almost incredible length of dismissing the atrocity as a "demonstration." Well, the word somehow fits. It was indeed a demonstration of what civilization can come to in a region wherein there are no competent police, little save a simian self-seeking in public office, no apparent intelligence on the bench, and no courage and no decency in the local press.

The Eastern Shore, Mencken went on, was being run by "its poor white trash" who still accepted the "brutish imbecilities" of the Ku Klux Klan. Salisbury was the "Alsatia of morons." It was holding Maryland up to the contempt of the whole world by staging "a public obscenity worthy of cannibals." Eastern Shore people were stupid but, said Mencken, "probably less stupid than misinformed . . . They must depend for their ideas upon clowns in the pulpit, clowns on the stump, and clowns in the editorial chair. Certainly it would be irrational to ask for enlightenment in communities whose ideas are supplied by such pathetic sheets as the Cambridge *Daily Banner* and the Salisbury *Times*."

The *Times*, the *Banner*, and the *Worcester Democrat* all reprinted Mencken's column, knowing it would enrage almost every white on the Shore. Defending its omission of details, the *Times* replied: "Our handling of the situation has occasioned the congratulations of hundreds of Eastern Shore people, white and colored, as well as that of the editors of many metropolitan papers who have said we did the very best thing any newspaper could have done in a similar situation. The verdict on that is thousands to one."

The *Banner* responded by recalling that Mencken himself had once advocated "a polite form of lynching" when he proposed to take William Jennings

H. L. Mencken's famous column, "The Eastern Shore Kultur," as reprinted in the *Daily Banner*.

Bryan to the top of the Washington monument, disembowel him, and throw the remains into the Potomac.

"Everybody knows," the *Banner* added, ". . . that we deplore the unfortunate lynching that occurred last week, and we deeply resent the implication that the people of the Eastern Shore, either by silence or expression, give their approval to such lawless methods, but we also resent that form of publicity which day after day spreads propaganda that tends to incite the less responsible citizenship to violence and then, after having sown the seeds of violence, attempts to shift the responsibility for the crop produced."

The weekly *Marylander and Herald* of Princess Anne bluntly charged that Mencken was affiliated with "anarchist and communist groups, composed for the most part of men and women from the lowest strata of the mongrel breeds of European gutters." It continued with a gruesome attack which accused Mencken and *Sun* cartoonist Edmund Duffy of being jealous because they hadn't gotten to "enjoy" the lynching, and even of potential cannibalism. Mencken replied in a second column, entitled "Sound and Fury," in which he reprinted the *Marylander and Herald*'s vilification of him and expressed his scorn of the "low down politicians, prehensile town boomers, ignorant hedge preachers, and other such vermin" responsible for it. In a ghoulish display on his own part, he said parts of Williams' body "no doubt . . . now adorn the mantel piece of some humble and public-spirited Salisbury home, between the engrossed seashell from Ocean City and the family Peruna bottle."

After that the *Sun* office was bombarded with telegrams threatening to lynch Mencken or any other *Sun* staffer who set foot on the Eastern Shore. Two

Sun trucks en route to Salisbury were halted, their drivers beaten, and their contents dumped into the bay. Salisbury merchants organized a boycott, pledging to do no more business with anyone in Baltimore until Mencken, the *Sun*, and all the ministers in the city apologized. Stickers reading "I am an EASTERN SHOREMAN and proud of it" appeared on cars throughout the Shore.

The age-old question of Eastern Shore secession from Maryland was taken out of mothballs and seriously debated at a public meeting in Salisbury. This inspired the editor of the *Federalsburg Times* to a paean of praise for what he envisioned as the "State of Delmarva."

> . . . We are ready and willing to sever what broken ties may remain with the Western Shore and Baltimore city, and form a state of our own across the bay. We are certainly not proud of everything Baltimore city has done and we are just a trifle weary of its meddling in our affairs.
>
> What a splendid state this Delmarva Peninsula would make. A rich country, close to city markets, but far enough away to avoid its contamination, and its political influence. A unified people with common interests, ideals and aspirations. What a great "free state" we could have—a state with more than one-half million people, with no dominating large cities—fourteen rich, prosperous counties in the best section of America.

Fortunately (or unfortunately, depending on the point of view) this new cry for Eastern Shore secession got no further than all its predecessors had. But bitterness against Baltimore and the *Sunpapers* would continue for many years. Half a century later, some Eastern Shore residents still speak with scorn of H. L. Mencken.

Replying to claims in the *Sun* that "every school child" in Salisbury knew the names of the lynch leaders, the *Times* said editorially that "we do not know any members of the mob who took part in the affair. Nor do we know anyone who knows, or whose friends know, any members of the mob." If Mencken or the *Sun*'s editorial writers had such knowledge, they should give it to the investigating authorities. Truitt did not reveal at that time that he had witnessed the lynching, but has said since that he did not recognize any of the participants.

That same ignorance was professed by everyone else who had been onlookers. After hearing testimony from 124 witnesses, the Wicomico County Grand Jury reported in March, 1932: "There is absolutely no evidence that can remotely connect anyone with the instigation or perpetration of the murder of Matthew Williams." That brought a final blast from Mencken. "The lynching," he wrote, "was a sort of transcendental event, taking place in secular space but only dimly visible to mortal eyes. A large crowd turned out to enjoy it, but no one could make out who was running it."

No investigation was ever conducted into the Elliott shooting. If Williams was actually innocent of the murder, as has since been suggested, few people on the Shore wanted to know about it.

The third link in the chain of horror came almost two years later. On October 18, 1933, George Armwood, a black resident of Princess Anne, was accused of raping a seventy-two-year-old white woman. He was arrested by State Police and first placed in the Baltimore city jail but soon afterward was returned to Princess Anne. That night he was taken from the jail and hanged.

The *Marylander and Herald* showed no such restraint in reporting the story as had the *Times* in the Salisbury lynching. In its issue of October 20, 1933, it gave the occurrence a double banner headline reading "Crowd of 3,000 Storm Jail, Lynch, Burn Negro," and described the lynching in gruesome detail. Editorially the paper expressed only mild regret over the tragedy and blamed it on public indignation over the Yuel Lee case. "The taking of this man to Baltimore, too vividly recalled to the citizens of this section the Yuel Lee case, and many other cases where the man charged with such crimes had been carried away . . . Lee confessed his crime—but through the manipulations of court technicalities he has not been punished to this day. Us, and we are glad to use the word 'us,' Eastern Shoremen resent the delay."

At the time, Lee was under sentence of death but, more than two years after his arrest for the Davis murders, was still alive. He had been convicted by a Towson jury on January 20, 1932, and sentenced to hang. In July, the Maryland Court of Appeals had reversed the verdict on grounds no blacks were included in the panel from which the jury was chosen. In a second Towson trial in December, he was again found guilty. Ades then appealed to the United States Supreme Court, which refused to review the case. Executive clemency by Governor Albert C. Ritchie was also denied. Nine days after the Princess Anne lynching, on October 27, 1933, Lee was hanged in Baltimore City jail. Throughout the case, Ades argued that his client's rights must be protected and that a hurried trial without a thorough defense was nothing less than "legal lynching."

After the Armwood lynching the wrath of the metropolitan press again descended on the Shore. Mencken erupted in typical virulence. In his weekly column, "Ramblings of an Editor," James E. Byrd of the *Marylander and Herald* replied indignantly that most of what the *Sun* had printed about the affair had come from the "drunken brain and imagination" of a staff writer who "arrived in Princess Anne absolutely drunk and stayed drunk every minute he was here." The man had been involved in a fight, and had "landed in the Salisbury jail on Friday. There he remained until Saturday, when another representative of the *Sun* arrived to pay his fine and escort him back to Baltimore." The Salisbury *Times* also carried this item, adding that the *Sun* reporter had received a black eye. The *Times* facetiously asked who it was that "launched the well-aimed smack to the optic? A public presentation of a medal for meritorious services rendered might be arranged."

For both papers, it was not a very subtle way of telling readers they couldn't believe anything they read in the *Sun*.

Even more indicative of the Shore's resentment of "outsiders" was the headline the *Marylander and Herald* put on a letter from a Reisterstown, Maryland, man who urged the paper to "make a vigorous stand in favor of stern prosecution of the members of that murderous band." The paper gave the letter prominent display, but instead of agreeing that the lynchers should be punished captioned it: "Another Outsider Butts In . . . Still Thinking that the Eastern Shore Can't Take Care of Its Own Business."

Soon afterward came a far more spectacular case of "butting in" on what the lower Shore insisted was its own business.

On the night of November 27 Governor Ritchie, acting on information that local authorities had refused to arrest known suspects, dispatched a detail of State Police and three hundred members of the Baltimore-based Fifth National Guard Regiment to Salisbury. They set up headquarters in the National Guard Armory, cut telephone lines in the area, and took four men into custody. After the arrests there was a clash between Guardsmen and a crowd in which the troops used tear gas.

The contrast in the treatment of this incident by the Salisbury *Times* and the *Sun* provides a classic study in journalistic bias. Both carried huge headlines, but the *Times* banner read "Ritchie Orders Invasion of Shore; Troops Use Tear Gas," while the first edition of the morning *Sun* said "4 Lynch Suspects in City Jail After Troops Battle Mobs."

Details in the two papers were equally at odds. The *Sun* said the troops had been assaulted "by 2,000 Salisbury rioters" and that tear gas and fixed bayonets had not been employed until after the mob had stormed the Armory in an attempt to free the prisoners by force. The *Times* said the "spectators were as orderly as a crowd at a baseball game. There was no effort to rush the Armory or the National Guard. There was nothing more severe in the crowd's attitude than 'boos' until tear gas was suddenly hurled into the crowd." The angry clash came after the tear gas was used, not before, according to the *Times*.

The difference in the two versions was far more than merely a question of detail. If the *Sun* was right, an angry and riotous mob had attacked the Guardsmen, who used tear gas in self-defense. If the *Times* was right, a sullen but orderly crowd had been provoked into anger by needless use of gas on the

Contrasting headlines in the *Morning Sun* and the Salisbury *Times*.

part of the Guard. Which version was believed depended pretty much on where one lived.

Later the crowd vented its anger and frustration on the "outside press." A dozen newsmen from Baltimore, Washington, and Philadelphia were roughed up or threatened; cameras were smashed, two automobiles were burned, and a movie sound truck was sunk in the waters of the Wicomico River. For a time the journalists were beleaguered in Salisbury's leading hotel, the Wicomico. They wrote dramatic accounts of hiding out in an eighth floor ballroom and hearing shouts of "Lynch them! Kill the newspapermen!" However, all escaped safely in taxis from a side door.

Governor Ritchie issued a statement saying he had sent in the Guard "only when local officials failed to perform their duty" after they had been furnished with names of suspects and "substantial evidence" against them. "It is my plain duty as Governor of Maryland to see that the law is supreme," he said.

He received high praise from the metropolitan press. But there was no doubt where Eastern Shore newspapers stood. To them it had been an unwarranted invasion, and they were almost unanimous in denouncing Ritchie in the strongest possible terms. Some examples:

The *Crisfield Times:* "Is the action of Governor Ritchie the action of a man in his dotage or a man insane? There can be no explanation for this outrage . . . The people of the Eastern Shore can not forget, nor will they forgive, this dastardly act."

The *Chestertown Enterprise:* "Governor Ritchie, influenced by the Sunpapers and Communistic groups, fell in line with the wishes of [Attorney General W. Preston] Lane."

The *Centreville Observer:* "Governor Albert C. Ritchie has made the most disastrous mistake of his entire public career."

The *Centreville Times:* "To send great hordes of armed troops to arrest men merely suspected of committing a crime sets up a new and altogether dangerous course of action."

The *Marylander and Herald:* "When mad dogs run at large on our highways, they are shot. When a person loses his mental balance, so that he becomes a menace to society, we lock him in an insane asylum. Governor Ritchie seems to have lost his mind. He should be treated just as we would treat any other insane person."

The Salisbury *Times* also described Ritchie's action as "mad" and compared him with such dictators as Hitler, Stalin, and Mussolini. It carried a statement by a local black leader, President T. H. Kiah of the segregated state college at Princess Anne, that "Communists are at work among my people in this vicinity and it is their apparent aim to stir up race hatred and even warfare . . . Both white and Negro have been cruelly misrepresented in some newspapers . . . It has been my observation that Negroes are better off and happier in these Eastern Shore counties than in any other place I have been."

The contention of the Eastern Shore press that Ritchie's action had been needless was supported when a hearing was held for the four arrested men Wednesday, November 29, in Princess Anne. According to the *Marylander and Herald*, "it took exactly eight minutes for the case to be dismissed by Judges John R. Pattison and Robert F. Duer . . . Evidence in the case was totally lacking; the men had been held without due authority, no warrants had been issued, and really there was no reason for the hearing at all." A hearing in another jurisdiction might have ended differently, but under Maryland law prosecution of a case could not be pursued outside the county in which the crime was committed.

No further arrests were ever made. In fact, the only major casualty in the affair—aside from George Armwood—was Governor Ritchie. Within a week after the troops had left, stickers produced in the commercial job printing plant of the *Times* began appearing in windows and on auto windshields all over the Shore. They were exact duplicates of the red, white, and blue emblems then being widely displayed in support of President Roosevelt's National Recovery Administration—except that on the Eastern Shore stickers, the letters NRA were spelled out in smaller type as "Never Ritchie Again." And when Ritchie ran for a fourth term as governor, he was defeated, with a heavy Shore vote against him.

In retrospect, it seems to this writer that both the Eastern Shore press and the *Sunpapers* were remiss in their handling of the entire related series of events. Certainly the Salisbury *Times* failed to face up to the primary responsibility of any newspaper—to inform its readers of the facts, no matter how unpleasant. The city dailies, on the other hand, were undeniably guilty of sensationalism and slanted reporting in their zeal to see the mob leaders punished. By the same token, Shore papers were too quick to defend the lynchers' motives; none of them ever took a vigorous stand in favor of finding and punishing the guilty parties. Mencken, ever the exponent of outrageous exaggeration, sinned, if in nothing else, by tarring the entire Eastern Shore with one crude brush. His target was the lower Shore—the area he called Transchoptankiana. But his savage language smeared the reputation of decent and intelligent people throughout the Eastern Shore as well as those who deserved it. The wounds he inflicted have been a long time in healing.

Entirely by coincidence, an altogether different kind of tragedy again focused national attention on the Lower Eastern Shore and on Salisbury *Times* managing editor Charles J. Truitt in the summer of 1933. This time the object of the nation's concern was not the ugliness of racism, but one of Eastern Shore history's most devastating storms. And this time there was no question that Truitt played a heroic role. However controversial his newspaper's stand might have been in connection with the two lynchings, he undoubtedly acted in the finest tradition of journalism in his reporting of the savage winds and floods which virtually isolated the Lower Shore in August of that year. For his work in getting news of the storm's effects to the outside world by "ham" radio when all other communications were cut off, Truitt received honorable mention for the Pulitzer Prize, American journalism's most prestigious award. It was the highest honor ever attained by an Eastern Shore reporter.

The tropical storm—technically not a hurricane because by the time it reached Maryland its winds were less than seventy-five miles an hour—struck the Eastern Shore with full fury early on the morning of August 23. Heavy rain had been falling for two days, and the renewed downpour, plus extremely high tides, produced the worst flooding in the peninsula's history. Most of lower Dorchester County was under water; Talbot's Tilghman Island was cut temporarily into a string of islets; livestock perished by the thousands; shore installations such as canneries and boatyards were washed away.

Most severely stricken of all were eastern Wicomico and Worcester counties. At Ocean City the Atlantic swept across the sands of upper Assateague peninsula, and the piled-up waters of Sinepuxent Bay cut a deep waterway to the sea, creating the island and channel which still exist today. Everywhere dams were washed out, highways inundated, bridges destroyed, vast acreages flooded. Numerous towns were without lights as electric lines were broken and power service failed. By 9 A.M. on August 23, telephone and telegraph service from the area was disrupted entirely. At the coastal resort centers of Rehoboth Beach, Ocean City, and Chincoteague, thousands of vacationers from Philadelphia and Baltimore were trapped and had to be evacuated by boat.

As Associated Press correspondent for the area, as well as "stringer" for the *Philadelphia Evening Bulletin*, Truitt knew how important it was to get news of the storm's effects and the evacuation efforts out to relatives and friends of the vacationers. He made a personal survey of the scene, driving through mud, water, and debris over miles of seemingly impassable roads. But on his return to Salisbury he found that, with telephone and telegraph lines knocked out, there appeared to be no way to get his first-hand report to the outside world.

At this juncture two amateur radio operators—familiarly known as "hams"—came to the rescue. They provided a radio transmitter which, with a portable gasoline-powered generator, was set up in English's diner on Main Street. The street outside was knee-deep in water, and even the diner's floor was flooded. While Truitt stood by with his prepared copy, the hams started calling, asking especially for responses from fellow amateurs in the Philadelphia or Baltimore vicinities. A reply came from a New Jersey man, who agreed to take down Truitt's account and transmit it to the *Bulletin*. From there it went out on the AP wire—the first detailed report of conditions in the stricken area. Newspapers all over the country gave it page one play.

Announcing the Pulitzer awards in the spring of 1934, the prize committee singled Truitt for an honorable mention. His coverage was described as "a distinguished example of a reporter's work . . . commanding public attention and respect." He was an invited guest at the dinner at Columbia University in New York City where the Pulitzer presentations were made May 7, 1934.

Because of the coincidence in dates, the legend has grown in Salisbury that Truitt received the honor for his coverage of the lynchings as AP correspondent. But that was not the case. As he later pointed out, it was pure happenstance that the great storm and Governor Ritchie's much criticized "invasion" of Salisbury both occurred in 1933.

In ensuing years the almost paranoid anger of some segments of the Eastern Shore press against "outside meddlers" remained strong. "Communists" and "radicals" who sought to change the Shore's way of doing things were favorite targets. When union agents attempted to organize workers at the Phillips Packing Company in Cambridge in 1937, the weekly *Democrat and News* attacked them in "extras" with large headlines. The issue of July 17 asked in ninety-six point type,

> Does Cambridge Want the "CIO"
> To Come Here with its Red Program
> Of Communism Bloodshed and Ruin?

Follow-up headlines answered the question.

> Cambridge Workers Fully Capable
> Of Running Own Affairs
>
> Communism Not Needed
> in City of Cambridge

Other Shore newspapers were less vociferous in their attitude toward unions; but they almost unanimously opposed union organization on the peninsula, especially in their own shops. To this day no union has succeeded in organizing an Eastern Shore newspaper, either among mechanical or editorial employees. Management of most papers also ignored such government-ordered innovations as the forty-hour week and fair employment practices. Reporters were—and in some cases still are—expected to work nights and weekends without compensating time off. Publishers have argued that they could not survive if they adhered strictly to federal and state employment standards. And there are few black reporters on Shore papers, no matter what the law says about "equal opportunity."

Ten years after the Ritchie incident, another Lower Shore editor took on the assembled might of Maryland's political hierarchy. This time, however, the overtones were more hilarious than ugly.

With wartime gasoline rationing at its tightest and most irritating, editor Rives Matthews of the *Somerset News* discovered in the spring of 1943 that Comptroller of the Treasury J. Millard Tawes (later governor) had used a state car and state gas for a trip to Georgia to attend the wedding of his son. Matthews published this tidbit and added a fictitious radiogram addressed to Tawes and purportedly signed by Dr. Josef Goebbels, Hitler's minister of propaganda. It congratulated Tawes on helping Germany defeat America by using motor fuel that might have been employed in the war.

Tawes, attempting to justify the junket, pulled a blooper. He actually was on official business, he explained, because in the course of the trip he had paid visits to several Southern state capitals, including "Augusta, Georgia." Matthews gleefully pointed out that Atlanta, not Augusta, was the capital of Georgia; Augusta was the capital of Maine. So much for Tawes' "official business" even though the Office of Price Administration, which administered gasoline rationing, had said it was all right for him to drive to Georgia for a wedding if there was no other way of getting there.

Most people thought all this was pretty funny, and that Tawes, an immensely popular Somerset Countian, had been fairly caught with his hand in the gas tank. But Prentiss W. Evans of Crisfield, Somerset County State's Attorney and a Tawes supporter, was not amused. He had Matthews arrested on a charge of criminal libel, claiming the *Somerset News* was guilty of creating "civil discontent" and that it was "bad for the boys in the service to read such things."

Evans said Tawes himself had had no hand in the arrest. "I took action on my own initiative," he said. "If I see a violation of the law, it's my duty to see that it is punished. I've been watching Matthews and his newspaper for a long time. His articles are creating a lot of civil discontent and have caused many complaints to this office.

When Matthews was released on twenty-five hundred dollars bail to await grand jury action, his plight received widespread publicity. Editors of the nation's major dailies were not amused either; they saw it as the John Peter Zenger case all over again, a direct attack on their hard-won freedom of the press. The *Washington Post* called the arrest "stupid." The *Washington Times-Herald* said that as a blow at press freedom it was "one of the most unusual in

CONFLICT AND SURVIVAL

> **RADIOGRAM**
>
> Dear Herr und Frau Tawes: Der Feuhrer was highly pleased to hear of your violation of the pleasure-driving ban. Aside from your using gas that won't be used against Him, it is a great help to His Cause for people of your standing in America to show your international Jewish leaders in Washington you are behind Der Feuhrer!
> Heil Hitler!
>
> **DR. JOSEF GOEBBELS**

Fictitious radiogram in the *Somerset News*, addressed to Comptroller General J. Millard Tawes, caused the arrest of editor Rives Matthews on a charge of criminal libel.

> **THANKS, BROTHERS:**
>
> Sometimes we have to wait almost a lifetime for a real demonstration of the spiritual things to which many of us give merely lip-service. Among these things, for a newspaper man, are the freedom of the press and the power of that far-flung fraternity of newspapermen which is ever ready to spring to the defense of one of its members.
>
> Brothers of the U. S. Press, the events of the past two weeks have been a demonstration for me. I stand in the presence of a miracle and I thank you from the depths of a heart which never doubted, from the cortex of a mind that never wavered in its belief in these cardinal and sacred things.
>
> *Rives Matthews.*

Editor Matthews took the entire front page of the *Somerset News* of June 17, 1943, to thank fellow journalists who had rallied to his support after his arrest.

the legal history of the forty-eight states." The *St. Louis Post Dispatch* theorized that if the radiogram was ruled libelous by the courts, "it will be dangerous for newspapers and individuals to mention help to the enemy in expressing their opinion of a person's conduct. Such a verdict would drastically restrict the use of an effective weapon in bringing reckless strike leaders and other offenders to their senses."

Harold Godwin of NBC radio's Blue Network did a national broadcast on the affair. "If it comes to the point where an American editor cannot make a charge against a state official without suffering libel accusations, then indeed 'it CAN happen here,' and we are little better off than Fascist Italy or Nazi Germany," Goodwin said. He described Matthews as "a fighting Maryland editor" with the "state bureaucracy stacked against him—and if he loses, he will be one more American martyr in a free cause."

In the *Somerset News* of June 24, 1943, Matthews published an entire page of messages he had received from all parts of the country praising his stand. Typical comment, from a Washington, D.C., secretary: "I wish we had a few more good souls to speak right up and follow through with their ideas of right and wrong."

Tawes' hometown paper, the *Crisfield Times*, was one of the few newspapers to defend Evans' action. Egbert Quinn, then editor of the *Times*, disdainfully referred to Matthews by his middle name of "Skinker." "Just mind you don't slip in a 't' by mistake," Matthews shot back at Quinn. The *Marylander and Herald*, rival weekly of the *News* in Princess Anne, also backed Evans, commenting that "the State's Attorney's action has the hearty approval of many people here." But outside Somerset County, few felt that way.

Faced with such near unanimous cries of outrage in the national press, Evans had second thoughts. Eventually the charge was quietly withdrawn. However, as Matthews pointed out, it had at least one good effect: Thousands of Americans who had never before heard of Somerset County now knew where it was.

As for Tawes, clearly no fault was found with his role in the affair. Attending a son's wedding, no matter the circumstances, was an action Maryland voters apparently could understand, forgive, and forget. With resounding majorities, they returned the genial Somerset Countian to Annapolis for two additional tours as comptroller and then elected him to the maximum two terms as governor. Still later he served as state treasurer, thus becoming the only Marylander in history to hold all three of what were then considered the state's top political offices.

The Eastern Shore's agony over racial problems did not end with the lynchings of the 1930s. One more chapter remained to be written, as the peninsula's blacks—a fifth of its population—became a part of the national struggle to achieve the basic human rights so long denied them. White resistance to an end of segregation in schools and public accommodations brought repeated clashes in which the Eastern Shore press played an important—and, on the whole, responsible—moderating role.

An early flare-up came in Talbot County, probably the most liberal (or least illiberal) area of the Shore as far as racial relations were concerned. There school officials decided, immediately after the Supreme Court decision of 1954, to make a start toward integration of the public schools. The plan adopted called for gradual desegregation, beginning with open enrollment in the first three primary grades. On September 5, 1956—significantly, a full year before the showdown at Little Rock, Arkansas, which galvanized the nation—six black children were enrolled at the Hanson Street primary school in Easton and two at Oxford's primary school.

There had been rumblings of resistance, and a hastily organized White Citizens Committee began holding nightly meetings in an Easton warehouse to rally public opposition. Spearheading the drive was Bryant Bowles, a spellbinding segregationist orator brought in from Delaware, where he and his cohorts had been successful in blocking school desegregation. He urged white parents to fight back by keeping their children out of school. By September 11, absenteeism at the Hanson Street school totaled ninety-seven, one quarter of the enrollment. At Oxford, however, there were only four absentees, three from one family.

Norman Harrington, editor of the *Easton Star-Democrat*, was informed that the Talbot County School Board planned to make a strong statement cracking down on absenteeism, which was illegal under state law. On this basis he wrote and published an editorial supporting the school board's supposed stand in the strongest possible terms.

Entitled "A Call to Reason," it challenged the parents directly. Was it fair, Harrington asked

> to keep the children out of school, to inject them as pawns into a situation they cannot comprehend at their age for the sake of indulging in a protest that is doomed to failure?
> ... And for what? It is a battle that cannot possibly be won; yet the children, not the parents, will be the losers.
> In the final analysis, we either live under a system of laws, or we live in anarchy.
> ... Reason must and will prevail.

The editorial charged that the opposition had been stirred up by "out of state agitators" and hate mongers"—meaning Bowles and his group. It raised the

Norman Harrington.

age-old Eastern Shore cry against outsiders. "Heretofore, Talbot Countians had always prided themselves on being able to deal with their own problems in their own way, working in the framework of the law . . . No outside influences should now be permitted to tarnish our heritage by stirring us to actions we would eternally regret. We can and must keep our present rendezvous with history in a manner marked by honor, dignity, wisdom and temperate action."

"No matter how one may feel about segregation, or integration, the law is the law."

This was strong stuff for any Eastern Shore newspaper to print, even in relatively moderate Talbot County. To make matters worse, the School Board

Open house at the *Easton Star-Democrat*'s new building, June, 1949. The pressman was Ed Kimmelshue. (Courtesy Laird Wise)

backed down and issued no statement on the subject. There were even reports it was considering a return to segregated schools.

"I was left out on a limb," Harrington has recalled since then. "The editorial was the only public statement bearing on the issue from any source. It was read from the pulpit in several churches that Sunday, and the *Star-Democrat* was praised—and condemned—for its outspokenness."

The issue carrying the editorial appeared Friday morning, September 14. That same morning a brick was thrown through the front window of the *Star-Democrat* building and landed on Harrington's desk. Luckily, he was out of the room; he came back to find the brick and shattered glass on the floor. The incident was reported to the police, but nothing was printed about it in the paper. "We were trying to be very restrained—perhaps too much so, in retrospect—and avoid anything which might further stir up an extremely delicate situation," Harrington says.

Eventually the "reason" for which Harrington had called did prevail in Talbot County, although full desegregation there lagged behind other Shore counties. Credit for heading off violence belongs to many sources—but not least to the *Star-Democrat* and to editor Harrington's firm stand.

School desegregation was also an issue in the rioting which thrust Cambridge into the national spotlight in the summer of 1963. But there the central focus was on the even more explosive issue of desegregation of restaurants, theaters, drugstores, and other public accommodations. And, as in Talbot County, cool and well-reasoned editorials in the *Daily Banner* played a part in eventual solution of the crisis.

From the beginning of demonstrations to end segregation in December, 1961, the *Banner* supported the blacks' basic goals although it condemned the violent methods resorted to as the struggle grew more heated. Cambridge blacks deserved "a better break," according to the *Banner*. The root of the trouble was "the unwillingness of Cambridge and Dorchester County to make concessions to Negroes in the face of a visible social revolution now sweeping the country . . . On the one hand the city wants to live in peace; on the other, it rejects the very conditions which will bring about peace." At the height of the disturbances in June, 1963, while National Guard troops were patrolling the city to maintain order, the *Banner* published a very strong procivil rights editorial cartoon. Under the caption, "Knock and It Shall be Opened—When?" it showed a black fist knocking at a closed door labeled "fair housing and employment."

However, the paper also made crystal clear that it disapproved of the tactics adopted by the "reckless leadership" of the Cambridge civil rights movement, and especially the intrusion of "outside demonstrators" such as the Freedom Riders, black comedian Dick Gregory, and others. The *Banner* blamed these "outsiders" for most of the violence and charged they were holding Cambridge blacks in a "reign of terror." Throughout the troubled period, the paper called for common sense and willingness to negotiate by both sides. Sometimes it seemed to be the only voice in Cambridge expressing this view.

The Salisbury *Times* on at least two occasions came to the aid of its sister paper. In editorials which the *Banner* reprinted, the *Times* pointed up the fact that Salisbury had worked out an agreement to desegregate peaceably, "before passions became inflamed," while Birmingham, Alabama, then in the national headlines, had exploded in bombings and bloodshed. "Our friends in Cambridge, white and Negro, should look well at Birmingham," the *Times* said. "The Birmingham story could have been Salisbury's story. It can yet be the Cambridge story . . . Birmingham's story can be repeated anywhere unless both races are willing to seek gains instead of headlines."

Maurice Rimpo, former editor of the *Banner*, was managing editor and chief reporter during the Cambridge racial troubles of the 1960s.

The *Times'* warning was heeded in Talbot County if not in Dorchester. At the height of the Cambridge troubles, the *Easton Star-Democrat* called for a voluntary end to restaurant segregation in Talbot "in an atmosphere of calm and dignity" instead of "a forced progress that would arouse tempers, incite anarchy, and could even be marked by violence." A month later the paper was happy to announce that fifteen Easton businesses, including variety stores, drugstores, restaurants, and the Tidewater Inn, had agreed to end all segregation, and that St. Michaels' four downtown eating places had joined them.

One journalistic aspect of the crisis which brought repeated complaints from the *Banner* was allegedly biased reporting by the national press. It charged such major newspapers as the *New York Times*, the *Washington Post*, and the *Sun* with "scandalous irresponsibility." The *Times*, the *Banner* said, had carried a story which "deliberately" omitted salient facts in order "to present only one side," while the *Post* had "converted a report on racial progress into a vicious editorial blasting Cambridge." In a later editorial the *Banner* conceded there had been factual and fair reporting by some national papers but said half the reporters in Cambridge had become sociologists and were "trying to find out what makes the town tick" instead of doing their jobs.

When a compromise agreement was finally worked out at the Justice Department in Washington under the watchful eyes of Attorney General Robert F. Kennedy, the *Banner* felt its middle-of-the-road course had been justified. Now Cambridge could get on with the real business of improving black housing and opportunities. The paper emphasized that the agreement itself was "only a starting point" and that making it work would "require of both Negroes and whites, good judgment, confidence, faith and the willingness to treat the other man the way we would like to be treated . . . Everything hinges on the good sense of every single citizen."

Unhappily, within four years racial fires would flare again in Cambridge. In 1967 a brief but violent episode centering around Rap Brown, a true "outside agitator" of national reputation, resulted in the burning of a school. The town and the state, with then Governor Spiro T. Agnew in the forefront, reacted swiftly and angrily. Brown was arrested two days later on charges of inciting to riot and arson.

The governor's prompt action did not pass unnoticed. In his narrative history, *The Glory and the Dream*, author William Manchester observed, ". . . Governor Agnew's resolute handling of the [Cambridge] incident had attracted the attention of the Republican party's national leadership, winning him the admiration of, among others, Richard M. Nixon." A year later Nixon picked the relatively obscure Agnew as running mate in his successful 1968 presidential campaign.

On less emotional issues, Eastern Shore newspapers of the modern era have favored most anything they thought would help the Shore. The Emerson C. Harrington causeway and bridge across the Choptank at Cambridge, which firmly linked the upper and lower Shores together, won enthusiastic approval. When President Roosevelt dedicated it in August, 1935, by sailing through the drawbridge in his yacht, the *Sequoia*, the event made headlines throughout the Shore. Most newspapers thought it would do more to restore prosperity than in fact it did. And despite some grumblings, as in the *Chestertown Enterprise*, that the proposed Chesapeake Bay bridge would bring "the trash of East Baltimore" to "overrun the Shore," the Eastern Shore press generally supported that bridge also and welcomed it when it was completed in July, 1952. The changes it produced on the Eastern Shore in the next few years, with slow

Opening of the Bay Bridge, July 30, 1952, received headline treatment in the Eastern Shore press.

but steady population growth and thousands of tourists and transients, were accepted with equanimity if not with cheers. They might disrupt the age-old patterns of Shore life, but they at least were bringing in fresh money and pushing up land values.

CHAPTER SEVEN

Today and Tomorrow
1960 TO 1985

BY THE 1960s the face of the Eastern Shore press itself was changing rapidly. Not only was it acquiring a new appearance thanks to the introduction of the photo-offset method of printing, but its ownership was shifting. Soon it no longer could be said that Shore newspapers were published "for home folks and by home folks." By 1984, especially in the middle-Shore counties, they were being published principally for relatively new residents by nonowner editors, and their ownership had passed from local publishers almost entirely to chains or newspaper groups based outside Maryland.

As of 1984, only fourteen paid-circulation newspapers still were being published on the Eastern Shore, out of nearly three hundred whose names are listed in this volume. And only one—the *News & Farmer* of Preston in Caroline County—was published by a resident of the county in which it appeared, or even by a Marylander. All the others had been bought up by newspaper chains based in places as far off as New York City, Charleston, South Carolina, and Toronto, Canada.

The chain ownerships, it is true, reflect a worldwide trend, and in some cases the introduction of outside capital has improved the papers as far as plant and equipment are concerned. But it has not necessarily resulted in a better editorial product, especially when editors and reporters unfamiliar with their communities were brought in. Fortunately, this has not proved a major problem.

The man most responsible both for the changing appearance of Eastern Shore papers and for the introduction of outside ownership, E. Ralph Hostetter, got his own start in the old tradition. Born in Cecil County near Rowlandville, he became managing editor of the *Cecil Whig* on his twenty-fifth birthday, January 14, 1947. Ten years later, after service in Korea and a short but successful business career, he bought the *Whig*. That was the beginning of the end for the Shore journalism's ancient ways.

A Harvard graduate with an engineering degree, Hostetter pioneered in technical developments which revolutionized newspaper production and completely changed the look of Shore newspapers. He introduced the photo-offset method of printing, which did away with dependence on "hot type" and zinc engravings, and thus enabled weekly papers to choose from a variety of type styles and use as many pictures as they had room for. In photo-offset there is no typesetting in the old sense of the word. Both headlines and body type are created photographically and reproduced on paper strips which are then pasted onto cardboard page forms. Pictures are converted into screened prints which can also be pasted up with the type. These are photographed and a metal plate produced which is used for the actual press run.

The extent to which this development has changed the look, if not the content, of the Eastern Shore press can be illustrated by a single comparison. The *Centreville Record* for August 18, 1923, contained only two small photo-engravings—a one-column "head shot" of a local political candidate and a two-column picture of a field of soy beans, then a novelty on the Eastern Shore. The *Record*'s successor, the *Queen Anne's Record-Observer*, on the same date in 1982 published eighteen large photographs occupying nearly half the total editorial space in the paper, and picturing local activities ranging from a rodeo to weddings and engagements. On the other hand, the 1923 *Record*, employing small headlines, managed to report twenty-one local news events on page one; the 1982 *Record-Observer*, with more of its space devoted to headlines and photos, had only five. Yet there was little difference in the *kind* of news presented by the two papers: county fairs, politics, petty crime, births and deaths, church activities, and vacation travels apparently were just as interesting to Queen Anne's Countians in 1982 as they had been fifty-nine years earlier.

When the *Cecil Whig*'s photo-offset plant opened September 1, 1960, it was the first in Maryland and one of the first on the East Coast. Since then many newspapers, not only on the Eastern Shore but throughout the country, have followed Hostetter's lead.

Soon he began expanding into what became a "little empire." In 1962 he bought the *Federalsburg Times*, in 1964 the *Easton Star-Democrat*, for which he outbid the A. S. Abell Company, publishers of the *Sunpapers* in Baltimore. By the 1970s the Hostetter-controlled Chesapeake Publishing Corporation owned nine Eastern Shore newspapers plus seven others in Maryland and Delaware. North of the Choptank it had a near monopoly, with the *Cecil Whig* and *Cecil Democrat* in Elkton, the *Kent County News* in Chestertown, the *Queen Anne's Record-Observer* in Centreville, the *Bay Times* in Stevensville, and the *County Record* in Denton, in addition to the *Star-Democrat* and *Federalsburg Times*. Several of the smaller papers were printed at the *Star-Democrat*'s Easton plant. South of the Choptank Hostetter's only holding was the struggling *Dorchester News*.

In April, 1973, the Cambridge *Banner* established a daily Talbot County edition of its paper in competition with the weekly *Star-Democrat*, which then had more than 10,000 circulation and was widely regarded as the best county weekly in Maryland. Convinced his weekly could not survive, Hostetter converted the *Star-Democrat* into a daily in August, 1974. For the next four years Talbot County had two daily papers to serve an area of less than thirty thousand people, a situation probably unmatched anywhere in America. The costly competition ended when the Evening Post Publishing Company of Charleston, S.C., owners of the *Banner*, gave up and turned their Talbot edition into a free distribution weekly in March, 1979.

In 1975 Hostetter sold his majority interest in Chesapeake Publishing Corporation to the Whitney Communications Corporation of New York City. The Whitney group, owned by the family which had formerly published the *New York Herald-Tribune*, converted the *Dorchester News* into a free distribution weekly, and closed down the century-old *Cecil Democrat* after one issue as a quarterly. There was also attrition among the independents: the *Journal* of Denton and the *Queen Anne's Journal* of Centreville, both launched in 1977, ceased publication at the end of July, 1980.

In the lower counties as well, outside ownership was becoming the rule. Brush-Moore Newspapers, Inc., of Canton, Ohio, which had bought the Salisbury *Times* as early as 1940, sold it in 1967 to Thomson Newspapers, Inc., a huge chain with more than a hundred papers based in Toronto, Canada. Independent Newspapers, Inc., of Dover, Delaware, acquired the *Crisfield Times* and the *Advertiser* of Salisbury in 1970, turning the latter into a free distribution weekly tabloid.

Hostetter's counterpart on the Lower Shore was George N. McMath, president of Atlantic Publications, Inc., of Accomac, Virginia. McMath, a native of the Virginia Shore and a newspaperman by background and training, started his career as coeditor, along with Ben D. Byrd, of the *Eastern Shore News* of Onancock and later Onley, which they bought in 1957. After acquiring several other Virginia papers, they moved into the Maryland Eastern Shore field in 1969 by purchasing the *Worcester Democrat* of Pocomoke City. In 1973 they bought the *Democrat Messenger* of Snow Hill, the Worcester County

---

Opposite, the "revolution" started by Ralph Hostetter is illustrated by these contrasting pictures. *Above*, the *Easton Star-Democrat*'s composing room in the days of "hot lead," and, *below*, the paste-up department of the 1981 *Daily Times*, Salisbury.

seat, and merged it with the *Worcester Democrat* to form the *Worcester County Messenger*.

Other Maryland purchases followed until by November, 1984, McMath's company—renamed Atlantic Publications, Inc., in 1977—owned four paid circulation weeklies on the Maryland Shore. These were, in addition to the *Worcester County Messenger*, the *Eastern Shore Times* and the *Maryland Coast Press*, both of Ocean City, and the *Marylander & Herald* of Princess Anne, acquired in 1984 from its long-time owner-publishers, the Byrd family. Atlantic also publishes a free distribution weekly, the *Beachcomber*, in Ocean City, and has a string of some fifteen other papers in Virginia, Delaware, and North Carolina.

These, then, were the survivors among Eastern Shore newspapers as of December, 1984:

Daily and Sunday

> *Times*, Salisbury

Daily (five days)

> *Banner*, Cambridge
> *Star-Democrat*, Easton[1]

Paid-Circulation Weeklies

> *Bay Times*, Stevensville[1]
> *Cecil Whig*, Elkton[1]
> *Kent County News*, Chestertown[1]
> *Queen Anne's Record-Observer*, Centreville[1]
> Caroline County *Times-Record*, Denton[1]
> *News & Farmer*, Preston
> *Marylander & Herald*, Princess Anne[2]
> *Crisfield Times*
> *Eastern Shore Times*, Ocean City[2]
> *Maryland Coast Press*, Ocean City[2]
> *Worcester County Messenger*, Pocomoke City[2]

Free Distribution Weeklies

> *Talbot Banner*, Easton
> *Dorchester News*, Cambridge[1]
> *Salisbury Advertiser*, Salisbury
> *Beachcomber* (separate summer and winter editions), Ocean City[2]
> *Maryland Coast Dispatch*, Berlin

1 Whitney group papers, published by Chesapeake Bay Publishing Corporation.
2 Atlantic Publications papers.

Whitney also owns the *Delmarva Farmer,* a paid-circulation weekly edited by Bruce Hotchkiss and specializing in agricultural interests throughout the Delmarva peninsula. It is produced at the *Star-Democrat* plant in Easton.

An overall look at Eastern Shore journalism as it nears the start of its third century indicates that the era of outside corporate ownership has brought surprisingly little change. Shore newspapers are still conservative in politics, still supporters of the social *status quo,* still determinedly provincial in their outlook on the world beyond the Eastern Shore. They remain boosters rather than critics of their communities; the new "advocacy journalism" so ardently embraced since Watergate by the metropolitan media has found no foothold in this area. Little or no investigative reporting into possible crime or unsavory situations is ever done.

Among the weeklies the time-honored maxim that local names are what make news appears to be as strong as ever. Checked at random, the *Kent County News* for August 18, 1982, was found to contain the names of 1,394 persons, nearly all of them Kent Countians. That is more than eight percent of the county's entire population of 17,000. President Reagan was mentioned only casually, and Maryland Governor Harry Hughes only in connection with local events; but weddings, funerals, births, hospitalizations, anniversaries, amateur sports, horse shows, church meetings, social visits, vacations, crab feasts, business news, turkey shoots, and court cases were covered in detail and down to the last name. By-lined columns told what, if anything, was going on in such places as Still Pond, Rock Hall, Betterton, Millington, Locust Grove, Georgetown, Lynch, and Galena as well as reporting who had been "seen on the street in Chestertown."

Such saturation coverage helps explain why the *Kent County News* is among the most successful Eastern Shore papers, with a circulation of 8,000 in a county of only 17,000 people. It may in fact point the way toward future survival of the rural press throughout America; editor-publisher H. Hurtt Deringer's operation has been cited at the American Press Institute as an outstanding example of what a weekly can do to remain strong in the face of challenges by television, radio, and the dailies.

Deringer readily admits that almost everybody in Kent County can expect to see his or her name in the paper at least once during any given year. "That's exactly what we'd like to do," he says. "Reading about themselves and their friends is the one thing a county weekly can give people that they can't get anywhere else." Like the *Dorchester News* of a generation ago, the *Kent County News* of the 1980s may contain little or nothing of interest to a stranger; but it contains a great deal to interest people who live in Kent County. And despite their New York City background, the Whitney group which now controls the paper has found it both profitable and wise to let the *News* continue in its traditional ways.

The Shore's three dailies also strive to retain the "local" image even though all three are corporate-owned and have access to national and world news through press association wires and feature syndicates. The *Star-Democrat* goes furthest in this respect; it almost never publishes a story of national interest on page one. When an Easton Little League baseball team reached that sport's "World Series," it produced a paroxysm of page one headlines, photos, feature articles, congratulatory editorials, and special sections. The siege of Beirut, which was going on at the same time, received routine inside-the-paper treatment in the *Star-Democrat,* and was never mentioned in the weekly *Talbot Banner.* The Salisbury and Cambridge dailies do not go quite to this extreme, but both consistently choose local stories for display over national or international ones.

While it is true that most of the traditional owner-editors of the Eastern Shore press have been replaced by corporate hirelings, many editors still present the "home-grown" look Frank Goodwin found so characteristic of the 1930s. By no means all have journalism degrees, and relatively few have had any newspaper experience away from the Eastern Shore. After some initial experimenting, the new ownership in general has appeared to recognize that "Eastern Shoreness" is a salable commodity, and that in so history-conscious a region, small town editors should not be regarded as interchangeable pawns. Here are brief sketches of the current editors of the Shore's fourteen paid-circulation newspapers and their backgrounds:

—Mel Toadvine, editor-in-chief (and also managing editor) of the daily and Sunday *Times* in Salisbury, is a native of that city and a graduate of Wicomico High School. He takes pride in the fact that the Toadvine family settled on the Eastern Shore in the seventeenth century. All his journalistic experience has been on the *Times*, where he started in 1961 as a photographer and feature writer.

—Denise Perry of the *Star-Democrat* in Easton also comes from an old-line Eastern Shore family. She is one of the few women ever to edit an Eastern Shore newspaper and the first to be named editor of a daily. She is also one of the few Shore editors to hold a degree in journalism, which she earned at the University of Maryland after graduation from Easton High School. Before joining the *Star-Democrat* staff, Ms. Perry served as editor of the *Queen Anne's Record-Observer* for several years.

—H. Hurtt Deringer, editor and publisher of the *Kent County News*, is a descendant of the inventor of the famous dueling pistol and, on his mother's side, of a family which has lived in Kent County for centuries. A product of Chestertown High School and the local Washington College, he started his

E. Ralph Hostetter.

Melvin Toadvine.

newspaper career on the old *Chester River Press*. All his subsequent experience has been in Kent County journalism.

—William H. Kerbin of the *Worcester County Messenger* is another native Eastern Shoreman. He grew up in Snow Hill, where his family had owned the *Democrat Messenger* before it was combined with the *Worcester Democrat* and moved to Pocomoke City under new ownership in 1973.

—James E. Pokrandt, Jr., became editor of the *Daily Banner* of Cambridge early in 1984 after the retirement of Maurice Rimpo, who had served with the *Banner* for more than thirty years as reporter, city editor, managing editor and editor. By coincidence, both Pokrandt and Rimpo are natives of New Jersey, although neither had newspaper experience in that state. Pokrandt joined the *Banner* staff as a reporter on his graduation from the University of Maryland in 1975. In 1979 he accepted the post of city editor on a paper in Martinsburg, West Virginia. He remained there until he was invited to return to Cambridge as editor.

—William A. Martin, Jr., of the *Crisfield Times* was born in Carroll County on the Western Shore but has lived in Crisfield so long most people there think of him as a native. As of 1985 he is starting his forty-eighth year with the paper. He began in 1938 as a Linotype operator, a job he says is "now as obsolete as the horse and buggy." He became editor in 1970.

—Donald Herring of the *Cecil Whig* was born in Kentucky and gained his early newspaper experience at the *Indianapolis Star*. He has been editor of the *Whig* since 1971.

—Michael Mills, a native of Baltimore, was named editor of the *Marylander & Herald*, Princess Anne, in September, 1984, when Atlantic Publications, Inc., acquired the paper from the Byrd family, which had published it for three generations. A 1983 graduate of the University of Maryland with a degree in journalism, Mills worked for the Salisbury *Times* and the *Eastern Shore Times* before taking over the *Marylander & Herald*.

—Paul V. McKnight, editor of the *Queen Anne's Record-Observer* since December, 1982, started his newspaper career as a reporter-photographer with the Newark (Delaware) *Weekly Post* in 1967. He became farm editor of the *Cecil Whig* in January, 1979, and moved from there to the *Record-Observer*. He also had editorial responsibility for the *Bay Times* of Stevensville.

—Richard Polk became editor of the *Caroline County Times-Record* in October, 1983, shortly after it was formed by the merger of the *Federalsburg Times* with the *County Record* of Denton. A journalism graduate of the University of Tennessee, Polk spent ten years on the staff of the *Enterprise* of Lexington Park, Maryland, as reporter and feature-photo editor.

—Gee Williams, general editorial manager of the Ocean City-based Atlantic Publications group of newspapers which includes the *Eastern Shore Times*, the *Maryland Coast Press*, and the *Beachcomber*, considers himself a native of Berlin in Worcester County although he was actually born in the hospital at Salisbury ("because that was the only hospital in the area," he explains). A graduate of Chesapeake College and the University of Maryland with a journalism degree, which he received in 1971, he has worked in various capacities for Atlantic Publications papers since then.

—Thomas Parker, editor of the *Eastern Shore Times* of Ocean City, which Atlantic Publications purchased November 21, 1984, is a native of Salisbury. After high school and a stint in the Air Force, he worked as a reporter and photographer for the Salisbury *Times* while attending Salisbury State College, then earned a journalism degree at the University of Maryland. He edited free distribution weeklies, tried public relations and sales, then returned to the newspaper field, becoming editor of the *Maryland Coast Press* under its former owner, Richard V. Lohmeyer, in February, 1984.

—Stewart Dobson, installed as editor of the *Maryland Coast Press* in November, 1984, is the son of Emory Dobson, for many years editor of the old *County Record* in Denton. A native of Denton, young Dobson began with the

The composing room of the *Marylander & Herald* in 1981, reminiscent of the early 1900s.

Federalsburg Times and later worked on the *County Record* with his father. Other jobs followed, including some time spent on the West Coast, before he returned to the Eastern Shore to assume the editorship of the *Times*.

—D. Scott Warehime of the *News & Farmer* of Preston deserves special mention as the last remaining Eastern Shore editor who is also president and publisher of his paper. He is also the last publisher to live in the county in which his paper circulates, and the last remaining Marylander to serve as publisher. Thus he alone represents what was once the standard in these respects. A native of Carroll County on the Western Shore, Warehime moved to Caroline County when he bought the *News & Farmer* in 1980, at the age of twenty-two, from its founder and long-time publisher, Max Chambers.

Special mention should also be made of Emory Dobson, one of the last of the true country editors, who died October 29, 1980, after a career which spanned more than three decades in Caroline County. Dobson helped to found two newspapers, the *County Record* and the *Journal*, served as mayor and commissioner of Denton, and held numerous civic posts reflecting his dedication to his home community. But it was for his craftsmanship in the fading traditions of old-time newspapering that he is best remembered. As a colleague, Bud Hutton of the *County Record*, put it in a page one tribute at the time of Dobson's death:

> He could do it all . . . He could go out and report a story, photograph it, go back to the office and write the story and develop the photos, all on his own. Then he could

sit down and edit story and photos as objectively and professionally as if he'd never seen them before.

Well, some old fashioned newsmen could do all of that, true. But then Emory could (and did) go out to the mechanical department, sit down at a Linotype machine, and set in type what he had written, process the photos into engravings, set into type the headlines on another machine, assemble all of it into a page form and put it on the press.

And if he had to, Emory Dobson could run the press, too, and finally deliver the fresh-lined product to the readers.

That, I submit, is being a very professional newsman.

Hutton's salute to Dobson was at the same time a salute to the old-time country editors all over America who had built the nation's press into a potent force but whose time had passed. America no longer needed journalists who could operate a Linotype or process a photograph as routinely as they could cover a Lions' Club meeting. The day of electronic journalism, of specialists in every field, had reached even such backwater regions as the Maryland Eastern Shore.

What lies in the future? "More attrition, and 'a dish on the roof,'" says Mel Toadvine of the *Times* in Salisbury. The *Times*, in 1982, had a circulation of 30,000, nearly three times greater than the Shore's second paper, the *Star-Democrat*, which had a circulation of 10,200.

"The weaker county weeklies are going to have a tough time surviving," Toadvine predicts. "Some of them are bound to go under, or be forced to consolidate. It's an unhappy situation, but you have to face economic realities."

The *Daily Times* office already has the look of the future. In both editorial and advertising departments, everything is done by computer. The familiar typewriter, copy paper, paste pot, and editor's blue pencil all have vanished; instead, each reporter has a computer terminal at his desk. He writes his story on a keyboard which feeds the copy into the main computer. The editor then calls it up on his own terminal, edits it, trims it if necessary, corrects errors, writes headlines—all without ever touching a pencil to paper. The computer sends the stories to electronic typesetting machines, and the finished product comes out at the other end neatly printed and ready for "paste-up."

Opposite, above, the *Marylander & Herald* pressroom, 1981, and *below,* the *Marylander & Herald* office, 1981. [Dickson Preston is at the right.]

Here, at the *Daily Times*, Salisbury, reporters type their stories into video display terminals, or VDTs. Reporters and editors can edit and write headlines on their terminals before transmitting them to electronic typesetting equipment.

Above, reporters just before deadline are shown filing their last minute stories into their video display terminals. Scene is the newsroom of the *Daily Times*. *Below*, Jackie Moore, a long-time employee of the *Daily Times*, pastes up classified ads on a page prior to going to press.

Above, the high-speed Goss offset press prints 30,000 papers in less than a half hour. The new presses are operated by complicated electronic equipment and are capable of printing in several colors. *Below*, employees assemble and bundle copies of *The Daily Times* minutes after they come off the press. These people work in the *Times* mail room and also insert special advertising supplements.

Even the wire service copy arrives by computer—and that's where Toadvine's "dish on the roof" comes in. "We get our AP copy by satellite. We feed news copy to all the radio and television stations on the Lower Shore. The dish is large and sits just outside the building, but new technology is coming, and it will mean a smaller dish, probably on top of the roof."

Toadvine says papers are still receiving their wirephotos through telephone lines. "It won't be long before photographs will also be sent to us via satellite," Toadvine said.

For those who can afford such complex and expensive equipment it's a brave new world. For those who can't, it's the end of the road, after nearly two hundred years of Eastern Shore newspaper history.

Directory of Eastern Shore Newspapers

Directory of Eastern Shore Newspapers
HOW TO USE THIS DIRECTORY

THE directory on the following pages lists, as nearly as possible, every known issue of every weekly newspaper ever published on the Eastern Shore of Maryland, and where each edition may be found. For space reasons, some daily newspaper tabulations have been summarized.

The newspaper listings are presented by counties, and by towns and cities within each county. They are also listed in alphabetical order in the index. Because many Eastern Shore papers changed their names frequently over the years, every name used by a newspaper has been included, with a reference to the chief name under which the publication is listed.

The newspaper names are presented in boldface type. Under each, in italics, are given the various repositories in which editions are located, with the years and dates of known existing issues. [Since this Directory was completed the Hall of Records became an independent agency of the State of Maryland in 1984 and is now known as the Maryland State Archives. The Archives has a continuing program to microfilm Maryland newspapers and as a consequence will have added titles to its collection which were not available there when the Directory was compiled.] Full addresses for the repositories appear on pages 198-99.

The data are presented in summary form by years of issue. A dash between dates indicates that every edition published between the two dates is included in the repository's collection. A comma or semicolon indicates that no editions published between the dates are included.

For example, the listing for the *American Union* (Denton, Caroline County) at the Enoch Pratt Free Library for 1860 reads:

1860: July 17-September 25; October 2-November 29; December 13, 20

This means that no issues before July 17, 1860, are available at the Pratt Library; that all editions from July 17 to September 25 and from October 2 to November 29, inclusive, can be found there, and that the only existing issues for December are dated the 13th and the 20th.

In many cases the tabulations in this directory necessarily were reproduced from file cards or from lists of collections provided by the repositories. Since it was impossible to check each listing individually, the editor and publishers cannot attest to the accuracy or completeness of every listing. We apologize for that, as well as for any errors or omissions of our making which may be found in the tables.

ADDRESSES OF REPOSITORIES
(Addresses of private collections are omitted.)

American Antiquarian Society, 185 Salisbury Street, Worcester, Massachusetts 01609

Bay Times Office, Love Point Road, Stevensville, Maryland 21666

Caroline County Public Library, Market Street, Denton, Maryland 21629

Cecil County Historical Society, 135 East Main Street, Elkton, Maryland 21921

Cecil County Library, 135 East Main Street, Elkton, Maryland 21921

Chesapeake College Library, Wye Mills, Maryland 21679

Clements Library, University of Michigan, Ann Arbor, Michigan 48104

County Record Office, 219 North Market Street, Denton, Maryland 21629

Daily Banner Office, 302 High Street, Cambridge, Maryland 21613

Dorchester County Historical Society, 904 LaGrange Street, Cambridge, Maryland 21613

Dorchester County Public Library, 303 Gay Street, Cambridge, Maryland 21613

Dorchester News, P. O. Box 176, Cambridge, Maryland 21613

Eastern Shore Times Office, 3316 Coastal Highway, Ocean City, Maryland 21842

Enoch Pratt Free Library, 400 Cathedral Street, Baltimore, Maryland 21201

Hall of Records, Box 828, Annapolis, Maryland 21404

Houghton Library, Harvard University, Cambridge, Massachusetts 02138

Huntington Library, San Marino, California 91108

Julia A. Purnell Museum, 208 West Market, Snow Hill, Maryland 21862

Kent County News Office, High Street, Chestertown, Maryland 21620

Library Company of Philadelphia, 1314 Locust Street, Philadelphia, Pennsylvania 19107

DIRECTORY OF EASTERN SHORE NEWSPAPERS   199

The Library of Congress, Washington, D. C. 20540

Maryland Coast Dispatch Office, P. O. Box 467, Berlin, Maryland 21811

Marylander & Herald Office, P. O. Box 310, Princess Anne, Maryland 21853

Maryland Historical Society, 201 West Monument Street, Baltimore, Maryland 21201

News & Farmer Office, Main Street and Noble Avenue, Preston, Maryland 21655

New-York Historical Society, 170 Central Park West, New York, New York 10024

Oxford Museum, Inc., Morris and Market Streets, Oxford, Maryland 21654

Queen Anne's County Free Library, Commerce Street, Centreville, Maryland 21617

Queen Anne's County Historical Society, Tucker House, 120 South Commerce Street, Centreville, Maryland 21617

Queen Anne's Record-Observer Office, 114 Broadway Avenue, Centreville, Maryland 21617

Salisbury Advertiser Office, 1619 North Division Street, Salisbury, Maryland 21801

Salisbury State College Library, Salisbury, Maryland 21801

Somerset County Historical Society, Teackle Mansion, Mansion Street, Princess Anne, Maryland 21853

Star-Democrat Office, Air Park Drive, Easton, Maryland 21601

Talbot Banner, 26 South Washington Street, Easton, Maryland 21601

Talbot County Free Library, Easton, Maryland 21601

Theodore R. McKeldin Library, University of Maryland, College Park, Maryland 20742

Times-Record, P. O. Box 160, Denton, Maryland 21629

University of Delaware Library, Newark, Delaware 19711

University of Illinois Library, Urbana, Illinois 61801

Washington College Library, Chestertown, Maryland 21620

Wicomico County Free Library, 122 South Division Street, Salisbury, Maryland 21801

Wisconsin Historical Society, 816 State Street, Madison, Wisconsin 53706

Worcester County Library, 307 North Washington Street, Snow Hill, Maryland 21863

Worcester County Messenger Office, 129 Market Street, Pocomoke City, Maryland 21851

Caroline

DENTON

American Union, 1860-1932

Weekly. First known issue July 17, 1860. Said to have been a successor to *The Pearl*. Name changed May 13, 1926, to *The Independent*, June 16, 1927, to *Caroline Independent*. Last known issue July 1, 1932.

American Antiquarian Society
1876: June 15

Enoch Pratt Free Library (under *Caroline Independent*)
(Chesapeake College Library has same on microfilm)
1860: July 17-September 25; October 2-November 29; December 13, 20
1861: June 27
1864: August 25; September 1
1867: January 17-August 15, 29-December 12
1869: January 7-December 16
1870: January 6-May 5, 19, 26; June 9-December 22
1871: January 19-August 10, 24-November 23
1875: January 14-August 5, 19-December 23
1877: January 4-August 2, 16-December 13
1880: February 19-July 8; December 16-30
1885: January 8-November 19; December 3-17
1892: June 23-December 15
1898: Complete
1899: April 6-20; May 4-June 8, 22-December 28
1902: June 19-December 25
1903: Complete
1904: January 7-August 11; September 8-November 3
1910: January 20-April 7; May 12-September 29; October 13-November 3
1912: January 11-June 13
1913: January 2-December 6
1915: September 23
1918: November 21-December 26
1919-1924: Complete
1925: January 1-June 4, 18-August 13, 27-December 3, 17-31
1926: Complete
1927: June 2-December 30
1928: Complete
1929: January 4-December 20
1930: January 3-April 25; May 16-July 4, 25-October 3
1931: Complete
1932: January 1-July 1

Maryland Historical Society
1884: December 11 (under *Caroline Independent*)

News & Farmer
1914: July 2
1923: May 19

University of Delaware Library
1879: June 5

Caroline Advocate, 1834-1837(?)

Weekly. Established May 6, 1834, by Thomas E. Martin. Later published by Henry Vanderford, who moved it to Centreville about 1837.

Library of Congress
1834: May 6

Caroline Democrat, 1879-1885

Weekly.

Enoch Pratt Free Library
1885: February 17; March 3; June 16-30; July 7-21; August 4, 11

Caroline Independent

See *American Union*

County Record, 1952-1983

Weekly. Established May 22, 1952, by print shop operators Charles T. Baker and Clyde R. Bell. Absorbed *Caroline Sun* 1959. Merged with *The Times* Federalsburg, to become the *Times-Record* August 1983. Owned 1981 by Whitney Communications Corporation, New York City.

County Record

1957: August 1-December 26
1958: Complete
1959: January 1, 15; May 14-December 31
1960 to date: Complete

Enoch Pratt Free Library

1952: May 22 to date, complete (missing December 24, 1959)

News & Farmer

1952: May 22-June 12; July 10; August 14

Denton Journal, 1847-1965

Weekly. Established December 11(?), 1847. Ceased publication May 6, 1965.

American Antiquarian Society

1876: July 15

Caroline County Public Library

1870: April 2
1871: September 9
1872: February 3-24; July 6
1873: January 4-18; February 1-15; March 1-15, 29; April 5, 19-26; May 10, 24; June 7, 21-28; July 12, 26; August 9-16, 30; September 6-20; October 4, 18-25; November 8, 22-29; December 6-13, 27
1875: January 9, 23-30; February 6, 20-27; March 6-May 1, 15-29; July 3-17; August 14-21; September 4, 18-25; October 16-30; December 11-18
1876: November 18-25; December 9-23
1880: January 10; April 20
1912-1919: Complete
1921-1964: Complete
1965: January 7-May 6

Chesapeake College Library

Microfilm

1870: April 2
1871: September 9
1872: February 3-24; July 6
1873: January 4-18; February 1-15; March 1-15, 29; April 5, 19-26; May 10, 24; June 7, 21, 28; July 12, 26; August 9-16, 30; September 20; October 4, 18-25; November 8, 22; December 13, 27
1875: January 9, 23; February 6, 20; May 1, 15, 29; July 3, 17; August 14, 21; September 4, 18, 25; October 16, 30; December 11, 18
1876: November 18; December 30
1877: January 6; March 17, 31-September 8, 22-December 29
1878: January 5-July 27; August 10-October 5, 26-December 28
1879: Complete
1880: January 10-December 25
1881: January 8-April 2, 16-August 20, September 3-December 31
1882-1883: Complete
1884: January 5-August 9, 23-December 27
1885: January 3-March 7, 21-September 12, 26-December 12, 16
1886: January 2-July 3, 17-December 26
1887: January 1-November 26, December 10, 31
1888-1889: Complete
1890: January 4-April 26; May 10-December 27
1891-1912: Complete

Enoch Pratt Free Library

1850: November 23
1864: October 1
1866: April 28
1868: January 4, 18; February 29; March 14-June 20; July 4, 18-August 8, 29-September 19; October 3-31; November 14, 21; December 5-12
1869: January 9-February 27; March 13; June 12-19; July 24-31
1876: January 8, 22; March 11; April 1-22; May 20; June, 3-10; July 15-22; August 5-12; September 16, 30; November 18-December 30
1877: January 6-March 17, 31-September 8, 22-December 29
1878: January 5-July 27; August 10-October 5, 26-December 28
1879: Complete
1880: January 10-December 25
1881: January 8-April 2, 16-December 31
1882: Complete
1883: January 6-December 22
1884: January 5-August 9, 23-December 27
1885: January 3-March 7, 21-September 12, 26-December 12, 26

1886: January 2-May 1, 15-July 3, 17-December 25
1887: January 1-November 26; December 10-31
1888-1889: Complete
1890: January 4-April 26; May 10-December 27
1891-1903: Complete
1904: January 9-December 31
1905: January 14-October 21; November 4, 18-December 30
1906-11: Complete
1927: August 20
1934: June 16-December 29
1935-1964: Complete
1965: January 7-May 6

Maryland Historical Society
1891: August 1
1937: April 21

News & Farmer
1882: January 28
1917: September 8
1935: April 6

New-York Historical Society
1873: April 12

Denton Pearl, 1840-1846(?)

Weekly. Established September 23, 1840. Title varies; at some point called simply *The Pearl*. Said to have been a predecessor of the *American Union*.

Enoch Pratt Free Library
1840: September 30
1846: March 28

The Independent

See *American Union*

Journal [sic], 1976-1980

Weekly. Established January 6, 1976, expired July 30, 1980.

Caroline County Public Library
1976-1980: Complete

The Pearl

See *Denton Pearl*

Times-Record, 1983 to date

Weekly. Established August 1983. Formed by a merger of *The Times*, Federalsburg, and *County Record*, Denton. Owned by Whitney Communications Corporation, New York City.

FEDERALSBURG

Courier and Farmer

See *Federalsburg Courier*

Federalsburg Courier, 1872-1932

Weekly. Established February 7, 1872, as *Maryland Courier*. Name changed 1883(?) to *Courier and Farmer*; April 5, 1884, to *Federalsburg Courier*. Last known issue June 10, 1932.

American Antiquarian Society
1876: August 9

Caroline County Public Library
1917: February 3

Dorchester County Historical Society
1877: June 2

Enoch Pratt Free Library
1872: February 7-April 17; May 1-December 25
1873: January 8-December 24
1874: January 7-December 23
1875: February 3-December 22
1876-1882: Complete
1883: January 6-February 17; March 3-June 23
1884: April 5-December 20
1885: January 3-June 6, 20-September 5
1927: July 29
1931: January 2-June 12, 26-December 25
1932: January 1-June 10

Library of Congress
1877: December 8
1882: February 4-December 30
1883: January 6-June 23

Maryland Historical Society
1877: November 3
1883: April 7

Federalsburg Times, 1929-1983

Weekly. Established July 26, 1929. Absorbed *Upper Dorchester News*, Hurlock, September 19,

1963. Published as *The Times*, with Federalsburg and Denton editions, February 1963-February 1964. Merged with *County Record*, Denton, to become the *Times-Record* August 1983. Owned 1981 by Whitney Communications Corporation, New York City.

County Record

1936: May 1-December 25
1937-1938: Complete

Enoch Pratt Free Library

1933: April 7-May 19; June 2-October 27; November 10, 24-December 29
1934: January 5-May 4
1935: April 5-June 28; July 19-December 27
1936 to date: Complete

Federalsburg Times

1973 to date: Complete

Maryland Historical Society

1937: April 20

News & Farmer

1934: September 28; October 12
1935: September 13
1945: November 30

Times-Record

1934-1935: Complete
1944: Complete
1974: Complete
1983: January-July

Maryland Courier

See *Federalsburg Courier*

The Times

See *Federalsburg Times*

GREENSBORO [GREENSBOROUGH]

The Enterprise, 1918-1942

Weekly. Established June 20, 1918, by W. Thomas Thornton, operator of the Model Printery. Final issue April 23, 1942.

Caroline County Historical Society

1926: June 10-December 30

1927: January 6-June 2
1928: June 13-December 27
1929-1930: Complete
1931: January 1-June 18

Enoch Pratt Free Library

1933: December 21
1934: January 4; September 13; October 18; November 1-December 27
1935-1941: Complete
1942: January 1-April 23

Free Press, 1881(?)-19--(?)

Weekly. Established by Risdon Plummer in January(?) 1881, published by Plummer family many years. In early years named *Greensborough Free Press*. Expired after June 9, 1911.

Caroline County Historical Society

1887: January 7
1900: March 23

Enoch Pratt Free Library

1885: February 20; March 13; April 3, 24; June 19, 26; July 3, 17-31; August 7, 14

Robert H. Taylor

1897: June 4

HILLSBORO [HILLSBOROUGH]

Caroline Intelligencer, 1831-?

Weekly. Established 1831 by the Lucas brothers; said to have been Caroline County's first newspaper. Soon moved to Denton.

Enoch Pratt Free Library

1831: August 30

PRESTON

Farm and Home

Weekly? Mentioned in *Preston News* September 16, 1937, as a successor paper to the *Preston Times*. Nothing else known.

New Farm, early 1900s

Weekly? An issue dated June 8, 1901, in extremely poor condition, was found in files of the *News & Farmer*. Nothing else known.

News & Farmer, 1937 to date

Weekly. Established by Max Chambers September 16, 1937, as *Preston News*. From February 19, 1942, to February 1, 1962, title was *Preston News and the Bay Country Farmer*. Partly subsidized through paid subscriptions by American Farm Bureau Federation chapters in seven Eastern Shore counties. Owner-publisher 1981 Scott Warehime.

Enoch Pratt Free Library

1937: September 16-October 28; November 11-December 30
1938: January 6-May 5, 19-June 9, 23-30; July 14-December 29
1939 to date: Complete

Library of Congress

1945: April 19
1946: October 24

News & Farmer

1937 to date: Complete

News Letter, 1867-?

Weekly? Named as a "new paper published in Preston" in the *Easton Journal* October 10, 1867. Nothing else known.

Preston Echo, 1866-?

Weekly. Established July 28, 1866, judging from issue of November 3, 1866, which is Volume I, No. 15. Only a facsimile of this issue, reproduced November 5, 1942, in *Preston News*, now exists. Original, owned by American Antiquarian Society, has been lost. Nothing else known.

Preston News and the Bay Country Farmer

See *News & Farmer*

Preston News I, 1905-1912(?)

Weekly. Established December 16, 1905, judging from issue of November 10, 1906, which was Volume I, No. 48. Last known issue November 9, 1912. No relation except locale to later *Preston News*.

News & Farmer

1906: January 13-March 3, 17-24; April 28; May 26; June 2, 16-23; July 7-September 29; October 13-27; November 10, 24; December 15-22
1908: January 4-18; February 1-15, 29; March 7-21; April 4-25; May 23; July 11-August 8; August 22-September 12, 26; October 17, 31; November 14; December 5, 19
1909: January 2-9, 23; February 20-April 3, 17; May 22-29; June 19-26; July 4(?)-10, 24-August 28; September 18; October 2-16; November 6-December 4, 18, 25
1910: January 22; February 5; March 26; April 2; June 8; September 10; October 15, 29
1911: February 11; March 4-June 10, 24; July 8; August 5; September 2-9, 23; November 18-December 16
1912: February 17; March 9; April 16; May 25-June 8; July 6; August 3, 17-31; September 14-October 4; November 9

Preston News II, 1937-1942

See *News & Farmer*

Preston Times, 1890-?

Weekly. Published in 1890s by a Mr. Rogers. Established November 23, 1890, judging from issue of February 26, 1891, which is No. 15. Nothing else known.

News & Farmer

1891: February 26

RIDGELY

Caroline Sun, 1902-1959

Weekly. Established March 15, 1902, by Dr. W.

W. Goldsborough, but soon acquired by Henry Wilkinson, whose family continued publication for many years. Merged with *County Record* and closed down after final issue April 25, 1959.

County Record
1927: March 19-December 31
1928-1955: Complete
1956: January 7-28
1957: April 6-December 29
1958: Complete
1959: January 3-February 28

Enoch Pratt Free Library
1921: April 2
1929: January 19-26; August 17

1933: May 13; August 19-26; September 23; October 21-November 4, 18-December 30
1934: January 6-February 17; March 10, 17, 31-April 14; May 5-August 25; September 8-29; October 13-December 29
1935-1958: Complete except March 11, 1944, and September 1, 1951
1959: January 3-April 25

Maryland Historical Society
1912: June 22
1917: May 22
1937: April 24

News & Farmer
1959: April 25

Cecil

CHESAPEAKE CITY

Chesapeake Chesapike, 1876-1879

Weekly. Founded 1876 by Harry Moss, who named it "for a fighting fish of the Chesapeake Bay." Name changed to *Chesapeake Record* March 23(?), 1878. Moved to North East as *North East Record* December 1879.

Enoch Pratt Free Library
1876: December 2
1878: March 30 (as *Chesapeake Record*)

Chesapeake Record

See *Chesapeake Chesapike*

ELKTON

The Appeal

See *Elkton Appeal*

Cecil County Advocate, 1840s

Weekly. Nothing else known.

Enoch Pratt Free Library
1848: April 19

Cecil County News, 1880-1937

Weekly. Established September 1(?), 1880, by Dr.

J. H. Frazer. Absorbed by *Cecil Democrat* February 13, 1937.

Cecil County Historical Society

1880: September 1
1900-1935: Complete
1936: December 23
1937: February 3

Enoch Pratt Free Library

1898: November 9
1900: May 23
1903: April 22; July 22; October 14
1905: November 1, 8
1909: November 10 (partial)
1930: September 17; October 15; November 5, 12
1931: April 15-29
1932: October 5
1934: September 19

Maryland Historical Society

1919: January 29

Cecil County Star, 1882-1940

Weekly. Published in North East July 29, 1882-September (?) 1929; in Elkton until March 1940. Succeeded *North East Record.* Various titles: as *North East Star* until 1885; as *Cecil Star* until 1927(?); as *Cecil County Star* until 1940. Merged into *Cecil Times* March, 1940.

Cecil County Historical Society

1918: November 2
1921: October 15-22; November 26
1922: June 17; July 1
1923: January 27; June 2-9, 23; December 8
1924: February 2; April 26; September 6; October 11
1925: July 4; December 5
1926: January 23; May 29; July 17; August 28
1927: April 2

Enoch Pratt Free Library

1882: July 29
1886: October 23; November 6-December 25
1887: January 8-29; February 5, 19, 26; March 5-July 9, 23-December 31
1888: January 7-July 7; August 4-December 15, 29
1889: January 5-February 9, 23; March 2-July 27; November 2-30; December 7
1890: January 4-November 1, 15-December 27
1891: January 3-May 23; August 8, 22-December 12, 26
1892: January 2-June 4, 18, 25; July 16; October 8-November 26; December 10-31
1893: January 14-21; February 11-December 30
1894: Complete
1895: January 5-February 9, 23-May 4; August 24-December 28
1896-1897: Complete
1898: January 1-May 7; July 16, 23; August 6-December 31
1899: January 7-September 30
1900: March 17-July 21
1903: April 4, 18, 25; May 16-30; October 31
1906: October 27-December 29
1907: January 5-September 7
1908: January 4-May 2
1910: May 7-October 22; November 5-December 31
1911: January 7-August 12, 26-December 2
1912-1914: Complete
1915: January 2-March 6; September 18; October 16, 30-December 25
1916: Complete
1917: January 6-March 24; April 7-June 2, 3
1930: March 20
1931: August 20; December 17
1932: January 7-May 20
1934: June 21-December 27
1935-1939: Complete

Maryland Historical Society

1937: April 29

Cecil Democrat, 1842-1981

Weekly. Continued *Cecil Gazette.* First issue February 19, 1842, as *Cecil Democrat and Farmers' Journal.* Shortened to *Cecil Democrat* June 1, 1850. Absorbed *Cecil County News* February 13, 1937. Owned 1981 by Whitney Communications Corporation, New York City.

American Antiquarian Society
1876: September 9, 23

Cecil County Historical Society
1843: November 4
1848-1873: Complete
1874: January 3-24
1877: February 3-December 29
1878-1938: Complete
1940-1959: Complete
1961-1964: Complete

Cecil County Library
1975 to date: Nearly complete

Enoch Pratt Free Library
1843: April 8; September 2; October 21
1844: September 21
1845: February 8
1846: January 3
1853: September 17; December 17
1860: March 24
1861: November 23
1862: January 18; October 18
1864: February 20; December 3
1868: May 2
1871: April 1
1877: December 29
1879: January 18
1882: January 28; July 15; August 5; September 23
1885: November 21
1887: April 30
1888: December 15
1889: February 16; April 27
1895: June 29
1899: April 22
1903: April 18, 25; May 30; June 20; July 4; October 31
1904: January 16
1905: November 11 (pages 1-2)
1907: May 25
1909: November 6 (pages 3-6)
1911: November 11
1912: November 9
1920: October 2-December 25
1921-1925: Complete
1926: January 2-December 18
1927: January 8-April 2, 16-May 21; June 4-August 20; September 10-December 17, 31
1928: January 7-August 18; September 1-15, 29-October 13, 27-December 29
1929: January 5-August 17, 31-December 28
1930 to date: Complete

Library of Congress
1842: July 23

Maryland Historical Society
1845: April 2
1865: November 4
1876: November 11

New-York Historical Society
1873: April 26

Cecil Democrat and Farmers' Journal

See *Cecil Democrat*

Cecil Gazette and Farmers' and Mechanics' Advertiser, 1834-1842

Weekly. Established as Democratic Party organ August 23, 1834. Name changed to *Cecil Democrat* February 19, 1842.

Cecil County Historical Society
1837: March 18
1839: May 25

Enoch Pratt Free Library
1834: August 23-December 27
1835: January 4-February 14
1837: May 27; July 1, 8; September 23-30; October 14; November 4, 25; December 2-30
1838: January 6-April 21; May 5, 12; November 24-December 29
1839: January 5-May 11
1840: September 12
1841: May 22, November 6
1842: January 15; February 5

Cecil Republican and Farmers' and Mechanics' Advertiser, 1832-1834

Weekly. Established May 12, 1832, with Richard P. Bayley as editor. May have been superseded by *Cecil Gazette.*

Enoch Pratt Free Library
1833: December 14

Library of Congress
1833: October 19

Maryland Historical Society

1832: December 22
1833: April 20-May 4, 18, 25

Cecil Times, 1940-1942

Weekly. Succeeded *Cecil County Star*.

Enoch Pratt Free Library

1940: April 18-December 26
1941: Complete
1942: January 1-November 5

Cecil Whig, 1841 to date

Weekly. No connection with earlier *Cecil Whig* of Port Deposit. Established August 7, 1841; first editor Palmer C. Ricketts. Absorbed *Midland Journal* January 15, 1948. Whig, pro-Union, Republican in politics. Owned 1981 by Whitney Communications Corporation, New York City.

American Antiquarian Society

1841: August 14, 21
1842: January 22; September 10; December 10
1843: March 4; April 22, 29; May 12; June 3; July 1, 15, 29; October 7; December 2
1844: January 20; February 3, 24; March 30; April 6; June 15; September 7; October 12; November 9
1845: August 30
1846: April 25; July 4
1847: April 24; May 8
1848: July 15; September 23, 30; October 28
1849: March 24; August 18
1850: February 2; April 13; May 18; June 15; August 17; September 28; October 19, 25; November 2, 16
1851: January 25; March 15; April 12, 19; May 3; June 21, 28; August 30; September 13
1852: January 31; February 7; August 21
1854: April 22; October 7
1855: August 11
1856: February 9; November 1; December 20
1857: August 15
1859: March 5; October 15, 22; November 19
1860: February 25; March 10, 17; September 15
1862: September 1
1866: September 1

Cecil County Historical Society

1841: August 7 (replica)
1845: July 26
1847: June 5
1853: May 14
1862: April 26
1863: November 14
1878: April 27
1880: September 11
1887: July 23
1891: January 3, 10
1903: March 14
1908: January 4
1911: June 10
1915: October 15
1916: July 1
1921-1946: Complete
1949: Complete

Cecil County Library

1975 to date: Complete

Enoch Pratt Free Library

Original issues
1920-1945: Complete
1948: Complete
1950-1956: Complete
1958:-1959: Complete
1961 to date: Complete
Microfilm (Cecil County Library has same microfilm)
1841: August 7-December 25
1842-1916: Complete *except* for scattered issues
1919: January 18-October 11, 25-December 27
1920-1926: Complete

Library of Congress

1843: November 4
1847: April 3
1855: September 22
1860: March 17

Maryland Historical Society

1842: March 12; June 4; July 16; October 15; December 31
1843: January 7, 21-28; February 25-March 4, 18; April 1, 22-29; May 13; June 10, 24; July 15-29; August 26; September 9; October 14; November 25; December 2, 16
1844: February 17; October 26-November 5; December 28
1845: January 11; February 8; April 26-May 3, 17; June 7; July 19; August 16, 30-September 13;

October 4, 25; November 15-22; December 27
1846: February 21; April 4-25; May 16; June 13-20; August 1, 15-22
1847: February 27-March 13; April 10-17; May 1, 29; June 12-August 14, 28-October 2, 23-November 13; December 4-25
1848: January 1-May 20; June 10-July 1, 15, 29; August 19-September 9, 23-December 16
1849: January 6, 20; February 3-10, 24-March 17, 31-June 30; July 14-August 18; October 13, 27-November 3; December 8-15
1850: January 5-12; February 9-April 13; May 4-25; June 8, 29-August 24; September 7-28; October 12, 26-November 16, 30-December 7
1851: January 4-February 8, 22-March 8, 22; April 12-May 3, 31-September 6, 20-27; October 11-November 1, 15, 29-December 20
1852: January 3-10, 31-February 7; April 17; May 8, 22; June 12-26; July 10-31; August 14-21; September 4-11, 25-October 2, 23-30; November 13-December 4
1853: January 8-22; February 5-26; March 12-19; April 23; May 14; July 2-9, 23-August 13, 27-October 8, 22; November 12-19; December 3, 17-31
1854: January 14; February 4-11, 25-March 25; April 8-June 10, 23-August 5, 19-September 30; October 14-21; November 4-18; December 23
1855: January 20-27; February 17; April 28-May 5; June 2-July 21; August 4, 18-September 15, 29-October 6, 27-November 3, 17-24; December 15-29
1856: January 5-February 2, 16-23; March 8-April 5, 19-May 17, 31-July 12, 26-September 15; October 18-December 27
1857: January 3-April 4, 25-May 16; June 6-July 11, 25-August 8, 29-October 17, 31-November 7, 21-December 26
1858: January 2-9; February 6-20; March 13, 27-April 17; May 8-22; June 5-19; July 31-August 14; September 4-11; October 2, 30-November 6, 20; December 4-18
1860: January 14, 28; February 11-18; March 3, 24; April 7-May 19; June 9, 23; July 21-August 25; September 8, 22-29; October 20; November 3, 17; December 1
1861: January 19-March 23; April 6, 20-May 11; June 1-8, 22-August 3, 17, 31-September 7; October 19; November 2, 16-December 7
1862: January 18-February 1, 15; March 15; August 23; September 20-27

1863: January 31-April 4; May 30; July 18
1864: January 2, 16; February 20; March 26-April 2, 23
1865: January 21-28; February 25; September 2; December 2
1872: August 17

New-York Historical Society
1873: May 17

Elkton Appeal, 1884-1907

Weekly. First titled *The Appeal*. Established April 9, 1884. Last known issue January 2, 1907.

Cecil County Historical Society
1903: April 15
1904: August 31
1906: February 14

Enoch Pratt Free Libary
1884: April 9-December 31
1885-1891: Complete
1892: January 6-September 7, 21-December 28
1893: January 4-July 12, 26-November 1, 22-December 27
1895: May 8-December 25
1896: January 1-December 2, 16-30
1897: January 6-November 10; December 22
1898: January 12-December 21
1899: January 4-October 11, 25; November 8-December 20
1900: January 10-April 18; May 2-June 27; July 18-December 26
1901: January 16-June 19; July 10-November 27
1902-1906: Complete
1907: January 2

Elkton Courier, 1836-1837(?)

Weekly. Established as Whig Party organ September 3(?), 1836. Last known issue November 4, 1837.

Cecil County Historical Society
1837: January 21

Enoch Pratt Free Libary
1836: September 24
1837: May 12; November 4

Elkton Mechanic, 1842-?

Semimonthly.

Enoch Pratt Free Library
1842: November 26

Elkton Press, 1823-1832(?)

Weekly. First Cecil County newspaper; established July 5, 1823, by John McCord. Name lengthened to *Elkton Press and Cecil County Advertiser* March 14, 1829. Expired shortly after presidential election of 1832.

American Antiquarian Society
1828: June 21

Cecil County Historical Society
1827: June 16
1831: October 22

Enoch Pratt Free Library
1828: August 30
1829: January 10; February 14-March 21; April 4-11; May 2, 16; June 6-13; July 4-August 1, 15, 22; September 5, 19-26; October 10-17, 31; November 21; December 12, 26
1830: January 23-February 20; March 6, 20-27; May 1-8

Library of Congress
1824: February 14; November 13
1827: September 1
1828: July 19-August 2, 16-30; September 13-27; October 25; November 1, 8
1829: July 11; September 12, 26; October 3
1830: January 2; September 18; November 16; December 25
1831: July 23; August 6

Maryland Historical Society
1823: July 5, 26-August 30; September 13-20; November 8-29; December 13, 27
1824: January 3-10; February 14, 28; March 13; April 17; May 1-29; June 12
1826: May 6 (photostat)
1828: November 1-22; December 6-27
1829: January 10-February 7, 21-March 7, 21-April 4

Elkton Press and Cecil County Advertiser

See *Elkton Press*

Jackson Picket Guard, 1856

Weekly. Established July 16, 1856, to support Buchanan for president. Soon absorbed by *Cecil Democrat*.

American Antiquarian Society
1856: September 24

New-York Historical Society
1856: September 3

Temperance Banner, 1848-1850

Weekly. Established as antiliquor paper by Thomas M. Coleman 1848. No surviving issues known.

Union Reformer, 1855

Weekly. Established 1855 by William Jones and Charles Haines as organ of ultranationalist Know-Nothing Party. Soon absorbed by *Cecil Whig*.

NORTH EAST

Advertiser and Perryville News

See *North East Advertiser*

Cecil Star

See *Cecil County Star*, Elkton

Maryland Pythian, 1897-?

Monthly. Published in the interest of the Knights of Pythias lodge.

Enoch Pratt Free Library
1897: March-May

North East Advertiser, 1929-1955

Weekly. Established 1929 by Charles O. McCauley, Jr. Soon merged with *Perryville News*; published as *Advertiser and Perryville News* until 1955, when it was absorbed by *Cecil Democrat*.

North East Record, 1878-1882(?)

Weekly. Succeeded *Chesapeake Record* December 21, 1878, when Dr. D. H. B. Bower, publisher, moved plant from Chesapeake City to North East. Last known issue December 17, 1881. Succeeded by *North East Star*.

Cecil County Historical Society
1878: December 21
1879: January 11-18

Enoch Pratt Free Library
1878: December 28
1879: January 4; February 8, 15; July 12
1880: July 17; September 25
1881: December 17

North East Star

See *Cecil County Star*, Elkton

PERRYVILLE

Perryville News, 1930s

Weekly. Combined with *North East Advertiser* to form the *Advertiser and Perryville News* some time after 1929. Nothing else known.

Perryville Record, 1893-1906

Biweekly, weekly. Established as biweekly January 4, 1893; became weekly January 2, 1895. Expired 1906.

Cecil County Historical Society
1903: January 7-28; February 11; April 8, 22; May 27

Enoch Pratt Free Library
1893: Complete
1894: January 3-May 9; June 6-September 12; October 10-December 19
1895: January 2-February 27; March 13-May 1, 15-June 26; July 10-November 6, 20-December 25
1896-1900: Complete
1901: January 2-May 29; August 21-28; September 11, 25-October 16, 30-November 6, 20-December 25
1902: January 1-March 5, 19-June 18; July 2-September 24; October 8-22; November 5-December 31
1903: Complete
1904: Complete except December 14

PORT DEPOSIT

The Call, 1880s

Weekly. May also have been called *Cecil Call*.

Enoch Pratt Free Library
1887: April 28

Cecil Whig and Port Deposit Weekly Courier, 1835-1836

Weekly. No connection with later *Cecil Whig*. Succeeded *Central Courant* July 1835 as Cecil County's only newspaper. Succeeded by *Elkton Courier* August 1836.

Library of Congress
1836: May 5

Maryland Historical Society
1835: December 26

Central Courant and Port Deposit Intelligencer, 1822-1835

Weekly. Established March 29(?), 1833, by L. A. Wilmer. Succeeded 1835 by *Cecil Whig and Port Deposit Courier*.

Cecil County Historical Society
1833: October 11

Enoch Pratt Free Library
1834: January 3, 24; April 11-25

Library of Congress
1833: May 3; June 28; July 12; August 2
1834: January 31

The News, 1945-1946(?)

Weekly. Established July 14, 1945, judging from

issue of May 18, 1946, which is Volume I, No. 45. Nothing else known.

Cecil County Historical Society
1946: May 18

Port Deposit Journal, 1928-1929

Weekly. Issued by the Port Deposit Board of Trade December 14, 1928, to May 7, 1929.

Port Deposit Rock and Cecil County Commercial Advertiser, 1839-1840

Weekly. Established August 6(?), 1839, by George Keating; strongly Whig in politics. Expired August 1840.

Cecil County Historical Society
1840: July 17

Enoch Pratt Free Library
1839: August 20, 27; September 17; October 1; November 26; December 3, 31
1840: January 7, 14; February 12, 19; March 4-18; April 8-24; May 8-22; June 19; July 17; August 7

RISING SUN

Home Journal

See *Midland Journal*

Maryland News

See *Maryland News-Courier*

Maryland News-Courier, 1947-1951

Weekly. Established July 4, 1947, as *Maryland News* by the Oxford (Pennsylvania) Printing Company. Name changed to *Maryland News-Courier* August 29, 1947. Last known issue March 2, 1951.

Cecil County Historical Society
1947: July 4-December 26

1948-1950: Complete
1951: January 5-March 2

Midland Journal, 1878-1948

Weekly. Established as *Home Journal* October 26, 1878, by William H. Pennington. Name changed April 24, 1880, to *Rising Sun Journal* and July 1885 to *Midland Journal*. Absorbed by *Cecil Whig* January 15, 1948.

Cecil County Historical Society
1893: March 17
1898: March 4
1937-1944: Complete
1946: Complete

Enoch Pratt Free Library
1878: November 2-December 28
1879: January 4-April 19; May 3-December 20
1880: January 3-March 6, 20-December 25
1881: January 8-February 12, 26-March 19; April 2-July 30; August 13-20; September 3-December 24
1882: January 7-February 18; March 4-June 10; July 8, 15, 29-October 7, 21-November 11, 25-December 30
1883: January 6-June 2, 16-July 28; August 11-December 22
1884: January 5-March 22; April 5-June 14, 28; July 12-October 18; November 1-29; December 13-27
1885: January 10-December 25
1886-1946: Complete
1947: January 3-June 27; July 18-December 25
1948: January 1-8

Rising Sun Commercial, 1878-1879(?)

Said to have been sponsored by local merchant; printed at Rising Sun at first, later at office of *Oxford* (Pennsylvania) *Press*. How often published is not known.

Library of Congress
1879: September 13; October 11

Rising Sun Journal

See *Midland Journal*

Dorchester

CAMBRIDGE

American Eagle, 1855-1864(?)

Weekly. Established May 2, 1855, Reuben S. Tall, publisher. A new owner, Levin E. Straughn, changed its name to the *Intelligencer* about 1864.

Dorchester County Historical Society
1856: May 14; October 15

Enoch Pratt Free Library
1856: July 23; September 24; October 22-November 26; December 10, 24
1857: January 14; February 25; March 18; May 13-June 3; July 15-August 12

Banner

See *Daily Banner*

Bay Star, 1971

Weekly. Established July 21, 1971, by Elwood J. Pliescott, Jr. Ceased publication with issue of October 6, 1971.

News & Farmer
1971: October 6

Salisbury State College Library
1971: July 21, 28

Talbot County Free Library
1971: July 21-September 8

Cambridge Chronicle and Maryland Weekly Advertiser

See *Cambridge Chronicle I*

Cambridge Chronicle I, 1822-1855

Weekly. No apparent connection with later *Cambridge Chronicle*. Established April 20 (?), 1822; said to have been first Dorchester County newspaper. Title varies: as *Cambridge Chronicle and Maryland Weekly Advertiser* October 27, 1827-May 17, 1828; as *Cambridge Weekly Chronicle and Farmers Register* January-June 1839. Last known issue March 14, 1855.

American Antiquarian Society
1828: August 30; September 6, 20, 27
1830: December 25
1831: July 23
1836: January 9

Enoch Pratt Free Library
1824: December 25
1825: February 12-26; March 12; April 23; May 21
1826: March 25; August 19
1829: January 24
1830: October 30
1831: January 1
1832: February 25; March 31; May 19
1836: March 12
1846: September 5, 19; October 3, 10, 31; November 28-December 19
1847: January 2-23; February 13; March 26; April 24; May 1, 8; July 3, 24; September 4-October 9; November 13; December 18
1848: January 15-29; February 12-26; March 11, 18; April 1-May 6, 20-June 24; July 15, 22; August 5, 12; September 23; October 14; December 9, 23
1849: February 24; March 17; April 28; June 2, 9, 30; August 11, 18
1850: November 23
1851: February 1
1852: March 20; September 4
1854: January 21, 28; February 11, 25; March 25; September 16

Hall of Records
Microfilm (Dorchester County Historical Society has same microfilm)
1830: December 25
1843: September 23, 30; November 18, 25
1844: February 17-March 2, 16, 23; April 13-May 18; June 1, 22; September 28; October 12, 26

1845: April 5, 26; May 17, 24; June 7-28; July 26; August 2, 16-30; September 6-27; October 11-December 13, 27
1846: January 10, 24
1855: March 14

Library of Congress
1826: April 29; August 5; September 23; October 14; November 11
1827: October 27-December 29
1828-1831: Complete
1832: January 7-May 19; June 30; July 28; September 15
1833: May 25; June 1, 15; October 12-December 28
1834-1839: Complete
1840: January 4-April 25; December 25

Maryland Historical Society
1828: November 8
1830: August 7
1852: July 3

Cambridge Chronicle II, 1870-1906(?)

Weekly. No apparent connection with earlier *Cambridge Chronicle*. Established January 15, 1870, as *Cambridge Telegraph* by William H. Bowdle. Name changed to *Cambridge Chronicle* April 5 (?), 1871. Absorbed by *Daily Banner* 1906(?).

American Antiquarian Society
1876: June 14

Enoch Pratt Free Library
1870: January 15, 29-February 26; March 12-April 23; May 7-December 29
1871: January 5-19; April 12-June 7, 21-August 9, 23-October 25; November 15-December 27
1872: January 3-March 13; April 3-September 4, 18-December 25
1873: January 8-February 12, 26-March 12; April 2-30; May 14-July 2, 16-August 20; September 10-17; October 1-December 17
1874: January 7-December 23
1875: January 6-September 22; October 27-December 22
1876: January 5-December 20
1877: January 3-June 13, 27-August 15, 29-October 3, 17-December 26
1878: January 2-April 17; May 1-15, 22-June 12, 26-July 31; August 21-28; September 11-December 25
1879: January 1-October 1, 15-December 31
1880-1883: Complete

1884: January 2-August 21
1885: June 25; July 2, 16-23; August 13-20
1887: February 10-December 29
1889: Complete
1890: January 2-October 23; November 6-December 25
1891-1897: Complete

Hall of Records
Microfilm (Dorchester County Historical Society has same microfilm)
1896: May 18
1900: May 17
1903: January 29
1904: April 28; May 5; September 22
1905: August 3

Maryland Historical Society
1891: July 30

Cambridge Democrat, 1845-1866(?)

Weekly. Established as *Democrat and Dorchester Advertiser* November 19, 1845, by John T. Taylor. Name later changed to *Cambridge Democrat* under publisher W. H. Bowdle. Merged with *Cambridge Herald* to form the *Democrat and Herald* some time before May 16, 1868.

American Antiquarian Society
1852: October 20, 27; November 24

Dorchester County Historical Society
1845: December 3, 10
1854: October 4
1858: April 14
1860: October 24

Enoch Pratt Free Library
1851: August 27; November 26-December 24
1852: January 7-November 10, 24; December 1-22
1853: January 5-August 24; September 7-14
1855: October 8-22; November 21-December 19
1856: January 2-September 3

Hall of Records
1852: August 4
1853: November 16
1864: January 13

Maryland Historical Society
1853: November 16

Cambridge Democrat and News

See *Democrat and News*

Cambridge Era

See *Dorchester Era*

Cambridge Herald, 1859-1866(?)

Weekly. Established by W. H. Bowdle about 1859. Merged with *Cambridge Democrat* to become *Democrat and Herald*.

Dorchester County Historical Society
1862: February 2

Enoch Pratt Free Library
1859: July 23-December 24
1860: January 7, 21-June 2; July 21-December 22
1861: January 5-February 16; March 2-June 29; July 20; August 3-October 30; November 13-December 25
1862: January 7-July 9; August 27-September 17; October 1-December 24
1863: January 7-July 1

Maryland Historical Society
1862: November 6

Cambridge Intelligencer, 1863-?

Weekly. Established March 21 (?), 1863. Continued the *American Eagle*. Ceased publication some time after 1868.

American Antiquarian Society
1866: June 30

Library of Congress
1865: January 28

Maryland Historical Society
1868: October 24

Cambridge Journal, circa 1910

Weekly? Existed 1910. Nothing else known.

Dorchester County Historical Society
1910: March 18

Cambridge Record, 1905-1941

Tri-weekly. Established September 11(?), 1905. Merged with *Daily Banner* to form *Daily Banner and Cambridge Record* February 3, 1941.

Enoch Pratt Free Library
1908: Christmas Number, Historical and Industrial
1911: October 11
1912: January 12-22, 29-February 9, 16, 21-23, 28-March 4, 8-15, 22-25, 29-April 10, 15-May 3, 10-13, 17-20, 27-June 21, 28-July 19, 24, 29-August 19, 26-September 4, 9-October 9, 14-November 4, 8-December 30
1913: January 3-March 10, 14-26, 31-April 9, 14-23, 28-May 5, 9-21, 26-June 9, 13-30
1915: January 11-20, 25-27; February 3, 8-12, 17, 22-24; March 1-3, 8-10, 15-17, 22, 29; April 5, 12, 19, 26; May 3-June 7, 11-28; July 7-October 4, 8-18, 22-December 31
1916: January 3-February 28; March 3-April 19, 24-October 20, 25-November 17, 22-December 1, 6-27
1917: January 3-29; February 2-June 29
1918: January 2-March 4, 8-April 15, 19-May 22, 27-June 7, 12-July 8, 15-26; August 2, 7-November 5, 8, 13, 20-22, 29; December 27
1919: January 6-8, 13, 17-May 12, 16-July 30; August 4-October 17, 22-November 5, 10-December 10, 15-17, 22-31
1920: January 2-16, 21-26; February 4-March 1, 5-April 19, 23-May 10, 14-17, 21-24, 31-June 14, 18-July 21, 26-September 1, 6-17, 22-October 13, 18-November 3, 8, 12-December 17, 22-24, 29-31
1921: January 3-26, 31-February 4, 9-May 2, 6-June 20, 24-July 27; August 1-26, 31-November 2, 7-December 30
1922: January 11-18, 23-25, 30-March 15, 22-April 21, 26-May 1, 5-June 23; July 3-7, 12-September 13, 22-October 27; November 15-17
1923: January 3-24, 29-February 5, 9, 14-16, 21-March 2, 7-June 29
1924: January 2-June 20, 25-30
1925: January 2-June 3, 8-July 24, 29-August 12, 17-28; September 2-November 2, 6-9, 13-16, 20-December 30
1926: January 4-April 23; May 3-June 30; July 26-August 13, 25-December 31
1927: January 3-May 4, 9-December 30
1928: January 4-April 6, 11-November 23, 28-December 31
1929: January 2-March 6, 11-December 30
1930: Complete
1931: April 1-June 29
1932: January 1-February 19, 24-March 30; April

4-September 2, 7-October 7, 12-December 30
1933: January 2-February 8, 13-July 28; August 2-September 1, 6-October 6, 11-December 29
1934: January 1-February 28; August 1-31; September 5-12, 17-December 31
1935: June 3-August 30; September 4-December 30
1937: June 23-December 24, 29-31
1938-1940: Complete
1941: January 1-31

Hall of Records

Microfilm (Dorchester County Historical Society has same microfilm)

1905: September 11; October 27; November 20
1907: November 8
1908: July 10
1912: May 22
1913: February 24
1924: February 4; August 8 (both partial)
1925: July 29
1928: June 1
1929: January 30; February 1; March 22; December 30
1930: February 12; October 24; November 10; December 22
1931: February 16; April 7; May 13, 18; July 17; December 16, 28, 30
1932: March 21; April 8, 20, 27; May 2, 16, 25, 30; June 13, 15; August 19; September 14; November 4, 11, 28
1933: February 10; May 22; August 28
1934: October 22
1935: April 5, 22; May 6, 13, 27, 29; July 12; August 7, 14; September 9, 20
1936: February 26; May 4-8, 15
1938: May 27; June 8, 13, 17; August 22; September 9, 12, 14, 21; November 25-30; December 7-30
1939: January 2-6, 18, 23-27; February 3-13, 20-March 3, 17-22; April 7, 14, 17; July 19, 21, 31; August 4; October 16; November 20, 24; December 1-8, 13, 15, 22
1940: January 3, 5; February 12, 21; June 3, 12; September 13; October 2; November 11, 27, 29; December 2, 6, 8
1941: January 24

Maryland Historical Society

1908: December 25
1937: April 26, 30

Cambridge Telegraph

See *Cambridge Chronicle II*

Cambridge Tribune, 1936-1948

Weekly. Established January 2, 1936. Last known issue March 26, 1948.

Enoch Pratt Free Library

1936: September 3-10, 24-December 31
1937: Complete
1938: January 6-May 12
1939: September 21-December 28
1940: Complete
1941: January 3-May 23; June 6-December 26
1942: January 2-May 29; June 19-December 25
1943-1946: Complete *except* September 7, 1945
1947: January 3-24

Hall of Records

Microfilm (Dorchester County Historical Society has same microfilm)

1937: March 25; November 11
1938: May 26; June 30; September 1, 8; November 24; December 1-15, 29
1939: January 19, 26; February 23; March 2-16; April 6, 20; August 3; November 9, 30; December 14, 21
1940: February 16; May 17; November 1, 29; December 6
1941: February 21; March 14-28; April 11, 18
1942: January 30; May 1-15, 29; June 12-July 17; August 14; December 11, 25
1943: January 1, 29; May 7; June 4; October 15; November 5, 12
1944: June 2; August 25
1945: February 23; March 2; June 15; August 31; November 23
1946: January 18; May 3; October 4
1947: April 11-May 9; June 13, 20; July 4; September 5, 19; October 10, 24; December 26
1948: January 9, 23, 30-February 20; March 5, 12, 26

Talbot County Free Library

1936: September 3-17
1937: May 6, 27; August 26; September 2
1938: February 10

Cambridge Weekly Chronicle and Farmers' Register

See *Cambridge Chronicle I*

Daily Banner, 1897 to date

Daily. Established September 21, 1897, by Lindsay C. Marshall and Armistead R. Michie. Absorbed *Cambridge Chronicle II* about 1906 and merged with *Cambridge Record* February 3, 1941. Known as *Daily Banner and Cambridge Record* for some years afterward. Owned 1981 by Evening Post Publishing Company, Charleston, South Carolina.

(Complete files of the *Daily Banner* from September 1954 to date are available on microfilm at the *Daily Banner* office, the Dorchester County Public Library, and at some other repositories. Extensive though not complete earlier files dating from 1902 to 1955, also on microfilm, are available in the Dorchester County Historical Society's collection at the Dorchester County Public Library. Details are omitted for space reasons; listings by dates are available at the Dorchester County Public Library. Extensive files of original issues, beginning June 1, 1907, and virtually complete from 1921 to September 1954, are available at Enoch Pratt Free Library. Exact dates of these also are omitted for space reasons.)

Daily Banner and Cambridge Record

See *Daily Banner*

Democrat and Dorchester Advertiser

See *Cambridge Democrat*

Democrat and Herald, 1866(?)-1870

Formed by merger of *Cambridge Democrat* and *Cambridge Herald* circa 1866. Merged with *Dorchester News I* 1870 to form *Democrat and News*.

Democrat and News, 1870(?)-1966

Weekly. Formed by merger of *Democrat and Herald* with *Dorchester News I* about 1870. First owner, Joseph H. Johnson. Merged with *North Dorchester News* (Hurlock) to form *Dorchester News II* January 5, 1966.

American Antiquarian Society

1876: June 3

Dorchester County Historical Society

Original issues
1929: March 15, 29
1938: January 6
1950: June 8
1957: August 29

Microfilm
(Hall of Records has same microfilm)

1872: January 20, 27; February 17, 24; March 16, 30; April 6, 20; May 4, 11, 25; June 1-August 31; September 14, 21; October 12-26; November 9-December 21
1873: January 4-February 22; March 8, 22-April 5, 19; May 17-June 21; July 19, 26; August 9-23
1880: January 3-December 18
1881: January 1-November 5
1882: January 7-December 23
1883: January 6, 13; March 3-December 1, 15, 22
1884: January 5-April 19; May 3-24; June 14, 28; July 5-19; August 2-December 20
1885: January 3-April 18; May 30-December 26
1886: January 2-December 11
1887: January 8-October 29
1888: January 7-August 11, 25-December 1
1889: January 1, 12-December 21
1890: January 4-October 11; November 29; December 6
1891: January 2, 17-June 20; July 4-August 1
1892: January 9, 23-February 6, 20-September 10, 24-November 19
1893-1894: Complete
1895: January 5-June 1, 15-December 28
1896: January 4-November 7
1897-1900: Complete *except* issues of December 24, 1898, and December 23, 1899
1901: January 5-December 7
1902-1907: Complete
1908: January 4-September 26; October 19
1909: January 2-November 26
1910: Complete
1911: January 6-December 15
1912: Complete
1913: January 3-November 28; December 12, 19

Enoch Pratt Free Library

1885: June 6, 20; July 11-August 9
1927-1933: Complete *except* August 12, 1932
1934: January 5-19; February 2-23; March 9-23;

April 6-December 27
1935-1965: Complete *except* April 28, 1960

News & Farmer

1937: June 26; July 17 (extras)
1945: November 29

Dorchester Aurora, 1835-1840(?)

Weekly. Established July 13, 1835, by Richard Pattison of William. Said to have been Cambridge's second newspaper, following the *Cambridge Chronicle*. Later published by a Mr. Callahan. Last known issue April 27, 1840.

Library of Congress

1835: July 13-October 19; November 9, 23; December 28
1836: January 4-11, 25; February 1-29; March 14-June 20; July 4-October 10, 31-November 21; December 5-26
1837: January 9-February 27; March 27; April 3, 17; May 1-August 7, 21-December 25
1838: Complete *except* April 16, October 29
1839: January 7-May 6, 27; June 10-July 29; August 26-September 16; December 16
1840: March 16-April 27

Dorchester Community News

See *Dorchester News II*

Dorchester County Era

See *Dorchester Era*

Dorchester Era, 1878-1906(?)

Weekly. Established March 23, 1878, as the *Cambridge Era*. Name changed to *Dorchester Era* November 1882 and to *Dorchester County Era* 1900. Ceased publication about 1906.

Dorchester County Historical Society

1878: March 23-December 28
1879: Complete
1880: January 3-March 13
1884: August 9

Enoch Pratt Free Library

1878: March 23-December 21

1879-1881: Complete *except* January 3, 1880
1882: January 5-March 23
1885: June 20, 27; July 18, 25; August 15

Hall of Records

1903: April 11 (microfilm)

Dorchester News I, 1867-1870

Weekly. Established 1867. Merged with *Democrat and Herald* 1870 to form *Democrat and News*.

Dorchester News II, 1966 to date

Weekly. Formed by merger of *Democrat and News* with *North Dorchester News* (Hurlock) January 5, 1966. Name changed to *Dorchester Community News* March 14, 1979, when paper began free distribution. Owned 1981 by Whitney Communications Corporation, New York City.

Dorchester County Library

1973-1978: Complete
1979: January 3-March 7

Dorchester News

1966-1978: Complete
1979: January 3-March 7

Enoch Pratt Free Library

1966: January 5-March 9; August 10
1967: April 26-May 31; June 14-December 27
1968-1978: Complete
1979: January 3

Dorchester Standard, 1895-190-(?)

Weekly. Established 1895 by Phillips L. Goldsborough. Owned 1901 by Thomas S. Latimer. Nothing else known.

Dorchester County Historical Society

1902: July 19

The Intelligencer, 1864(?)-1869(?)

Weekly. Continued the *American Eagle*. Ceased publication some time after 1868.

American Antiquarian Society

1866: June 30

Library of Congress
1865: January 28

Maryland Historical Society
1868: October 24

The Item, 1894-1901

Monthly. Founded February 1894; ceased publication January 1901. E. P. Vinton was publisher. In 1935 he had a complete file, which now appears to have been lost.

Maryland Weekly Advertiser

See *Cambridge Chronicle I*

GLUCKHEIM

The Ruralist, circa 1900

Monthly. Published by "the Ruralist Company, Gluckheim," according to issue of June 1900. Printed by Stowell Printery, Federalsburg. Contained local ads but no local news.

C. W. Mowbray
1900: June
1901: April

HURLOCK

Dorchester News III (Hurlock)

See *Upper Dorchester News*

Hurlock Advance, 1898-19--(?)

Weekly. Established 1898, according to Mrs. Arthur McDaniel, quoted in Salisbury *Times* October 18, 1958. Name changed to *Upper Dorchester News* 1923. Nothing else known.

North Dorchester News, 1963-1965:

Weekly. Established December 5, 1963, by Town of Hurlock and Easton Publishing Company after demise of *Upper Dorchester News*. Absorbed after issue of December 29, 1965, by *Democrat and News* to form *Dorchester News II*.

Dorchester News (Cambridge)
1963: December 5-26
1964-1965: Complete

Upper Dorchester News, 1923-1963

Weekly. Continued *Hurlock Advance* (?). Became *Upper Dorchester News* February 2, 1923. Title varied: *Dorchester News* June 24, 1938-January 29, 1948. Absorbed by *Federalsburg Times* September 19, 1963.

Dorchester County Historical Society
1942: September 3

Enoch Pratt Free Library
1934: June 15; September 21; November 2-December 28
1935: January 4-June 28
1936: February 14-March 6, 20-December 25
1937-1941: Complete
1942: January 1-February 12, 26-June 11, 25-December 31
1943-1946: Complete
1947: January 2-August 14; October 3-December 24
1948-1962: Complete *except* March 4, 1954
1963: January 3-September 12

Kent

CHESTERTOWN

Apollo; or, Chestertown Spy, 1793

Semiweekly. Established March 19, 1793, judging from issue of March 26, 1793, which was Volume I, No. 3. First published by George Gerrish and Robert Saunders, Jr. Gerrish soon dropped out, and Saunders changed the title to *Chestertown Gazette* July 26, 1793. Last known issue December 31, 1793.

American Antiquarian Society
1793: May 10

Houghton Library, Harvard University
1793: July 23

Maryland Historical Society
1793: March 26-June 14, 21, 25; July 2-9, 16-19, 26-30; August 9-13, 30-September 6, 13-October 8, 15-18; November 1-15, 22-29; December 31

New-York Historical Society
1793: April 12

Chester River Press, 1962-1970

Semimonthly, weekly. Established July 1, 1962; final issue September 9, 1970. Semimonthly until January 1, 1963; weekly thereafter.

Enoch Pratt Free Library
1962: July 1-September 1; October 1-December 15
1963-1969: Complete *except* June 12, 1963
1970: January 1-September 9

Washington College Library
1962: July 1; August 1
1963: January 16-March 6, 20-December 25
1964-1969: Complete
1970: January 7-September 9

Chestertown Enterprise

See *The Enterprise*

Chestertown Gazette

See *Apollo; or, Chestertown Spy*

Chestertown Telegraph

See *The Telegraph*

Chestertown Transcript, 1862-1946

Weekly. Established May 20, 1862, reportedly by Eben F. Perkins. Merged with *Kent News* February 1, 1946, to form *Kent County News*.

American Antiquarian Society
1876: February 18

Enoch Pratt Free Library
1862: May 20-June 24; July 8-December 30
1863-1864: Complete
1865: January 7-February 25; March 11, 25-May 6, 20-December 30
1866: January 6-December 22
1867: January 5-November 16, 30-December 21
1868: Complete

1869: January 2-December 4
1870: January 8-December 31
1871-1872: Complete
1873: January 11-December 27
1874: January 3-May 2, 23-December 26
1875: Complete
1876: January 7-May 5, 19-December 29
1877: Complete
1878: January 4-April 26; May 21-December 31
1879: January 7-May 29; June 12-December 25
1880-1881: Complete
1882: January 5-April 13; June 1-December 28
1883: Complete
1884: January 23-December 25
1885: January 1-December 17
1886: Complete
1887: January 6-July 14, 28-December 29
1888: January 5-December 13
1889: January 10-December 26
1890-1897: Complete *except* January 7, 1892
1898: January 20-December 29
1899-1917: Complete *except* July 17, December 25, 1915
1918: January 5-March 23; April 13-August 17; September 7-December 28
1919: January 4-October 11
1920: January 10-December 25
1921-1933: Complete *except* December 22, 1923
1934: June 1-December 29
1935-1945: Complete
1946: January 4-25

L. P. Keating

1881: June 30
1883: January 11

Kent County News

1887-1900: Complete
1902: April 3-December 25
1903-1914: Complete
1918-1919: Complete
1922-1923: Complete

Library of Congress

1883: October 25

Maryland Historical Society

1866: November 10
1875: March 12-July 16, 30-December 31
1876: January 7-November 17; December 1-29
1877: January 5-March 30; April 13-November 16; December 21, 28
1878: January 4-18; February 8-May 10

1896: June 25-December 31
1897: January 7-July 29
1899: February 9; April 13-December 28
1900: January 4-March 17(?)
1937: May 1
1940: April 6, 13; May 4-18; June 15, 22

Washington College Library

1932-1944: Complete

The Enterprise, 1893-1955

Weekly. Established September 27, 1893, by L. Bates Russell. Absorbed by *Kent County News* February 4, 1955.

Enoch Pratt Free Library

1936-1954: Complete
1955: January 4-25

Talbot County Free Library

1936: February 19

Washington College Library

1894: June 6-December 26
1895-1898: Complete
1901-1916: Complete
1918: Complete
1920-1926: Complete
1928-1954: Complete

Freedmen's Journal, post-Civil War (?)

Reportedly published by R. Clay Crawford for several years after the Civil War. Nothing else known.

Kent Bugle, 1834-1840(?)

Weekly. May have succeeded *The Telegraph*. Established December 12(?), 1834. Name changed to *Kent News* circa 1840.

Enoch Pratt Free Library

1834: December 26
1835: May 8-29; July 31-August 28; November 6; December 11, 18

Maryland Historical Society

1837: July 22
1838: January 2, July 7

Kent Conservator, 1861-1863(?)

Existed 1861; nothing else known.

Maryland Historical Society
1861: February 9

Kent County News, 1840 to date

Weekly. Established May 2, 1840, as *Kent News;* claims "lineal" descent from *The Apollo, The Telegraph,* and *The Bugle.* Merged with *Chestertown Transcript* February 1, 1946, to form *Kent County News.* Owned 1981 by Whitney Communications Corporation, New York City.

American Antiquarian Society
1876: September 23

Enoch Pratt Free Library
1843: January 21
1858: January 16-March 20; April 3-December 25
1859: January 1-November 19; December 3-24
1860: Complete
1861: January 5-December 21
1862: January 4-May 17
1863: March 7
1875: April 24
1882: August 5
1885: May 2, October 31
1887: August 13
1890: March 15
1891: February 21
1892: April 30
1893: January 7
1900: October 20
1903: January 3-February 7, 21; March 7-October 3, 17-November 21; December 5-19
1904: January 2-September 10, 24-November 12, 26; December 3, 24, 31
1905: January 7, 28-March 25; April 8-May 13, 27-August 26; September 9-December 16
1906: January 20-March 24; April 7-August 4, 18, 25; September 8-December 29
1909-1911: Complete
1914: January 3
1915: May 22
1917-1918: Complete
1919: December 6 (industrial & war record edition)
1924: May 24
1934: June 9-December 29
1935-1945: Complete
1946: January 4-25
1947: January 3-December 4
1949: December 23
1950: June 30-December 29
1951 to date: Complete

Hall of Records
Microfilm
(*Kent County News* and Chesapeake College Library have same microfilm)
1845: May 3-December 28
1846-1857: Complete *except* for scattered issues
1860: November 24-December 29
1861-1863: Complete
1864: January 2-September 3; November 19-December 31
1865-1870: Complete
1871: January 7-April 22; December 2-30
1872-1875: Complete
1876: Complete *except* May 6
1877-1890: Complete except May 7, 1887
1904: September 24-December 31
1905: Complete
1906: February 3-December 29
1907: January 5-December 14
1908-1909: Complete
1912-1913: Complete

Kent County News
1914-1916: Complete
1918-1924: Complete
1926 to date: Complete

Library of Congress
1840: May 9, November 28

Maryland Historical Society
1851: June 7, 14
1857: March 14
1885: May 16
1894: February 17-April 21
1933: October 28
1964: August 26

Queen Anne's County Free Library
1953: September 25

Talbot County Free Library
1844: August 24
1850: December?
1892: April 30 (partial)
1909: January 23
1953: September 25

Washington College Library
1930-1936: Complete
1938-1944: Complete
1947 to date: Complete

Kent Independent, 1870s

Weekly. Existed 1879. Nothing else known.

Enoch Pratt Free Library
1879: November 1

Kent Inquirer, 1830-1834(?)

Weekly. Established November 12, 1830. Nothing else known.

Enoch Pratt Free Library
1830: November 12; December 3
1831: January 7; February 18; April 29; May 13-27; June 17; July 8, 29
1832: December 1
1833: February 2; June 29; September 14, 21; November 2-16

L. P. Keating
1832: April 27

The Telegraph, 1825-1830

Weekly. Established as *Chestertown Telegraph* October 21(?), 1825. Name shortened to *The Telegraph* October 27, 1826. Said to be a predecessor of *Kent News*. Last known issue July 16, 1830.

Enoch Pratt Free Library
1829: October 30; December 18

Hall of Records
Microfilm
(*Kent County News* and Chesapeake College Library have same microfilm)

1825: October 28-December 30
1826-1828: Complete *except* September 22, 1826; May 11, 1827; July 11, August 1, 1828
1829: January 2-February 27; March 13-July 4, 18-August 14, 28; September 11-25; October 9-23; November 6-13

Huntington Library
1830: July 16

L. P. Keating
1830: March 26

Library of Congress
1828: April 11-25; July 11, 25; August 1-29; September 5, 23, 26; October 3, 10; November 7-21; December 5
1829: July 10, 17; September 11, 25; October 2; November 27
1830: January 1, 8

Maryland Historical Society
1825: December 23
1826: December 1

Telescope, and Eastern Shore Advertiser, 1833-?

Weekly. Established December 13, 1833, by James R. Cann. Last known issue November 14, 1834. Said to have been succeeded by *Kent Bugle*.

Library of Congress
1833: December 20
1834: February 14

Maryland Historical Society
1834: November 14

Queen Anne's County Historical Society
1834: February 28

Queen Anne's

CENTREVILLE

Centreville Evening Times and Eastern Shore Publick Advertiser

See *Centreville Times I*

Centreville Observer, 1864-1936

Weekly. Succeeded *Centreville Times*. Established July 26, 1864, by William W. Busteed and Charles T. Loveday, as *The Observer*. Name changed to *Centreville Observer* August 23, 1864. Merged with *Queen Anne's Record* November 5, 1936, to form *Queen Anne's Record-Observer*.

American Antiquarian Society
1876: August 15

Enoch Pratt Free Library
1869: November 2
1870: September 27
1871: June 27
1873: January 21; April 29
1876: July 4
1896: January 7
1907: August 2, 16; November 4 (extra), 8; December 20
1908: January 10
1910: January 15
1914: June 20 (50th anniversary edition); October 3-10; November 21-28
1915: November 20, 27
1916: September 16, 30; November 25
1917: January 6, 27; February 3-March 31; April 14-May 26; July 7; August 4, 18, 25; September 8-October 20; November 10; December 1
1918: January 5, 19; February 2-March 16; April 6-May 25; June 1, 29; August 3, 17-31; September 7, 14, 28; October 5-26; November 9-December 7
1919: January 4-March 29; April 5, 19, 26; May 3, 17-31; June 14; July 5-12, 26; August 2-September 9; October 4-25; November 8-December 27
1920: January 3-March 27; April 3, 17, 24; May 1-29; June 5, 19; July 10-August 28; September 11-25; October 2, 9, 23, 30; November 13-27; December 4, 18, 25
1921: January 8, 22; February 5-April 2; May 21; July 23; August 13, 20; September 10, 17; October 8-22; November 5, 26; December 3, 10, 24, 31
1922: January 7-28; February 25; March 4, 18, 25; April 1-22; May 6-27; June 3, 17, 24; July 1, 8, 29; August 5, 26; September 2, 23; October 7; November 25; December 16, 30
1923: March 3-April 21; May 5-26; June 2, 9, 30; July 7-28; August 4, 11, 25; September 8-October 20; November 3, 17, 24; December 1-29
1924: January 5-26; February 9-September 13, 27-December 27
1925: January 10-February 28; March 7, 14, 28; April 4-25; May 2, 16-30; July 4, 18; August 1, 8; September 12, 19; October 10
1926: January 2-February 27; March 13, 27; April 3-17; May 22; June 5, 12, 26; July 17, 24; September 4, 25; October 2-16; November 13-27
1927: October 1-December 31

1928: January 7-June 30; July 14-November 24; December 15-29
1929: January 12-February 23; March 9, 16; April 13-27; May 11-October 5, 19-December 28
1930: January 4-April 24; May 8, 15, 29; June 5-November 6
1934: June 14-December 24
1935: January 3-December 19
1936: January 3-October 29

Maryland Historical Society

1891: May 21; August 13
1897: July 29
1921: June 11

New-York Historical Society

1873: March 25

Queen Anne's County Historical Society

1902: December 19
1911: June 17
1914: June 20
1916: October 7
1924: April 5
1926: September 18

Queen Anne's Record-Observer

1915-1924: Complete
1929: February 9-December 28
1933: March 23-December 28

Centreville Record, 1874-1932

Weekly. Established November 26, 1874, by R. G. Bordley and W. W. Cheezum. Expired April 14, 1932. Followed by *Queen Anne's Record*.

Enoch Pratt Free Library

1874: November 26; December 17-24
1875: January 7-February 25; March 11; April 1; May 6-August 12; November 25-December 30
1876-1877: Complete
1878: January 31-February 7, 28-September 5, 19-October 24; November 7-December 19
1879: January 23-November 13; December 18
1880: January 15-December 25
1881: November 17-December 29
1882: January 5-August 31; September 14, 28; October 5-November 9
1883: February 8-July 26
1884: February 7-November 27
1885: January 1-21; June 4-October 22
1886: January 7-March 4
1887: January 1-August 20
1888: January 7-July 21; August 4-November 24
1889: January 5-October 26
1890: January 18-September 6
1891: January 3, 24-May 23; June 6-September 12
1892: January 2-April 30; May 14-October 8
1893: January 7-December 2
1894: January 6-December 15
1895: Complete
1896: January 4-December 12, 26
1897-1902: Complete
1903: January 3-March 14, 28-August 15, 29-December 26
1904-1907: Complete
1908: January 4-February 15, 29-December 26
1909: January 16-March 20; April 3-December 25
1910: February 19-April 16, 30-July 30; August 13-October 1, 15; November 26; December 10-31
1911: January 7-July 22; August 5, 19-December 23
1912: January 6-June 8, 29-December 28
1913-1915: Complete
1916: January 1-April 15, 29-June 3, 17-December 30
1917: January 6-June 30; July 14-December 29
1918-1919: Complete
1920: January 3-March 27; April 10-December 25
1921: January 1-March 19; April 2-9, 23-December 31
1922: January 7-May 20
1923: Complete
1924: January 5-September 6, 20-October 4, 18-December 20
1925: January 8-15, 29-February 19; March 5-April 2, 16-July 23; August 6-13, 27-December 24
1926: January 1-November 4, 18-December 30
1927: January 6-December 15, 29
1928: January 12-December 27
1929: Complete
1930: January 2-July 17, 31-December 25
1931: January 1-October 1, 15-December 31
1932: January 7-April 14

Maryland Historical Society

1913: February 15
1921: June 11

Queen Anne's County Historical Society

1914: June 20
1926: September 16
1929: July 11

Queen Anne's Record-Observer
1898: Complete
1899: January 7-December 2

Talbot County Free Library
1894: January 5; March 17-December 15
1897: January 9-August 21; September 11-October 9
1898: December 3-17
1899-1900: Complete
1909: January 16-March 20; April 3-September 18; October 2-December 25
1910: April 2; May 7-21; June 4-18; July 2-9, 23; August 13, 27; September 3, 17-24; October 1, 15-22; November 5, 19-26; December 10, 24
1911: January 7, 21-28; February 4-18; March 4-11, 25; April 8, 22-29; May 6, 27; June 3, 17; July 1, 22; August 5; October 7
1912: February 17; March 9; April 20-May 11; August 24; October 5
1919: June 28; October 4-December 20
1920: January 3-31; February 14-28; March 6, 27; April 17; May 1-29; June 19-26; July 3-10, 24-September 11, 25; October 16; December 25
1923: January 27-May 5; May 19-August 25; September 8, 22-October 27; November 17-December 22
1924: January 5-May 17, 31; June 7-14, 28; July 5-September 6, 20-27; October 25-December 20
1925: May 14; October 15; December 24
1926: February 11; December 16
1928: November 1-8; December 6, 20-27
1929: January 10-24; March 28; June 20
1930: November 6

Centreville State Rights, 1857-1863

Weekly. Established April 6, 1857, by Thomas J. Keating as *State Rights Advocate and Maryland Sentinel*. Succeeded *Maryland Sentinel*. Became *Centreville State Rights* July 24, 1860. Expired after plant burned circa December 2, 1863. Vigorous supporter of secession.

Enoch Pratt Free Library
1860: December 4-25
1861: January 8-April 23; May 7-July 23; August 6-September 10
1863: January 31

Centreville Times and Eastern Shore Advertiser

See *Centreville Times I*

Centreville Times and Eastern Shore Public Advertiser

See *Centreville Times I*

Centreville Times I, 1824(?)-1864

Weekly. First Queen Anne's newspaper. Title varies. *Centreville Times and Eastern Shore Advertiser* 1826. *Centreville Evening Times and Eastern Shore Publick Advertiser* 1828; *Times and Public Advertiser* February 7, 1829-April 9, 1831; *Centreville Times and Eastern Shore Public Advertiser* at least until 1839; *Times and Advertiser* circa 1845; *Centreville Times* thereafter. Succeeded 1864 by *Centreville Observer*.

American Antiquarian Society
1827: February 3
1831: February 5, July 30

Enoch Pratt Free Library
1846: September 19

Library of Congress
1826: July 15, October 26
1828: June 21-November 22
1829: February 7-December 26
1830-1833: Complete *except* April 16, 1831
1834: January 4-October 4
1839: August 31
1845: March 29
1853: February 5

Maryland Historical Society
1863: May 16

Queen Anne's County Historical Society
1857: March 7

Centreville Times II, 1932-1934

Weekly. Published August 20, 1932, to November 1, 1934.

Enoch Pratt Free Library
1934 September 29

Freedom's Sentinel, 1839-1842

Weekly. Established as Democratic Party organ in 1839 by Henry Vanderford. Name changed to *Queen Anne's Telescope* October 1842.

Maryland Citizen, 1860-1876

Weekly. Established by John T. Hand January 5, 1860. Ceased publication August 1876. Republican in politics.

American Antiquarian Society
1863: April 9
1876: April 29

New-York Historical Society
1873: March 8

Queen Anne's County Historical Society
1863: December 17

Talbot County Free Library
1865: April 22

Maryland Sentinel, 1845-1857

Weekly. Succeeded *Queen Anne's Telescope* January 1845 under name of *Weekly Sentinel*. Published by J. H. Rowlenson. Name changed to *Weekly Sentinel and General Advertiser* September 29, 1846, and to *Maryland Sentinel* 1854. Succeeded by *State Rights Advocate* April 6, 1857.

Enoch Pratt Free Library
1846: September 29
1854: December 19

Library of Congress
1845: April 1

Maryland State News, 1970 to date

Weekly. Maryland edition of the *Delaware State News*, Dover, Delaware.

The Observer

See *Centreville Observer*

Queen Anne's Journal, 1977-1980

Weekly. First issue February 17, 1977; expired July 30, 1980.

Queen Anne's County Free Library
1977-1980: Complete

Queen Anne's Record, 1933-1936

Weekly. Established February 23, 1933, after demise of *Centreville Record*. Merged with *Centreville Observer* November 5, 1936, to form *Queen Anne's Record-Observer*.

Enoch Pratt Free Library (under *Queen Anne's Record-Observer*)
1933: Complete *except* October 12
1934: January 4-June 7, 21-July 26; August 30; September 20-October 25; November 29
1935: April 4-December 26
1936: Complete to October 29

Queen Anne's County Free Library
1933: February 23-December 28
1935: Complete
1936: Complete to October 29

Queen Anne's County Historical Society
1934: August 23

Queen Anne's Record-Observer, 1936 to date

Weekly. Established November 5, 1936, by merger of *Queen Anne's Record* and *Centreville Observer*. Name given as *Queen Anne's Record—The Centreville Observer* November 5-12, 1936, then shortened. Owned 1981 by Whitney Communications Corporation, New York City.

Enoch Pratt Free Library
1936: November 5-December 31
1937 to date: Complete *except* November 17, 1938; June 23-October 13, 27, 1960

Queen Anne's County Free Library
1937-1940: Complete
1944-1975: Complete
1977 to date: Complete

Queen Anne's County Historical Society
1946: April 4

1947: January 30; February 27; March 6, 20; May 29; September 4-18; November 13-20; December 4
1948: September 23
1949: April 14; May 12, 26; June 2-9; October 13; November 3; December 29
1950: May 4; August 17, 31; September 7-21
1951: January 4; March 15, 29; April 12; November 29
1952: February 14
1958: October 23
1959: December 10
1968: April 25; May 2
1974: January 2

Queen Anne's Record-Observer
1936: November 5-December 31
1937-1942: Complete
1946-1949: Complete
1963-1967: Complete
1969 to date: Complete

Queen Anne's Record—The Centreville Observer

See *Queen Anne's Record-Observer*

Queen Anne's Telescope, 1842-1845

Weekly. Succeeded *Freedom's Sentinel* October 1842. Followed by *Weekly Sentinel* January 1845. Proprietor, H. Manderville.

State Rights Advocate

See *Centreville State Rights*

Times and Advertiser

See *Centreville Times I*

Times and Public Advertiser

See *Centreville Times I*

Weekly Sentinel

See *Maryland Sentinel*

Weekly Sentinel and General Advertiser

See *Maryland Sentinel*

CHURCH HILL

Church Hill Air Line, circa 1870

Weekly? In existence 1870, according to Frederic Emory's *History of Queen Anne's County*. R. E. C. Downes, publisher, announced he was about to resume publication that year. Nothing else known.

Church Hill News, 1886-?

Monthly. Established August 1886 with offices at Church Hill, Sudlersville, and Millington. William Du Hamel, managing editor. Nothing else known.

CRUMPTON

Crumpton Gazette, 1865(?)-1869

Established 1865(?) by S. W. Herrick and J. C. Sheppard. Name changed to *Crumptonian* about 1867. Final issue December 17, 1869.

Crumptonian

See *Crumpton Gazette*

QUEENSTOWN

Queen Anne's News . . . and the Queenstown News

See *Queenstown News*

Queenstown News, 1882-1956

Weekly. Established "as an experiment" January 1, 1882, by J. M. and M. W. Aker. Regular publication began January 21, 1882. Name changed to *Queen Anne's News . . . and the Queenstown News*

October 28, 1939-May 3, 1940. Final issue June 22, 1956.

Enoch Pratt Free Library

1934: June 2-October 6, 20; November 3-December 29
1935: January 5-September 7, 21-December 28
1936-1939: Complete
1940: January 6-March 22; April 5-December 28
1941-1945: Complete
1946: January 4-August 16, 30-December 27
1947-1955: Complete
1956: January 6-June 22

Hall of Records

Microfilm
(Many issues are mutilated or have missing pages.)
1888: January 7-August 25; September 8-22
1890: September 27-December 6
1892: October 22-November 26
1897: January 30; February 6, 20, 27; March 6-June 5, 19, 26; July 3-November 6, 20, 27; December 4-18
1900: March 10-June 30; July 21-August 4; September 15-29; December 22, 29
1901: January 5, 26; February 2, 9, 23; March 2, 30; April 13, 20; May 4, 25; June 1, 15-29; July 13-27; August 24, 31; October 12; December 21, 28
1902: January 4-March 22; April 5-September 13, 27-November 8
1903: April 25-July 11
1905: December 23, 30
1906: January 6-August 4, 18-September 29; December 1-29
1907: January 5-19; February 2, 16-May 25; June 15, 22; July 6-September 14; October 19-November 2, 30; December 7, 21, 28
1908: January 4-February 15, 29; March 7-May 16, 30; June 6-August 22
1924: July 26-August 2
1925: November 21- December 26
1927: January 8-22; March 26; April 9-23; May 21
1929: January 26; September 28-December 28
1933: April 8; May 20; June 3; July 22
1935: April 13; May 4
1937: July 31; August 14
1943: January 1
1944: February 25; March 31; May 12; September 8, 29
1946: January 4-March 15; August 9, 16; September 6-27; October 18; November 1-December 13

1948: July 30-August 20
1949: November 11, 18
1951; January 5-19; February 2, 16, 23; March 2, 16-April 6; October 5, 29; November 16, 23; December 7, 14
1952: January 18-February 22; December 5, 26
1953: January 8; June 5-July 31; September 18-December 25
1954: January 1-August 20; September 3-November 19; December 24

Note: Albert V. Stant of the Queenstown Bank of Maryland, who salvaged the *Queenstown News* files when they were being thrown away, also has a copy of the Hall of Records microfilm.

STEVENSVILLE

Bay Times, 1963 to date

Weekly. Established November 22, 1963, by Christopher J. Rosendale, Sr. Sold May 1974 to Easton Publishing Company. Owned 1981 by Whitney Communications Corporation, New York City.

Bay Times
1966 to date: Complete

Enoch Pratt Free Library
1965: February 12, March-December 31
1966 to date: Complete

Queen Anne's County Free Library
1963: November 28-December 26
1964: Complete *except* February 27
1965: March 12-December 31
1966: Complete
1967: Complete *except* December 28
1968: Complete *except* December 26
1969: Complete *except* January 2
1970: January 8-July 19; August 20-27; September 24-November 19
1971: January 7, 21; February 18-March 11; April 8-May 13; May 27-December 30
1972: Complete *except* December 28
1973: Complete *except* December 27

1974: January 3-April 25

Queen Anne's Record-Observer
1971: Complete *except* December 30

Kent Island News, 1962-1963

Weekly. Established circa December 1962. Only a few issues published. Nothing else known.

Somerset

CRISFIELD

Crisfield Index, 1870s

Weekly. Existed 1872-1873. Nothing else known.

Enoch Pratt Free Library
1872: October 26-December 28
1873: January 4-February 1, 15-June 28; July 12, 19; August 2-September 6, 20-October 4, 18-25

Crisfield Leader, 1872-1908(?)

Weekly. Title varies: as *Crisfield Leader*, as *Somerset Republican* 1904(?); as *Crisfield Tribune* to about 1908. Described as Crisfield's "old established paper" in 1899.

American Antiquarian Society
1876: August 19

Marylander & Herald
1885: October 24

Crisfield News, 1915-(?)

Weekly. Established April 17, 1915, judging from the issue of January 22, 1916, which was identified as Volume I, No. 41. No other issue is known to exist.

Marylander & Herald
1916: January 22

Crisfield Post, 1935-1959(?)

Weekly. Established September 6, 1935. Absorbed *Somerset News* (Princess Anne) January 10, 1947.

Enoch Pratt Free Library
1935: October 4-November 8, 29-December 27
1936: January 3-10, 24-December 27
1937-1940: Complete (not published December 29, 1939)
1941: January 3-December 5, 19-26
1942-1947: Complete
1948: January 2-23

Library of Congress
1945: April 13

Crisfield Times, 1889 to date

Weekly. Established 1889 by Lorie C. Quinn, who moved plant from Pocomoke City, where he had published the *Eastern Shoreman*. Quinn served as editor more than 60 years. Owned 1981 by Independent Newspapers, Inc., Dover, Delaware.

Enoch Pratt Free Library
1925: September 19
1932: May 21
1934: May 25-September 21; October 5-December 21
1935-1943: Complete
1944: January 7-14, 28-to date *except* issue of March 11, 1966

Maryland Historical Society
1911: June 17: (historical supplement)
1937: April 16, 23

Talbot County Free Library
1954: August 27

Woodrow T. Wilson
1908 to date: Complete except for 1918

Note: Files are not available to the public except in special circumstances. Colonel Woodrow T. Wilson, local historian, has made abstracts of births, deaths, marriages, and major news events for the *Times* from 1908 to date. These are available on request from the editor of the *Crisfield Times*. Some specific requests to look at individual issues can also be honored.

Crisfield Tribune

See *Crisfield Leader*

Peninsula Press, 1947-1950(?)

Weekly. Established January 31, 1947, by John W. S. Justice, who reportedly operated his own Linotype and ran his press with a gasoline engine. Last known issue July 28, 1950.

Enoch Pratt Free Library
1947: January 31-December 26
1948: Complete
1949: January 7-July 22; August 5, 19-November 18; December 2-23
1950: January 6-13, 27-February 10, 24; April 28; May 12; July 28

Somerset Republican

See *Crisfield Leader*

MARION STATION

Eastern Shore Republican, 1939

See *Eastern Shore Republican*, Princess Anne

PRINCESS ANNE

Eastern Shore Republican 1928-1939

Weekly. Established at Princess Anne August 29, 1928. Published at Marion Station March 8, 1939, to October 4, 1939, when it expired.

Enoch Pratt Free Library
1935: September 17, 24; October 8-December 31
1936-1937: Complete
1938: January 4-December 20
1939: January 3-October 4

Maryland Historical Society
1937: April 27

The Herald

See *Somerset Herald I*

The Marylander

See *True Marylander*

Marylander & Herald, 1898 to date

Weekly. Established August 9, 1898, by merger of *The Marylander* and *Somerset Herald II*. Owned by the Byrd family since about 1930; said to be the last locally owned, locally printed paper on Eastern Shore of Maryland as of 1981. It was sold in 1984 to Atlantic Publications, Inc., and was to be renamed, in January 1985, the *Somerset Herald* [III].

Enoch Pratt Free Library
1915: August 17
1928: June 16
1930: January to date: Complete *except* March 10, April 28, May 14, 1933

Marylander & Herald
1898: August 23
1899: April 4; December 12
1901: March 19

1903: November 10
1909: February 9
1910: December 13
1911: February 7; June 6
1913: Complete
1914: January 6; April 12; December 29
1915 to date: Complete

Pathfinder, circa 1900-1905

Monthly. A publication of the Red Men lodge.

Marylander & Herald
1905: January

People's Press, 1836-1838(?)

Established October 4, 1836, by John S. Zieber. Nothing else known.

American Antiquarian Society
1838: January 23, 30

Library of Congress
1836: October 4, 11, 25; November 1, 15; December 6, 13
1837: January 3-February 14, 28; March 28; April 4, 18; May 16; June 6-July 25; August 8, 22, 29; September 12, 26; October 3, 17-November 28
1838: January 16-February 6; March 27-April 24

Marylander & Herald
1837: February 14 (partial photocopy)

Somerset Herald I, 1827-1846(?)

Weekly. No apparent connection with later *Somerset Herald*. Established by John S. Zieber as *Village Herald* April 3(?), 1827. Name changed to *The Herald* May 22, 1838, to *Somerset Herald* August 28, 1838. Last known issue August 4, 1846.

American Antiquarian Society
1827: July 3, 17, 31; October 23; November 6, 13; December 18, 25
1828: June 17, 24; July 29; August 26; September 16-23; October 14; November 11
1830: June 8, 29; July 6, 20; August 24
1831: January 4; June 7
1835: December 22
1836: January 26
1837: December 5
1839: August 13
1840: March 24

Clements Library, University of Michigan
1827: July 3; October 23
1828: August 5
1830: July 20

Dorchester County Historical Society
1840: December 1
1844: March 5

Library of Congress
1827: April 10-December 25
1828-1839: Complete *except* May 15, 1838
1840: January 7-November 24

Marylander & Herald
1827: September 11; October 9 (partial photocopies)
1832: December 25
1840: October 13 (replica)
1841: April 13
1846: June 9; August 4

Maryland Historical Society
1827: November 27
1828: July 8, 29; September 9
1830: August 17
1835: June 2-August 4
1838: May 22-June 26; July 10 December 25
1839: Complete
1840: January 7-June 30; July 14-October 6, 20-27; November 10-December 29
1841: January 5-June 22

Somerset County Historical Society
1832: December 25 (as *Village Herald*)

Somerset Herald II, 1861-1898

Weekly. No apparent connection with earlier *Somerset Herald*. Established June 11(?), 1861. Merged with *The Marylander* to form *Marylander and Herald* August 9, 1898.

American Antiquarian Society
1876: May 16

Marylander & Herald
1862: November 13 (extra)
1872: October 15
1876: December 5
1887: March 8
1892: September 27
1893: June 27
1894: October 9
1895: February 5; November 19
1896: September 29

New-York Historical Society
1873: March 25

Somerset County Historical Society
1861: October 29
1868: September 22

Somerset Herald III, 1985-

See *Marylander & Herald*

Somerset Iris and Messenger of Truth, 1828-1829

Weekly. Established June 13, 1828, with "George Brown, in Main Street," as publisher. Last known issue April 7, 1829.

American Antiquarian Society
1828: August 19

Enoch Pratt Free Library
1828: July 15

Library of Congress
1828: June 13-December 30
1829: January 6-April 7

Marylander & Herald
1828: October 28

Maryland Historical Society
1828: June 13; August 12, 19

New-York Historical Society
1829: March 31

Talbot County Free Library
1828: July 22

Somerset Journal, 1897-1903(?)

Weekly. Established January 16, 1897, judging from issue of May 28, 1898, which is Volume II, No. 14. Last known issue November 28, 1903.

Marylander & Herald
1898: May 28
1902: May 17
1903: November 28

Somerset News, 1925-1947

Weekly. Established March 25, 1925. Absorbed by *Crisfield Post* January 10, 1947.

Enoch Pratt Free Library
1934: May 19-December 29
1935-1946: Complete *except* December 17, 1942, and December 30, 1943
1947: January 2

Somerset Union, 1856(?)-1861(?)

Weekly. Established April (?) 1856. Last known issue November 5, 1861.

Enoch Pratt Free Library
1858: January 26
1860: July 3

Marylander & Herald
1861: May 21

Somerset County Historical Society
1861: November 5

True Marylander, 1866-1898

Weekly. Established January 2(?), 1866. Name changed to *The Marylander* 1881. Merged with *Somerset Herald II* August 9, 1898, to form *Marylander and Herald*.

American Antiquarian Society
1876: September 6

Enoch Pratt Free Library
1877: September 18
1879: June 10

Marylander & Herald
1867: May 14
1868: March 10

1882: May 30
1891: January 6
1895: December 31
1896: May 12; September 15, 29
1897: June 15; September 14

New-York Historical Society
1873: February 11

Village Herald

See *Somerset Herald I*

Talbot

EASTON

Delmarva Farmer, 1976 to date

Weekly. Established March 1976 as *Eastern Shore Farmer*. Name changed to *Delmarva Farmer* March 3, 1978. A publication of Chesapeake Publishing Corporation.

Star-Democrat
1976: March to date

The Democrat

See *Easton Democrat*

Eastern Shore Farmer

See *Delmarva Farmer*

Eastern Shore Journal, 1976

Weekly. Established January 8, 1976. Expired February 11, 1976.

Talbot County Free Library
1976: January 8-February 11

Eastern-Shore Star, 1841-1843

Weekly. Continued *Eastern-Shore Whig and People's Advocate* under new name. Established April 20, 1841, by George W. Sherwood after fire destroyed *Whig* office. Name changed May 23, 1843, to *Easton Star*.

Dorchester County Historical Society
1842: August 30

Maryland Historical Society (filed under *Easton Star-Democrat*)
1841: April 20-December 28
1842: Complete
1843: January 3-May 16

Eastern-Shore Whig and People's Advocate, 1828-1841

Weekly, semiweekly. Established September 9, 1828, to support radical or Jackson wing of Democratic Party, with John D. Green as first editor. Absorbed *Republican Star* June 1832. Published weekly September 9, 1828, to December 11, 1832; twice weekly during sessions of Congress December 15, 1832, to January 3, 1835; twice weekly full time to January 3, 1937; weekly thereafter. Not published March 23 to April 13, 1841, following disastrous fire. Reappeared April 20, 1841, under new name of *Eastern-Shore Star*.

Enoch Pratt Free Library
1837: January 31

Huntington Library
1830: September 7

Library of Congress
1828: November 11
1829: August 4

Maryland Historical Society
Microfilm (Talbot County Free Library and Theodore R. McKeldin Library, University of Maryland, have same microfilm)
1828: September 16, 23; October 21
1829: December 22
1830: March 9 (partial); July 13 (partial)-November 2, 16-December 21
1831: January 4-March 8, 22-April 19; May 3-July 26; August 9-September 13, 27-October 11, 25; November 1-December 27
1832: January 3, 17-31; February 7-April 3, 17; May 8-September 18; October 2-November 20; December 11-29
1833: January 5-29; February 5-April 2, 16-23; May 7-14, 28; June 4-December 31
1834: January 4-7, 14-28; February 1-December 30
1835: January 3-September 8, 15-26; October 3-December 8, 15-29
1836: January 2-23, 30; February 6-13, 20, 23-July 2, 9-August 20; September 3-17, 24-November 19, 29-December 6, 13, 20, 24
1837: January 3-31; February 21-March 7, 21-April 4, 18-October 21; November 7-December 26
1838: January 9-May 22; June 5-October 23; December 4-25
1839: January 1-November 12, 26; December 10-31
1840: January 7; February 4-April 28; May 12-June 2, 16-December 29
1841: January 5-March 2

Talbot County Free Library
1829: January 6, 20-27; March 3, 17; May 12, 26; June 30
1832: March 27
1833: March 16; July 23; September 24
1835: June 13
1838: May 1
1840: April 28; October 27

Easton Democrat, 1885-1896

Weekly. Established May 20, 1885, as *The Easton Independent*. Name changed November 27, 1886, to *The Democrat*, and June 15, 1889, to *Easton Democrat*. Merged with *Easton Star* February 12, 1896, to form *Star-Democrat*.

Maryland Historical Society
1886: January 20-May 12; June 9-November 10, 27-December 25
1887-1890: Complete
1891: January 3-September 12

Talbot County Free Library
1886: December 25
1887: January 8; June 18, July 16
1888: January 7-14
1890: March 29

Easton Enterprise

See *The Enterprise*

Easton Gazette, and Eastern Shore Intelligencer

See *Easton Gazette*

Easton Gazette, 1817-1929

Weekly. Established by Alexander Graham December 15, 1817, to support Federalist candidates. Several name changes: as *Easton Gazette and Eastern Shore Intelligencer* April 5, 1819, to November 6, 1824; as *Gazette-Democrat* November 9, 1901, to February 22, 1902; as *Easton Gazette* otherwise. Supported Union in Civil War, Republican Party afterward. Final issue November 1, 1929.

American Antiquarian Society
1818: July 6
1827: October 27
1837: July 14
1841: January 30
1842: June 18
1851: October 18
1860: October 13
1862: June 14
1866: June 30
1876: September 30

Enoch Pratt Free Library
1818: August 3
1819: April 5-26; December 6-13
1820: January 3-February 7, 21-March 11, 25-April 8, 29; May 13-October 7; December

9-30
1826: December 30
1886: July 24; October 2
1895: March 2-April 6, 27-December 28
1896: Complete
1897: January 2-September 11, 25-October 16
1900: February 3-November 10
1904: February 6-December 10
1910: September 17, 24; October 1-15; November 5-December 31
1913: July 9, 23
1914: January 7
1916: August 2-9; October 4; November 29
1917: April 4; June 27
1922: September 7
1924: November 6, 13
1925: October 22
1928: January 13

Library Company of Philadelphia
1850: November 30

Library of Congress
1821: March 3; July 28
1824: November 6
1826: January 14; September 9-October 21; December 16-30
1827: January 6-April 29; October 6-December 29
1828: January 5-November 15
1829: May 23; June 27: September 5-12, 26; October 3
1830: July 24; November 13
1831: July 30
1832: December 15
1840: November 7

Maryland Historical Society
Original issues
1886-1890: Complete
1891: February 14; April 14; May 16-August 22; September 5
1893: January 14-28
1897: December 11-25
1907: December 28
1911: April 8
1914: November 25
Microfilm (Talbot County Free Library has same microfilm)
1818: December 14-28
1819: Complete
1820: Complete *except* January 3
1821: Complete *except* January 13, 20

1822-1829: Complete *except* April 2, 1829
1831: February 12-October 8, 22-December 31
1832: Complete *except* August 25
1833: Complete *except* April 6, December 7, 14
1834-1865: Complete *except* for scattered issues
1866: January 27-November 3, 17-December 22
1867: January 19-December 21
1868: Complete
1869: Complete *except* November 27, December 18
1870: Complete *except* February 26, April 30, July 16
1871: January 7, 14, 28; February 4-March 11, 25-September 23; October 7-November 4, 18-December 23
1872-1873: Complete *except* December 20, 1873
1874: Complete to November 28
1875-1880: Complete *except* few issues
1881: May 28; June 4, 18-July 16
1882: March 4, 11; May 20-June 10
1885: January 2; July 25-December 26

New-York Historical Society
1873: April 5

Talbot County Free Library
Original issues
1818: January 24-December 28
1819: January 4-November 29
1820: March 6-May 27; July 1-29; November 11-December 2
1821: March 3; April 14
1822: March 30; December 21-28
1823-1828: Complete *except* January 18, November 29, 1823; October 7, 1826; July 5, 1828
1829: January 3-10
1831: October 8, 29
1832: January 14; March 17; April 7; May 12; July 14; August 4; September 15; November 10
1838: August 4
1839: December 21
1840: August 15
1842: July 16; September 3
1844: January 20; February 17-May 18; June 1-October 19; November 2-December 28
1847: January 2, 9, 23, 30; February 6-October 16; November 13; December 4-25
1848: April 22
1850: December 28
1851-1855: Complete *except* December 24-31, 1853
1856: January 5-July 12
1857: December 19-26

1858: February 20; May 1-8, 22; June 5-19; July 3, 24-31; August 7-October 2, 16-December 18
1859: January 1-February 26; March 12-April 2, 23-December 3, 17
1860: January 21; February 18-25; March 3, 24-31; April 21; May 5-19; June 9-16; July 14, 28; August 4, 18; September 8; November 3, 17; December 1-22
1861: January 5; March 23
1862: February 15; April 5, 26; May 17; July 12-19; August 2-16, 30; September 6; November 8; December 6
1864: May 7; December 17
1865: September 23
1867: January 26; February 16; April 6-August 10, 24-October 12, 26; November 16-30; December 21
1868: January 11-25; February 1-15; March 7-April 18; May 9-16, 30; June 6, 27; July 4-18; August 1, 15-29; September 12, 26; October 3; November 14-December 26
1869: January 9-March 6
1871: January 14
1880: March 20; April 3, 17-May 1, 22-June 26; July 10-October 23; November 13-December 18
1885: August 1, 15-December 26
1886-1892: Complete
1893: Complete to December 2
1896: February 15-December 26
1897-1908: Complete *except* December 29, 1900; December 28, 1901; October 25, 1902
1910: December 31
1916: December 20
1917: January 3, 17-24; February 7-14; April 11
1918: February 7
1920: September 30
1921: October 27
1926: January 7; February 11, 25; April 8; May 27; November 4

Microfilm
1818: December 18-25
1819-1829: Complete
1831: February 12-December 31
1832-1841: Complete
1842: January 1-March 5; May 12-December 31
1843-1847: Complete
1848: January 1-October 7
1854: May 27-December 30
1855-1860: Complete
1861: January 5-May 27; December 14
1862-1864: Complete

1865: January 4-December 2
1866: January 27-December 29
1867-1870: Complete
1871: January 7-28; November 11
1881: May 28-December 31
1882-1885: Complete
1891: August 1-December 26
1892-1898: Complete
1899: January 2-December 23

Theodore R. McKeldin Library, University of Maryland
Original issues
1846: January 24-December 26
1860: Complete *except* April 14
Microfilm
1818: December 14-28
1819-1824: Complete

Easton Independent

See *Easton Democrat*

Easton Journal I, 1863-1874

Weekly. Established August 4, 1863, by Arthur Brown as a substitute for *The Easton Star*, which had been suppressed for prosecession sentiments. Not published September 17 to October 15, 1874, when name was changed to *Easton Ledger*.

Maryland Historical Society
1863: August 4; October 13
1864: July 26
1865: August 29; September 26-December 26
1866: January 4-February 1, 15-May 17-August 9, 23-November 1, 15-22
1867: March 28-June 27; July 11-November 14, 28-December 5, 19
1868: January 9, 23; February 13, 27-April 23; May 7, 21-June 18; July 9-September 24; October 8, 22; November 19-December 31
1869: January 7; February 4, 18; March 11, 25-April 22; June 24; September 2
1870: March 3; May 18; June 9, 21-28; November 10
1871: March 16; October 12, 26-December 28
1872: January 11-February 1, 15-August 22; September 5-December 26
1873: January 2, 16-30

News & Farmer
1872: May 23

New-York Historical Society
1873: April 3

Talbot County Free Library
1865: October 3
1866: September 13; December 6-13
1867: January 10-February 21; March 7-May 9, 23-July 25; August 8-December 26
1868: January 9-June 25
1869: December 9-30
1870-1873: Complete
1874: January 1-September 10

Easton Journal II, 1874

Weekly. Published briefly by Jonathan Leonard September 24 to October 15, 1874, during a financial dispute with previous editor J. A. Johnson. The Leonard family had seized the *Journal* for nonpayment of a mortgage. Johnson changed the name to *Easton Ledger* and resumed publication. Leonard's *Journal* expired shortly.

Maryland Historical Society
1874: September 24; October 15 (under *Easton Ledger*)

Easton Journal III, 1931-1956

Weekly. Established August 20, 1931, with John H. Cook as president and J. Clayland Mullikin as editor. Name changed April 26, 1956, to *Mid-Shore Times*.

Enoch Pratt Free Library
1931: September 17
1933: June 22; September 28; October 12-26; December 7-14
1934: January 4-11; February 15; March 8-22; April 5-19; May 3-December 27
1935: January 3-February 21; March 7-July 25; August 8-October 17, 31-December 19
1936-1937: Complete
1938: January 6-May 12
1939: September 21-December 21
1940-1941: Complete
1942: January 1-8, 22-December 31
1943: January 7-December 30
1944-1945: Complete

1946: January 3-June 27; July 11-September 5, 26-December 26
1947: January 2-16; September 4-December 25
1948: Complete
1949: January 6-March 10, 24-December 29
1950-1955: Complete
1956: January 5-April 19

Maryland Historical Society
1934: May 31

Talbot County Free Library
1931: August 20-27; September 3-24; October 1-8, 22-29; November 5-19; December 3-10
1933: April 27 (partial)
1943: July 29-December 30; Complete *except* August 5
1944: Complete *except* January 20
1945: Complete *except* January 18
1946: Complete *except* June 13, July 18, December 26
1947: January 2-16, 30; February 6, 20; March 6-20; April 10-May 8, 22-July 10, 24-31; August 7; September 4-December 25
1948-1953: Complete
1954: Complete *except* November 11
1955: Complete
1956: Complete through March 1

Easton Ledger, 1874-1918(?)

Weekly. Continued *Easton Journal I*, starting October 15, 1874, after editor J. A. Johnson lost right to use name of *Journal* for nonpayment of mortgage. Last known issue July 19, 1917.

American Antiquarian Society
1876: October 5

Enoch Pratt Free Library
1885: June 11
1900: August 2
1903: November 19

Maryland Historical Society
1874: October 22-December 31
1875: January 7-March 18; April 1-May 6, 20-July 1, 15-October 14, 28-December 30
1876: January 6-April 20; May 4-25; June 8-December 28
1877: Complete
1878: Complete *except* December 12
1879: Complete *except* May 29, June 19
1880-1888: Complete

1889: Complete *except* September 19
1890: August 7; September 11
1891: February 5; March 26; May 21; June 4-18; July 2, 16-30; August 6-27; October 1, 8
1907: October 24
1913: August 14

Talbot County Free Library
1874: October 15-December 31
1875: Complete
1881: January 6, 20-April 7, 21-June 30; August 11-September 15, 29; October 6-December 22
1882: January 5-March 30; April 13-June 29; July 20-December 21
1883: January 4-11, 25; February 1-April 19; May 3-June 7, 21-July 26; August 16-December 27
1884: January 3-10, 24-31; February 14-28; March 13-April 3; May 8-June 12, 26-August 14; September 4-11, 25; October 2-December 25
1885: January 29-February 26; March 12-September 10, 24-November 12, 26; December 3-10
1886: March 11; April 8, 29; September 2, 16; November 11
1905: April 27; May 18
1912: February 29
1917: July 19

Easton Star, 1843-1896

Weekly. Continued *Eastern-Shore Star* under new name May 23, 1843. Suspended May 12, 1863-September 12, 1865, and editor Thomas K. Robson banished to Virginia for strong prosecessionist statements. Merged with *Easton Democrat* February 12, 1896, to form *Easton Star-Democrat*.

American Antiquarian Society
1872: October 24
1876: August 29

Dorchester County Historical Society
1843: September 19; October 3-10; December 5-26
1844: January 9, 23; February 13-March 26; May 21; June 4; July 9-August 13; November 5, 12, 26
1845: January 5; February 4; April 8, 15, 29; May 6, 13; 27; June 3-July 1, 22, 29; August 12-26; September 9-November 4, 18-December 30
1846: January 6, 13, 27

Enoch Pratt Free Library
Microfilm
(Talbot County Free Library and Hall of Records have same microfilm)

1870-1890: Complete
1891: February 24; April 14, 28; May 19-June 9; July 21-August 4; September 1-15, 29; October 6

Library of Congress
1845: April 1
1853: March 8-December 20
1859: Complete
1860: February 7-December 25

Maryland Historical Society (filed under *Easton Star-Democrat*)
1843-1862: Complete *except* for scattered issues
1863: January 6, 20, 27; February 3-17; March 24
1865: September 26
1866: March 27; April 10-October 23; November 6-December 4, 18
1867: March 19; April 2-May 21; June 4-November 5, 19-December 24
1868: Complete *except* January 7, 28; August 4, 11; September 29
1869: January 5-February 2, 16; March 23-April 13; June 22; August 3, 17; December 21
1870-1890: Complete
1891: February 24; April 14, 28; May 19-June 9; July 21-August 4; September 1-15, 29; October 6; December 27
1893: January 10

New-York Historical Society
1873: March 18

Talbot County Free Library
Original issues
1844: May 7
1848: June 6; July 4-August 29; September 12-December 26
1850: October 22
1851: March 25; May 27
1853: February 15; March 8
1854: September 26; October 17
1855: January 2; February 6, 20; May 8, 22-June 12, 26; July 3, 17-October 2, 16-23; November 6-December 4, 18
1856: January 1, 22-July 15; August 5; December 16-23
1857: January 13-February 3, 17-May 19; July 7; August 4-11, 25; September 1-15; October 6-13; November 3, 17; December 1, 15
1858: January 5-12; February 2-April 20; May 4-18; June 1; July 6-20; August 3-17; October 5, 19; December 14-21
1871: August 1-15; September 12, 26; October 3-10, 31; November 7-December 12-26

1872: January 2-April 9, 23; May 14-June 25; July 9, 30; September 17-October 15; November 12-December 31
1873: March 11-April 22; June 3-December 30
1874: May 19-November 3, 17-December 29
1875: January 5-February 16; March 2-April 27; May 18-June 22, July 6-November 2, 16, 30-December 28
1876: January 4-March 14, 28-May 30; June 13-27; July 11-25; October 10; November 7, 21-December 19
1877: January 30-April 10; May 1-November 6, 20-December 25
1878: Complete *except* September 10, October 1, December 31
1879: January 7-March 18; April 1-May 27; June 10-August 19; September 2-November 4, 18-December 30
1880: February 3-10, 24; April 20-May 4; August 17-November 30
1881: January 4-18; February 1, 15
1882: February 21; June 6-July 4
1883: July 5, 19
1885: January 1-8; August 11; September 1-8; December 24-31
1886: February 16; June 1; August 10; November 9
1887: July 12
1888: February 14-21; March 6-20
1889: October 22
1890: July 22, October 14; November 11, 25
1891: July 21; August 4; September 29

Theodore R. McKeldin Library, University of Maryland
1849-1854: Complete

University of Illinois Library
1844: January 9; February 27; September 3, 17, 24; October 15; November 5

Easton Star-Democrat

See *Star-Democrat*

The Enterprise, 1879-1883(?)

Monthly. "Devoted to the Interests of the New Academy of Music," according to its logo. Name also given as *Easton Enterprise*. Last known issue May 1883.

Maryland Historical Society
1879: July

Talbot County Free Library
1883: May

Gazette-Democrat

See *Easton Gazette*

General Advertiser

See *Republican Star*

Herald and Eastern Shore Intelligencer

See *Maryland Herald and Eastern Shore Intelligencer*

Maryland Censor, 1818-1819

Believed to have been an "alias" of the *People's Monitor* of Easton, which had supposedly gone out of existence December 1817. Nothing else known.

Maryland Historical Society
1818: January 6; September 9, 19 (extra), 30-December 30
1819: January 27-February 10; March 3, 10

Maryland Herald and Eastern Shore Intelligencer, 1790-1804

Weekly. Eastern Shore's first newspaper. Established May 11, 1790, by James Cowan. Title changed to *Herald and Eastern Shore Intelligencer* November 12, 1799. Final issue November 13, 1804

American Antiquarian Society
1790: May 18-August 17, 31; September 7, 21-28; October 5, 19; November 16; December 14-21
1791: March 8; April 12, 26; June 23; August 16, 30; September 6, 13; October 4
1792: January 24-February 7; May 8; June 19, 26; July 3, 17, 31; September 18
1793: February 12; March 12; July 16
1798: August 28
1804: January 17; March 13; June 26

Enoch Pratt Free Library
1790: October 12

1791: July 12
1800: February 25 (photostat)

Houghton Library, Harvard University

1791: June 7, 28; July 5, 19; November 15
1795: February 24; March 24; May 19; June 9, 16; November 10
1796: May 17, 24; June 7, 21; July 5-19; August 2-23; September 6-27; October 11-25; November 15-22; December 6-27
1797: January 10-24; February 14, 28; April 18

Library Company of Philadelphia

1795: October 27; November 3-10; December 1

Library of Congress

1792: July 24
1794: August 26
1798: August 7, 21, 28; September 4, 25; October 2; November 20-27; December 11
1799: July 30; November 19
1800: December 16
1801: October 20 (partial)
1803: January 4

Maryland Historical Society

Microfilm

1790: May 11-June 1; August 3-31; September 14-October 26; November 16-December 28
1791: January 4-June 14, 28-September 6; October 11; November 15
1792: May 1, 15, 29; June 12, 26; July 10, 24; August 7, 21; September 4, 18; October 2, 16; November 6-20; December 4, 18
1793: January 15, 29; February 12, 26; March 12, 26; April 9, 30-May 7; June 4; July 2, 23; August 27-September 7; October 1-15; November 5; December 10, 24
1794: January 4, 21; February 4; March 4; April 15-22; May 13-August 26; September 9-December 9, 30
1795: January 13, 27; February 10, 24; March 10-31; April 21; May 5, 19; June 2, 16, 30; July 14, 28; August 18; September 29; October 13, 27-November 10; December 8-15, 29
1796: January 5-February 16; March 8-29; April 12-September 20; October 11-November 8
1797: April 11-December 26
1798: January 2-23; March 6-June 12, 26-August 21; September 4-October 23; November 20-December 18
1799: January 22-September 3; November 5, 19-26; December 10-24
1800: January 21, 28-February 18; March 4-June 10, 24-October 28; November 11-18; December 2-9
1801: January 6-June 23; July 14-December 29
1802-1803: Complete
1804: January 10; February 7-14, 28; March 27-April 17; May 1-October 23; November 13

New-York Historical Society

1801: March 24

Somerset County Historical Society

1792: June 12
1803: October 25

Talbot County Free Library

1791: March 29; April 5; May 24
1793: November 5
1796: March 22; April 12; May 10
1801: March 3-10, 24-31; April 21-28
1802: January 26; February 9; March 2-9; May 25; June 29; August 3-17; September 14-October 12, 26; November 16-23; December 7
1803: March 1-April 19; May 3-10; June 21-28; July 19; August 2; September 6, 20-October 4; November 1-22
1804: March 13, 27-April 10; May 1-15; June 5, 19-July 3, 31; August 14-21; September 4-11

Wisconsin Historical Society

1795: March 19
1799: February 19-26; May 7; July 30-August 20; September 24-October 22

Maryland Independent, 1930-?

Weekly. Established March 13(?), 1930, by H. P. Brown to support local Republican candidates after the demise of the *Easton Gazette*. Published in the Stewart Building, Easton. The only known existing issue, that of June 5, 1930, is in the collection of Dr. Laurence G. Claggett, Easton, Maryland.

Mid-Shore Times, 1956-1959

Weekly. Continued *Easton Journal III* under a new name, adopted April 26, 1956. Absorbed by *Easton Star-Democrat* March 27, 1959.

Enoch Pratt Free Library

1956: April 26-December 27
1957-1958: Complete
1959: January 1-March 19

Talbot County Free Library
1956: April 26

Once a Month, 1868-1869

Monthly. Established May 15, 1868, as advertising sheet by hardware firm of Thomas C. Nicols & Co. Expired after issue of April 1869.

Peninsula Democrat, 1901

Weekly. Established in Easton May 9(?), 1901, by A. W. Lightbourn. Merged with *Easton Gazette* November 9, 1901, to form *Gazette-Democrat*.

Talbot County Free Library
1901: October 31

People's Advocate

See *Eastern-Shore Whig*

People's Monitor, 1809-1817(?)

Weekly. Established March 4, 1809, by Samuel B. Beach as Federalist Party organ. Later publishers were Henry W. Gibbs and Nicholas S. Rowlenson. Discontinued December (?) 1817 but may have been published 1818-1819 under "alias" of *Maryland Censor*. Succeeded by *Easton Gazette*.

American Antiquarian Society
1809: March 4-November 4, 18; December 2-30
1810: January 6-February 24; May 26; July 7, 14
1811: February 2, 23; April 13, 27
1812: January 18; June 6, 20; August 8, 15; September 12, 19; October 3, 10; December 26
1813: January 2, 9; February 27; December 4
1816: February 3

Enoch Pratt Free Library
1811: February 2

Houghton Library, Harvard University
1809: March 25, April 1

Maryland Historical Society
1809: April 1, 29; June 3, 17; November 4
1810: December 8
1814: June 11

Wisconsin Historical Society
1813: January 9-July 31; August 14-December 25

Public Monitor, 1858

Weekly. Established July 1, 1858, by William T. Rowlenson, former partner of Thomas K. Robson in the *Easton Star*. Last known issue November 25, 1858.

Maryland Historical Society
1858: July 8, 29; Agust 12, 19; September 16; November 11-25

Republican Star, 1799-1832

Weekly. Established August 27(?), 1799, by Thomas Perrin Smith, who served as editor until his death May 2, 1832. Various titles: *Republican Star; or, Eastern Shore Political Luminary* 1799-September 1802; *Republican Star; or, Eastern Shore General Advertiser* September 7, 1802-September 13, 1814; *Republican Star* September 20, 1814; *Republican Star; or, General Advertiser* September 27, 1814-1816; *Republican Star and General Advertiser* 1816-1832. Absorbed by *Eastern-Shore Whig* after Smith's death. Last known issue June 12, 1832.

American Antiquarian Society
1800: February 11
1802: February 2; March 9
1804: March 13; June 26
1805: January 15
1806: June 17; September 2; October 14
1810: July 10; October 2
1811: February 26; March 12; August 6
1812: February 11
1814: May 31; June 21, 28; July 26; August 2, 16, 23; September 13
1815: June 13
1822: November 12; December 3
1823: December 23
1824: February 10-June 29
1825: March 22-December 27
1826: January 3-August 15
1828: August 12-26; September 23-October 14; November 4, 18-25

Enoch Pratt Free Library
1803: October 11

1808: October 11
1816: March 5

Houghton Library, Harvard University
1804: October 16; November 13-December 25
1805: January 1-22; February 5-April 9, 30; May 7; June 4-25; July 9-November 19; December 3, 10, 24, 31
1806: January 28; April 1; June 24

Huntington Library
1830: September 14

Library of Congress
1800: December 23
1806: September 9-December 30
1807-1809: Complete
1810: January 2-August 28
1813: February 9; April 6; September 14; October 12-November 2, 30
1815: October 10
1818: March 17
1819-1824: Complete
1826: February 18, 25
1828: December 30
1829: September 1-29
1831: August 16

Maryland Historical Society
1801: March 24
1802: September 7-December 28
1803: January 4-March 22; April 5-December 13, 27
1804-1825: Complete *except* August 28, 1810, April 18, 1815, and April 21, 1818
1826: January 3-August 22; September 5, 19; October 3, 24-December 19
1827: January 2-April 3, 24-May 1, 15-June 19; July 3-August 7, 21-October 2, 16; November 6-27; December 11-25
1828: January 1-8; March 25-April 15, 29-July 29; August 12-October 28; November 11, 25-December 30
1829: January 6-20; February 3-10, 24-March 10, 24-June 30; July 14-August 11, 25-September 1, 22-November 17
1830: January 12-26; February 9-16; March 2-23; April 6; May 4-18; June 22-September 7; October 12; November 30

New-York Historical Society
1807: December 8-15
1808: January 26; February 2; March 15; April 5-12, 26; May 10, 24; June 14-28; July 5-December 27

1809: January 3-March 7, 21-December 26
1810: January 9, 23; February 6, 27-June 19; July 3-10, 24-December 25
1811: January 1-29; April 16; May 7-June 15; July 9-September 3, 17; October 1-8

Talbot County Free Library
1800: February 11 (photostat of page 1)
1802: September 7-December 28
1803: Complete *except* December 20
1804: Complete *except* June 12
1805: Complete
1806: January 7-August 26
1810: September 4-December 25
1811-1813: Complete
1814: Janaury 4-March 15, 29-August 9
1815: October 3-17
1817: August 5; October 7
1818: September 22
1821: February 6; September 11
1822: May 21
1824: April 20

Wisconsin Historical Society
1802: September 7-December 28
1803-1831: Complete *except* for scattered issues
1832: January 3-June 12

Republican Star; or, Eastern Shore General Advertiser

See *Republican Star*

Republican Star; or, Eastern Shore Political Luminary

See *Republican Star*

Republican Star; or, General Advertiser

See *Republican Star*

Republican Star and General Advertiser

See *Republican Star*

Sharp Shooter, 1864(?)

Weekly? Established by Captain Andrew J. Stafford as camp newspaper for Federal troops stationed at Camp Kirby, near Easton, during Civil War. Nothing else known.

Social Journal, 1860-1861(?)

Weekly. Established November 1, 1860, by F. H. Houston as a "neutral" newspaper in dispute which led to Civil War. Expired "soon after hostilities started," according to Dr. Samuel A. Harrison, because "neutrality of sentiment was regarded to be very like treason by both the disputants in the fight." Press later used to found *Easton Journal* August 4, 1863.

Star-Democrat, 1896 to date

Weekly, daily. Claims "direct descent" from *Republican Star*, founded 1799. Established February 12, 1896, by merger of *Easton Star* and *Easton Democrat*. Title was *Easton Star-Democrat* to June 2, 1961, *Star-Democrat* since. Absorbed *Mid-Shore Times* March 27, 1959. Became daily (five days weekly) August 28, 1974. Owned 1981 by Whitney Communications Corporation, New York City.

Dorchester County Historical Society
1926: October 23

Enoch Pratt Free Library
Original issues
1925: May 30; December 26
1927: December 24
1928: November 24; December 22
1933: May 5-12; December 22
1955 to date: Complete
Microfilm
1934: January 26-February 2; March 9-Apil 6, 27-December 28
1935-1954: Complete *except* for scattered issues

Maryland Historical Society
1911: March 25 (historical and industrial edition)

Talbot County Free Library
Original issues
1905: April 1, 22; May 6, 20
1913: December 20
1917: April 7
1921: October 29
1926: February 27; June 5, 19; July 3; November 6
1927: February 19; March 5, 26

1931: August 1
1933: September 28
1941: November 21-December 26
1942-1973: Complete
1974: January 2-August 21
Microfilm
1934: January 26-February 2; March 9-April 6, 27-December 28
1935-1940: Complete *except* for scattered issues

Worcester County Library
1974: August 21 (175th anniversary edition)

Talbot Banner, 1973 to date

Daily, weekly. Established April 2, 1973, as Talbot County edition of the *Daily Banner*, Cambridge. Titled *Talbot Banner* April 16, 1973, to April 1, 1975; *The Banner, Mid-Shore Edition*, to February 28, 1979. Became weekly *Talbot Banner* with free distribution March 14, 1979. Owned 1981 by Evening Post Publishing Company, Charleston, South Carolina.

Talbot Banner
Microfilm (Talbot County Free Library and *Daily Banner*, Cambridge, have same microfilm)
1973: April through December complete
1974-1978: Complete
1979: March 14 to date complete

Talbot County Record, 1935

Weekly. Published briefly in summer of 1935. Nothing else known.

Enoch Pratt Free Library
1935: June 21, 28

Talbot County Free Library
1935: June 21

Talbot Times

See *Talbot Times*, Trappe

OXFORD

Oxford Enterprise, 1880-?

Weekly? Established October 1880, judging from

issue of November 13, 1880, which is listed as No. 4. A. A. Christian was "proprietor." One source says it was published "in a house on the Strand" for about ten years. Nothing else is known.

Oxford Museum, Oxford, Maryland
1880: November 13

ST. MICHAELS

The Comet

See *St. Michaels Comet*

Comet and Advertiser

See *St. Michaels Comet*

New Comet

See *St. Michaels Comet*

St. Michaels Comet, 1866-1942 (not continuous)

Weekly. Started as an advertising sheet, *The Comet*, September 1, 1866, by St. Michaels merchants H. Clay Dobson and John T. Ford. Expanded to full newspaper; name changed to *St. Michaels Comet* December 22(?), 1866; to *Comet and Advertiser* January 4, 1868; to *Weekly Phenix* May-July 1870; back to *Comet and Advertiser* July 1870-1925; to *New Comet* 1928(?). Publication suspended several times. Last known issue October 30, 1942.

American Antiquarian Society
1870: September 10

Enoch Pratt Free Library
1866: September 15
1882: June 10
1888: June 10
1935: December 5-25
1936-1937: Complete
1938: January 14-December 23
1939-1941: Complete
1942: January 9-October 30

Maryland Historical Society
1866: December 22
1867: April 27
1868: January 4
1869: July 31
1870: May 14; July 16
1879: February 1
1913: August 2

Talbot County Free Library
1935: September 5, 26; October 24; November 7

Weekly Phenix

See *St. Michaels Comet*

TRAPPE

The Index, 1873-1874

Monthly. Established September 1873 by Robert T. Mullikin, storekeeper and postmaster. Last known issue June 15, 1874

Neva T. Jones
1873: December 15

Talbot County Free Library
1874: June 15

Talbot Times, 1885-1903

Weekly. Established October 7(?), 1885, by Reverend Burton S. Highley and Percival Mullikin. Succeeded *Trappe Enterprise*. Moved to Easton 1902. Last known issue March 11, 1903.

Neva T. Jones
1885: November 25

Talbot County Free Library
1901: June 13; August 29; September 12, 26; October 3
1903: March 11

Trappe Courier, no date

Appears to have been an advertising sheet for Merrick & Kemp, Trappe druggists.

Talbot County Free Library
One undated issue

Trappe Enterprise, 1883-1885

Weekly. Established March 7, 1883, by C. H. Kemp and Percival Mullikin. Last known issue July 22, 1885. Succeeded by *Talbot Times*.

Neva T. Jones
1883: March 7

Talbot County Free Library
1883: March 21-November 21; December 5-26
1884: January 2-30; February 13-November 19; December 3, 17
1885: January 14, 28; February 25; July 22

Wicomico

SALISBURY

Advocate

See *The Courier*

The Bachelor, 1870-1874

Weekly. Established in 1870 by R. Reese Morgan with Charles F. Holland and George W. Cooper, both bachelors, as co-editors. Featured articles poking fun at the institution of marriage and weekly gossip column lampooning Salisbury social life. Absorbed by *Salisbury Advertiser* November 1874.

New-York Historical Society
1873: February 5

The Courier, 1899-1919

Weekly. Established as a Republican Party organ April 19, 1899, by a group headed by William H. Jackson with Alan F. Benjamin as editor. Ceased publication April 1913 and reappeared May 3, 1913, as *The Advocate*. Again ceased August 8, 1913, but reappeared March 1914 as *Maryland Tribune*. Absorbed January 25, 1919, by *Wicomico Countian*.

Salisbury State College Library
Microfilm (same microfilm available at Theodore R. McKeldin Library, University of Maryland, and Wicomico County Free Library)
1905-1907: Complete
1909-1910: Complete

Daily and Sunday Times, 1923 to date

Daily and Sunday. Established December 3, 1923, by a group headed by Fred P. Adkins as *Evening Times*. No connection with Salisbury *Times I*. Name changed to Salisbury *Times II* May 27, 1927; to Salisbury *Times and the Wicomico News* January 18, 1938; to Salisbury *Times and Shoreman's Daily* January 9, 1939; to Salisbury *Times* again October 8, 1957; to *Daily Times*, December 12, 1964. Absorbed *Wicomico News* January 18, 1938. Began Sunday edition October 22, 1967. Owned 1981 by Thomson Newspapers, Inc., Toronto, Canada.

Enoch Pratt Free Library
Microfilm (Salisbury State College Library, Wicomico County Free Library, and Theodore R. McKeldin Library, University of Maryland, have same microfilm)
1923: December 3-31
1924 to date: Complete except May 27-June 5, September 23-30, 1929; May 26-June 4, 1930; June 1- September 29, 1933

Maryland Historical Society
1937: April 26, 28

Worcester County Library
1976: June 6; July 4
1979: February 28

Eastern Shoreman, 1868-1876(?)

Weekly. Established March 1868 by Charles A. Wailes and Joseph C. Bell. Merged with *Salisbury Advertiser* in 1876(?) to form *Salisbury Advertiser and Eastern Shoreman*. Last known issue August 5, 1876.

American Antiquarian Society
1876: June 10; August 5

Enoch Pratt Free Library
1872: April 20

New-York Historical Society
1873: January 25

Evening Times

See *Daily and Sunday Times*

Maryland Tribune

See *The Courier*

New Era 1868-18--(?)

Weekly. Established 1868 as a Republican organ by Owen T. Wharton. Soon expired and equipment was moved to Crisfield. Nothing else known.

Peninsula Patron, circa 1880

Weekly. Established "in the early eighties" by Captain Levin A. Parsons. After brief career it expired and plant was sold to a Laurel, Delaware, publisher. Nothing else known.

Salisbury Advertiser, 1867 to date

Weekly. Established 1867 by R. Reese Morgan and Samuel Q. Parker. Absorbed *Bachelor* November 1874; *Eastern Shoreman* 1876(?); *Wicomico Record* 1886. Merged with Salisbury *Times I* 1882 and with *Wicomico Countian* 1922. Purchased September 1977 by Independent Newspapers, Inc., Dover, Delaware, and converted into a free circulation tabloid.

Title varies: as *Salisbury Advertiser* 1867-1876(?); as *Salisbury Advertiser and the Eastern Shoreman* 1876(?)-1885; as *Salisbury Advertiser* again 1885-1922; as *Salisbury Advertiser and the Wicomico Countian* after 1922; as *Salisbury Advertiser* again in recent years.

American Antiquarian Society
1876: July 15

Enoch Pratt Free Library
1934: April 19-May 24; June 7-December 27
1935 to date: Complete *except* March 7, 1935, and September 22, 1960

Library of Congress
1945: April 19
1957: October 3

News & Farmer
1945: November 29

New-York Historical Society
1873: January 11
1943: December 30

Salisbury Advertiser
1932: February 4-December 29
1933: Complete
1934: January 4-February 22
1941: Complete
1952-1953: Complete
1967: Complete

Wicomico County Free Library
Microfilm (Salisbury State College Library and Theodore R. McKeldin Library, University of Maryland, have same microfilm. Hall of Records has same microfilm but only through December 14, 1918.)
1871: January 21-December 30
1872-1877: Complete *except* December 29, 1877
1883: March 10-December 28
1884-1896: Complete
1897: January 2-February 27; April 17-December 25
1898-1912: Complete
1914: August 15-December 12

1918: April 27-December 14
1924: January 5-December 20
1925: May 16-December 19
1926: January 9-June 29

Salisbury Advertiser and the Eastern Shoreman

See *Salisbury Advertiser*

Salisbury Advertiser and the Wicomico Countian

See *Salisbury Advertiser*

Salisbury Advocate

See *The Courier*

Salisbury Courier

See *The Courier*

Salisbury Times and Shoreman's Daily

See *Daily and Sunday Times*

Salisbury Times and the Wicomico News

See *Daily and Sunday Times*

Salisbury Times I, 1879-1882

Weekly. Established 1879 by Joseph A. Graham, who merged it with the *Salisbury Advertiser* 1882. No connection with later Salisbury *Times*.

Salisbury Times II

See *Daily and Sunday Times*

The Sentinel I, 1859-1861

Weekly. First Wicomico County newspaper. Established October 1, 1859, by John Morgan and R. Reese Morgan, father and son. Produced on a small hand press. Expired 1861 "when the younger Morgan went south to join confederate forces."

Thomas D. Irvin
1860: August 10

The Sentinel II, 1891-189-(?)

Weekly. No connection with earlier *Sentinel*. Established 1891 by Colonel Lemuel Malone to support Fusion ticket against Democrats, who won. Expired after six months.

Sharpshooter, 1864-186-(?)

Weekly. Established March 1864 at Camp Wallace just outside Salisbury for the Union troops stationed at the camp.

Times

See *Daily and Sunday Times*

Wicomico Countian, 1919-1922

Weekly. Established February 1919 as successor paper to *Maryland Tribune*. Publisher was Hooper S. Miles. Merged 1922 with *Salisbury Advertiser* to form *Salisbury Advertiser and the Wicomico Countian*.

Wicomico News, 1886-1938

Weekly. Established May 1886 by A. Lee Lankford as a prolabor newspaper. Acquired in 1887 by Marion V. and Harry L. Brewington, whose family owned the *News* for thirty-one years. On August 1, 1918, it was sold to the News Publishing Company, headed by Fred P. Adkins, and operated as a sister paper to the *Evening Times* (founded December 3, 1923) for a number of years. Absorbed by Salisbury *Times* January 18, 1938.

Enoch Pratt Free Library
Microfilm (Salisbury State College Library, Theodore R. McKeldin Library, University of Maryland, and Wicomico County Free Library have same microfilm)

1899: January 12-November 23
1900: Complete
1902-1908: Complete
1912-1922: Complete
1923: February 1- December 6
1924: January 24-December 18
1925-1932: Complete
1933: January 5-September 28
1934-1937: Complete

Wicomico Record, 1884-1886

Weekly. Established October 1884 by Thomas F. J. Rider and Clarence L. Vincent. Absorbed by *Salisbury Advertiser* 1886 after plants of both newspapers were destroyed by fire.

SHARPTOWN

Sharptown Herald

[Preston refers, on page 140, to "the only known issue . . . dated March 7, 1903," but unfortunately his notes do not disclose the whereabouts of that issue or any other facts about this newspaper.]

Sharptown Observer, 1907-19--(?)

Weekly? Established October 1907 judging from issue of November 16, 1907, which is volume I, No. 4. This issue, the only one known, is privately owned by a Sharptown resident.

Worcester

BERLIN

Berlin Advance, 1908(?)-1910(?)

Weekly. Existed circa 1910. Nothing else known.

Worcester County Library
1908: October 31
1910: April 22

Berlin-Ocean City News, 1929-1932

Weekly? Absorbed by *Eastern Shore Times* 1932. Nothing else known.

Berlin Times

See *Eastern Shore Times*, Ocean City

Eastern Shore Times, Berlin

See *Eastern Shore Times*, Ocean City

Maryland Coast Dispatch, 1984 to date

Weekly. Free distribution. Owned by Richard Lohmeyer, Berlin, Maryland.

OCEAN CITY

Beachcomber, 1960(?) to date

Weekly. Free distribution. Owned 1981 by Atlantic Publications, Inc., Accomac, Virginia.

Salisbury State College Library
1967: July 1

Worcester County Messenger
Extensive file, not indexed

Eastern Shore Times, 1872(?) to date

Weekly. Published in Berlin until after 1953, then moved to Ocean City as *Eastern Shore Times and Beachcomber*. Said to have been established 1872 under name of *Berlin Times*, but no issues from that era are known. Name of *Eastern Shore Times* adopted 1924(?). Owned 1981 by Atlantic Publications, Inc., Accomac, Virginia.

Eastern Shore Times
1976 to date

   Theodore R. McKeldin Library, University of Maryland
Microfilm
1977 to date: Complete

   Worcester County Library
1942: December 17
1970: April 23
1976: July 1

   Worcester County Messenger
1932: August 4-December 28
1933: January 5-July 27
1935: August 1-December 27
1936: Complete
1937: January 7-July 29
1954-1967: Complete
1969: Complete
1972-1975: Complete

Eastern Shore Times and Beachcomber

See *Eastern Shore Times*

Maryland Coast Press, 1969 to date

Semiweekly. Established August 1969 judging from issue of September 11, 1969, which is Volume I, No. 4. Owned 1981 by Resort Publications, Inc., Ocean City, Maryland. March 15, 1984, sold to Richard Lohmeyer, Berlin, Maryland.

   Enoch Pratt Free Library
1969: September 11
1975: January 1, 8; August 6-December 31
1976 to date: Complete

   Maryland Coast Dispatch
1970 to date: Complete

   Salisbury State College Library
1978: August 17

Oceana, 1978 to date

Weekly. Free distribution. Owned by Southswell Communications, Inc., Ocean City, Maryland.

Ocean City Post, 1950s

Weekly. Existed 1954. Nothing else known.

   Enoch Pratt Free Library
1954: September 24; October 1

Ocean City Week, 1974 to date

Weekly. Free distribution. Published by Resort Publications, Inc., Ocean City, Maryland.

   Salisbury State College Library
1978: May 21

POCOMOKE CITY

(Note: Pocomoke City was known as Newtown until April 5, 1878, when name was officially changed.)

Eastern Shoreman, 1887(?)-1889

Weekly. Established about 1887 by Lorie C. Quinn. In 1889 he moved the plant to Crisfield and resumed publication as the *Crisfield Times*.

   Worcester County Library
1890: August 30; September 27; October 4

Ledger-Enterprise, 1896-1920

Weekly. Established 1896 by merger of *Peninsula Ledger* and *Worcester Enterprise*. Merged with *Worcester Democrat* January 1920.

   Enoch Pratt Free Library
1898: July 2-September 17; October 1-December 10, 24-31
1899: Complete
1900: January 20-March 31; April 14-June 9; July 14-August 25; September 29-November 17; December 1
1901: March 16-June 15; July 6-November 30
1906: January 20-June 23; July 7-December 15
1907: June 29
1909: July 17-October 16, 30-December 25
1912: January 13-June 29
1913: July 5-December 27

1914: July 4-August 1, 15-September 5, 19; November 7, 28-December 26
1915: January 2-November 28; December 11-25
1919: January 4-July 19

Marylander and Herald
1901: November 30
1910: January 8

Worcester County Library
1905: January 28

Worcester County Messenger
1910: January 1-June 19
1912: July 13-December 28
1914: January 3-June 27

Newtown Gazette, 1869(?)-1871

Weekly. Established late 1860s by William D. Clark. Merged with *Newtown Record* to form *Newtown Record and Gazette* circa October 1871.

Newtown Record, 1865-1871

Weekly. Established 1965 by Albert J. Merrill. Merged with *Newtown Gazette* to form *Newtown Record and Gazette* circa October 1871.

Enoch Pratt Free Library (under *Record and Gazette*)
1866: June 30

Newtown Record and Gazette

See *Record and Gazette*

Peninsula Ledger, 1887(?)-1896

Weekly. Established late 1880 or early 1881 by Albert J. Merrill. (*Ledger-Enterprise* issue of November 30, 1901, which is Volume XXI, No. 48, indicated a founding date of January 8, 1881.) Merged with *Worcester Enterprise* 1896 to form *Ledger-Enterprise*.

Enoch Pratt Free Library (under *Ledger-Enterprise*)
1891: September 19-October 3

Worcester County Library
1896: July 4

Pocomoke City Times (or The Times), 1882-1888

Weekly. Established 1882 by J. Lloyd Wilkinson. Expired after plant was destroyed by fire November 22, 1888.

Pocomoke Progress, 1959

Weekly. Established March 12, 1959, by a group of businessmen from Accomac, Virginia. Expired July 30, 1959.

Worcester County Messenger
1959: March 12-July 30

Record and Gazette, 1871-1891

Weekly. Established circa October 1871 by merger of *Newtown Record* and *Newtown Gazette*. Publisher was Albert J. Merrill, owner of the *Record*. First named *Newtown Record and Gazette;* "Newtown" dropped circa April 5, 1878, when town's name was changed to Pocomoke City. In 1880s became official organ of the Prohibition Party of the Eastern Shore. Name changed to *Pocomoke Record and Gazette* circa 1889. Moved to Snow Hill 1890 and published there as *Record and Gazette*. Succeeded by *The Press* April 4, 1891.

American Antiquarian Society
1876: August 12

Enoch Pratt Free Library
1872: November 2-December 28
1873: January 4-June 28; July 12-October 25
1874: October 31; November 7, 21-December 26
1875: January 2-November 27; December 18, 25
1876: January 1-November 4
1877: October 27-December 30
1878: January 5-June 29; July 20-December 28
1879: January 4-March 22; April 12-July 12, 26-October 18

Worcester County Library
1875: March 20
1888: July 14-November 17; December 8-29

1889: January 5-June 22; July 6-December 28
1891 (as *Record and Gazette*, Snow Hill): March 28

Worcester County Messenger, 1973 to date

Weekly. Established March 1, 1973, by merger of *Worcester Democrat* of Pocomoke City and *Democratic Messenger* of Snow Hill. Owned 1981 by Atlantic Publications, Inc., Accomac, Virginia.

Enoch Pratt Free Library
1973: March 1 to date

Worcester County Library
1973: March 1

Worcester County Messenger
1973: March 1 to date

Worcester Democrat

See *Worcester Democrat and the Ledger-Enterprise*.

Worcester Democrat and the Ledger-Enterprise, 1898-1973

Weekly. Established 1898 by Samuel M. Crockett as *Worcester Democrat*. Merged with *Ledger-Enterprise* January 1920 to form *Worcester Democrat and the Ledger-Enterprise*. Merged with *Democratic Messenger* of Snow Hill March 1, 1973, to form *Worcester County Messenger*.

Enoch Pratt Free Library
1899: March 18-December 2
1906: January 13-December 15
1907: January 5-June 22; July 6-December 21
1908: January 4-December 26
1921: January 8-December 10, 24-31
1922: January 7-June 24; July 15-November 18; December 2-30
1923: January 20-August 25; September 8-December 15
1924: January 5-October 25; November 8; December 13-27
1925: Complete
1926: January 2-March 6, 27-June 26; July 10, 24-August 7, 21-December 25
1934: May 18-December 28
1935-1972: Complete *except* May 22, 1942; October 19, 1945; March 24, 1966; August 8-22, 1947
1973: January 4-February 22

Maryland Historical Society
1937: April 23

Salisbury State College Library
1955: June (no date), anniversary edition

Talbot County Free Library
1922: April 22

Worcester County Library
1922: April 22
1939: July 21
1953: November 26
1955: June 16 (75th anniversary edition); October 27; December 15, 22
1956: April 19; May 10
1958: March 27
1959: October 15
1960: June 16; July 7, 14, 28
1965: August 26; September 2 (Pocomoke City centennial)
1966: June 16 (progress edition)
1968: January 25; February 8, 15
1969: October 30
1970: April 30
1973: February 22 (last issue)

Worcester County Messenger
1929: Complete
1932-1972: Complete
1973: January 4-February 22

Worcester Enterprise, 1894-1896

Weekly. Established 1894 by a group of Pocomoke City businessmen. Merged with *Peninsula Ledger* circa 1896 to form the *Ledger-Enterprise*.

SNOW HILL

The Borderer, 1834-1835(?)

Weekly. Established February 11, 1834. Last known issue September 1, 1835. Nothing else known.

Enoch Pratt Free Library
Microfilm
1834: April 29-June 24; August 19-September 23
1835: January 6-13, 27; February 3, 17-May 5; June 23-August 4, 18; September 1

Democratic Messenger, 1869-1973

Weekly. Established January 30, 1869. Merged with *Worcester Democrat* to form *Worcester County Messenger* March 1, 1973.

American Antiquarian Society
1876: June 27

Enoch Pratt Free Library
1870: September 24
1928: September 1
1929: March 30; September 14
1930: May 17
1931: March 7
1932: December 29
1936: February 27-December 31
1937-1972: Complete *except* August 20 and October 8, 1964
1973: January 4-February 28

Julia A. Purnell Museum, Snow Hill, Maryland
1893: August 12
1920: April 10
1945: April 12

New-York Historical Society
1873: February 15

Worcester County Library
Original issues
1887: February 12
1893: July 22
1894: August 11
1895: March 16 (front page only); July 6
1897: August 28
1898: July 23
1899: November 4
1900: February 10
1908: February 1
1909: November 6
1915: December 4
1916: February 5
1917: October 6
1920: April 10
1926: February 20; August 14
1927: May 7

1922: March 16
1940: May 30 (partial)
1942: December 17
1943: February 11
1951: June 7 (partial)
1969: August 7 (centennial edition)
1970: April 22, 29

Microfilm (Enoch Pratt Library has same microfilm)
1888-1889: Complete except for scattered issues
1903-1906: Complete
1908: Complete
1909: Complete *except* January 2
1910-1913: Complete
1914: February 14-December 26
1915: Complete
1916: January 29-December 30
1917: March 10-December 29
1918: Complete
1919: February 1-December 27
1921-1923: Complete
1925: Complete
1926: January 23-December 30
1927-1930: Complete
1931: February 28-December 26

Worcester County Messenger
1946: Complete
1955-1972: Complete
1973: January 4-February 28

Peninsula Press, 1896(?)-1898(?)

Weekly. May have been successor to *The Press*. Last known issue May 26, 1898.

Julia A. Purnell Museum, Snow Hill, Maryland
1898: May 26

Worcester County Library
1896: December 12-26
1897: January 2; March 6; April 24; May 8, 22, 29; August 28; September 4, 25; November 27

The People, 1915(?)-1920(?)

Weekly. Existed in 1917-1920 period. Nothing else known.

Worcester County Library
1917: July 14
1918: June 8
1920: August 7

The Press, 1891-1896(?)

Weekly. Established April 4, 1891, as successor to *Record and Gazette*, Snow Hill. May have been succeeded by *Peninsula Press* circa 1896.

Worcester County Library
1891: April 4

Record and Gazette, 1890-1891

See *Record and Gazette*, Pocomoke City

Snow-Hill Messenger, 1827(?)-1834(?)

Weekly. Earliest known issue August 5, 1828. Name changed to *Snow-Hill Messenger and Worcester County Advertiser* September 13, 1830, when numbering started over as Volume I, No. 1. Last known issue March 11, 1834.

American Antiquarian Soceity
1832: May 14

Enoch Pratt Free Library
Microfilm
1830: September 13; November 8; December 14
1831: January 11, 25; February 1
1834: January 21

Snow-Hill Messenger and Worcester County Advertiser

See *Snow-Hill Messenger*

Worcester Advertiser (?)

Mentioned in *Worcester County, Maryland's Arcadia* (1976). Nothing else known.

Worcester Advocate, circa 1896

Weekly? Existed 1896. Nothing else known.

Worcester County Library
1896: May 16 (supplement only)

Worcester Banner, 1838-1840

Weekly. Established November 20(?), 1838. Last known issue November 10, 1840.

Enoch Pratt Free Library
Microfilm
1839: July 16-30; August 6, 20; September 24; October 1, 8; November 19; December 3
1840: January 21; June 23

Library of Congress
1840: November 10

Maryland Historical Society
1839: October 15

Talbot County Free Library
1839: November 26

Worcester County Shield, 1846-1890(?)

Weekly. Established January 6(?), 1846, as *Worcester County Shield and Farmer's Manual*. Numerous title changes: as *Worcester Shield, and Spirit of the Whig Press* October 20, 1846, to July (?), 1847; as *Worcester County Shield, Spirit of the Whig Press* to 1855; as *Worcester County Shield* to February 1856; as *Worcester Shield* to December 31, 1856; as *Worcester County Shield* again thereafter. Last known issue March 10, 1888.

American Antiquarian Society
1862: December 20
1876: June 10

Enoch Pratt Free Library
Microfilm
1846: May 19; October 6, 13, 20
1847: January 26; April 6, 20; June 1, 29; September 28; October 5
1848: February 29; July 11; December 26
1849: January 16, 23; February 20; August 21; October 30
1850: April 2; May 21; August 20
1851: January 14; February 25; July 29; October 21; November 4
1852: January 13; May 11; June 1; July 6; November 2, 16
1853: February 8, 15; April 5; May 10, 31; August 9; September 6, 13; November 1
1854: May 9, 30
1855: May 29; September 18
1856: February 13; June 10; December 30

1857: July 25
1858: September 25
1861: July 27
1863: August 22
1866: August 11
1867: June 29
1880: September 18
1881: May 14; July 2; September 10, 24; October 1, 8, 29; November 12
1882: March 4, 25; April 1; May 20; June 10, 17; July 1-15; August 5, 12, 26; September 2, 16; November 4-25
1883: January 6, 20, 27; February 3, 10, 24; March 3-May 5
1884: April 5-26; May 10-24; June 7, 21, 28; July 19, 26; August 16-October 18; November 1, 15-December 20
1885: January 17, 24; February 7, 21; March 7, 21, 28; April 4-25; May 2, 9, 30; June 27; July 4, 25; August 29; September 5, 12; October 17, 24; November 21, 28; December 5, 12, 19
1886: January 9, 23; February 6-20; March 6-April 24; May 8; June 19; July 10, 24, 31; August 7; September 11-October 2; December 25
1887: January 8, 15, 29; February 12-26; March 5, 19; April 2, 9, 23, 30; May 7-21; October 29; November 5, 26; December 17
1888: January 7, 14; February 25; March 10

Houghton Library, Harvard University
1847: July 27

Julia A. Purnell Museum, Snow Hill, Maryland
1868: September 19

Maryland Historical Society
1846: July 7
1851: November 18
1856: January 29
1857: July 18

Worcester County Shield; Spirit of the Whig Press

See *Worcester County Shield*

Worcester County Shield and Farmers' Manual

See *Worcester County Shield*

Worcester Palladium, circa 1838

Weekly? Quoted by *Baltimore Sun* September 20, 1838, in an article about a tragic boating accident in Chincoteague Bay. Nothing else known.

Worcester Sentinel and Farmers' and Mechanics' Shield, 1835-?

Weekly. Established October 16, 1835. May have been predecessor of *Worcester County Shield*. Last known issue April 18, 1837.

Enoch Pratt Free Library
Microfilm
1835: October 23
1836: March 25; July 26
1837: April 18

Worcester Shield

See *Worcester County Shield*

Worcester Shield, and Spirit of the Whig Press

See *Worcester County Shield*

Worcester Spy, circa 1838

Weekly? Quoted by *Baltimore American* September 19, 1838, in an article on a tragic boating accident in Chincoteague Bay. Nothing else known.

Bibliographical Notes

TWO monumental works on American newspapers provided the foundation on which the directory portion of this volume was built. The two complement each other, and between them provide a comprehensive tabulation of all extant files of newspapers known to the authors to have existed between 1690 and 1936. They are:

Brigham, Clarence S. *History and Bibliography of American Newspapers 1690-1820*, 2 vols. Worcester, Mass.: American Antiquarian Society, 1947.

Gregory, Winifred. *American Newspapers, 1821-1936: A Union List of Files Available in the United States and Canada.* New York: H. W. Wilson Company, 1937.

In the compilation of an Eastern Shore directory, the listings given by Brigham and Gregory were followed up in every possible case to determine (1) if their original tabulations were correct and (2) if the repository still possesses all the listed issues. In addition, a number of repositories unknown to the two authors were consulted; especially important among these were Eastern Shore libraries, newspaper offices, and historical societies not included in the earlier surveys. Finally, diligent efforts were made to ensure that the tabulation in this volume was as nearly as possible complete, accurate, and up to date.

Also useful, especially in the section on newspaper history, were the following:

PRINTING AND NEWSPAPER HISTORIES

Harrison, Dr. Samuel Alexander. "The Newspapers of Talbot," a series of articles published in the *Easton Star*, 1874-1878.

Hofstetter, Eleanore O. and Eustis, Marcella S. *Newspapers in Maryland Libraries: A Union List.* Baltimore: Maryland Department of Education, 1977.

Kobre, Sidney. *The Yellow Press and Gilded Age Journalism.* Tallahassee: Florida State University Press, 1964.

Minick, A. Rachel. *A History of Printing in Maryland 1791-1800.* Baltimore: Enoch Pratt Free Library, 1949.

Mullikin, James Clayland. *Story of the Easton Star-Democrat.* Easton: Easton Publishing Company, 1949.

Rutherfurd, Livingston. *John Peter Zenger: His Press, His Trial and a Bibliography of Zenger Imprints.* New York: Dodd, Mead, 1904; reprint ed., New York: Arno Press, 1970.

Wheeler, Joseph Towne. *The Maryland Press 1777-1790.* Baltimore: Maryland Historical Society, 1938.

Winchester, Paul, and Webb, Frank D. *Newspapers and Newspaper Men of Maryland Past and Present.* Baltimore: The Sibley Company, 1905.

LOCAL HISTORIES

Clark, Charles B., ed. *The Eastern Shore of Maryland and Virginia,* 3 vols. New York: Lewis Historical Publishing Company, 1950.

Emory, Frederic. *Queen Anne's County, Maryland; Its Early History and Development.* Baltimore: Maryland Historical Society, 1950; reprint ed., Queenstown: The Queen Anne Press, 1981.

Johnston, George. *History of Cecil County, Maryland.* Elkton, Md.: privately printed, 1881; reprinted ed., Baltimore: Regional Publishing Company, 1967.

Jones, Elias. *New Revised History of Dorchester County, Maryland.* Baltimore: Read-Taylor Press, 1925; reprint ed., Cambridge, Md.: Tidewater Publishers, 1966.

Noble, Edward M. and others. *History of Caroline County, Maryland, from Its Beginning.* Federalsburg, Md.: Printed by the Stowell Printing Company, 1920; reprint ed., Baltimore: Regional Publishing Company, 1971.

Tilghman, Oswald, comp. *History of Talbot County, Maryland 1661-1861.* Baltimore: Williams & Wilkins Company, 1915; reprint ed., Baltimore: Regional Publishing Company, 1967.

Truitt, Charles J. *Historic Salisbury, Maryland.* Garden City, N. Y.: Country Life Press, 1932.

Truitt, Reginald V. and Les Callette, Millard G. *Worcester County, Maryland's Arcadia.* Snow Hill, Md.: The Worcester County Historical Society, 1977.

Usilton, Fred G. *History of Kent County, Maryland 1630-1916*. Chestertown: no publisher, 1916.

Wagandt, Charles Lewis. *The Mighty Revolution: Negro Emancipation in Maryland, 1862-1864*. Baltimore: Johns Hopkins University Press, 1964.

Wilson, Woodrow T. *History of Crisfield and Surrounding Areas on Maryland's Eastern Shore*. Baltimore: Gateway Press, 1974.

Index

A. S. Abell Company, 179
Abolitionists, 72, 76, 84
Accomac, Va., 180, 250, 251, 252, 253
Acree, David, 133
Adams, John, 30
Adams, John Quincy, 40, 54, 55, 56
Ades, Bernard, 155, 161
Adkins, Fred P., 247, 249
Adler, 25
Advertiser and Perryville News, 211, 212
Advocate, 247
Agnew, Spiro T., 176
Agricultural Conservation Program of 1939, 149
Aker, H. M. & M. W., 125, 229
Aker, Mike, 125
Alexander, James, 7
American Eagle, 43, 70, 73, 76, 214, 216, 219
American Farm Bureau Federation, 152, 205
American Party, 69, 70
American Union, 76, 82-83, 98, 102, 110, 116, 128, 151, 201, 203
Andrews, William, 128-30
Annapolis, Md., 4, 5, 10, 11, 12, 170
Anne Arundel County, Md., 10
Apollo; or, Chestertown Spy, 12, 21-23, 24, 221, 223
Appeal, The. See *Elkton Appeal*
Appomattox Court House, 107
Ariel, 133
Armwood, George, 161, 165
Asby, General Turner, 94
Associated Press, 147, 156
Atlanta, Ga., 168

Atlantic Publications, Inc., 180, 182, 186, 232, 250, 251, 253
Aurora, 43, 219

Bachelor, 111, 121, 125, 142, 247, 248
Baker, Charles, 202
Balloon (steamer), 92, 94
Baltimore, Md., 11, 12, 26, 47, 54, 60, 61, 69, 84, 85, 94, 99, 104, 122, 128, 130, 131, 133, 134, 160, 164, 166
Baltimore American, 28, 59, 82, 88, 256
Baltimore and Ohio Railroad, 59
Baltimore Daily Gazette, 92
Baltimore Sun, 67, 118, 137, 155, 158, 159-60, 162-64, 165, 175, 179, 256
Bancker, Elizabeth, 21
Banner. See *Daily Banner*
Barroll, J. Leeds, 84, 92-93
Barroll, William, 33
Bayley, Richard P., 208
Bay Star, 214
Bay Times, 179, 182, 186, 230-31
Beach, Samuel B., 35, 62, 243
Beachcomber, 182, 186, 250
Beirut (Lebanon), 184
Bell, Clyde R., 202
Bell, John, 74, 75, 82
Bell, Joseph C., 248
Bell, Sidney, 142
Benjamin, Alan J., 142, 247
Benjamin, Mrs. D. A., 104
Benson, General Perry, 32
Berlin, Md., 182, 186, 250
Berlin Advance, 250
Berlin-Ocean City News, 151, 250
Berlin Times, 111, 250

Betterton, Md., 183
Birmingham, Ala., 174
Bishop, John L., 91
Black Tuesday, 151
Borderer, The, 42, 43, 52, 54, 253-54
Bordley, John Beale, 15
Bordley, R. G., 226
Boston, Mass., 99
Bowdle, William H., 215, 216
Bower, D. H. B., 124, 212
Bowles, Bryant, 171
Bradford, Andrew, 4
Bradford, William, 3
Bray, Clement E., 134
Breckinridge, John, 74, 75, 82, 109
Brewington, Harry L., 125, 249
Brewington, Marion V., 125, 249
Brown, Arthur, 96, 238
Brown, George, 54, 234
Brown, H. P., 242
Brown, Rap, 176
Brush-Moore Newspapers Inc., 180
Buchanan, James, 71
Bugle, The, 223
Busteed, William W., 225
Byrd, Ben D., 180
Byrd, James E., 161

Call, The, 212
Callahan, Mr., 219
Calvert, Charles, 4
Cambridge, Md., 27, 73, 75, 142, 155, 167, 174, 176, 180, 182, 185, 214-20
Cambridge Chronicle, 40, 51, 56-57, 70, 72, 214-15, 218, 219
Cambridge Chronicle and Maryland Weekly Advertiser, 214
Cambridge Daily Banner. See *Daily Banner*
Cambridge Democrat, 70, 74, 76, 82, 88, 110, 215, 216, 218
Cambridge Democrat and News, 215
Cambridge Era, 141, 142, 216, 219
Cambridge Herald, 98, 110, 215, 216, 218
Cambridge Intelligencer, 43, 110, 216
Cambridge Journal, 216
Cambridge Record, 216-17, 218
Cambridge Telegraph, 215, 217

Cambridge Tribune, 217
Cambridge Weekly Chronicle and Farmers' Register, 214, 218
Camp Kirby, 102
Camp Wallace, 99
Cann, James R., 224
Canton, Ohio, 180
Carmichael, Judge Richard Bennett, 88-91, 94, 97, 98
Caroline Advocate, 40, 201
Caroline County, Md., 12, 17, 40, 76, 83, 91, 97, 111, 140, 153, 154, 178, 187, 201-6
Caroline County Times-Record, 186, 203
Caroline Democrat, 201
Caroline Independent, 151, 201
Caroline Intelligencer, 40, 204
Caroline Sun, 111, 187, 202, 205-6
Carroll County, Md., 185, 187
Cathel, Levi, 61
Catholics. See Roman Catholics
Caton, Lewis, 42-43, 54
Cecil Call, 111, 212
Cecil County, Md., 40, 61, 67, 76, 98, 111, 124, 178, 206-13
Cecil County Advocate, 206
Cecil County News, 111, 151, 206-7
Cecil County Star, 207, 209
Cecil Democrat, 45, 61, 64, 65, 66-67, 76, 84, 88, 99, 106, 107, 109, 110, 111, 179, 180, 207-8, 211
Cecil Democrat and Farmers' Journal, 208
Cecil Gazette, 207, 208
Cecil Gazette and Farmers' and Mechanics' Advertiser, 45, 208
Cecil Republican and Farmers' and Mechanics' Advertiser, 208-9
Cecil Star, 207, 211
Cecil Times, 207, 209
Cecil Whig, 45, 64, 66, 67, 68, 70, 76, 110, 111, 117, 178, 179, 182, 186, 209-10, 211, 213
Cecil Whig and Port Deposit Weekly Courier, 212
Central Courant, 212
Central Courant and Port Deposit Intelligencer, 212
Centreville, Md., 17, 42, 78, 109, 110, 152, 179, 180, 182, 201, 225-29

INDEX

Centreville Evening Times and Eastern Shore Publick Advertiser, 225
Centreville Observer, 110, 152, 225-26, 227, 228
Centreville Record, 151-52, 179, 226-27, 228
Centreville State Rights, 62, 63, 76, 97, 227
Centreville Times, 40, 45, 47, 76, 130, 152, 225, 227
Centreville Times and Eastern Shore Advertiser, 227
Chalmers, George, 23
Chambers, Judge Ezekiel F., 84
Chambers, Max, 153-54, 187, 205
Charleston, S. C., 96, 107, 178, 180, 218, 245
Charleston Mercury, 83
Charlestown, Md., 98, 99
Cheezum, W. W., 226
Chesapeake and Delaware Canal, 61
Chesapeake and Ohio Canal, 59
Chesapeake Bay, 59, 150
Chesapeake Bay Bridge, 176-77
Chesapeake Bay Yacht Club, 130
Chesapeake Chesapike, 43, 124, 206
Chesapeake City, Md., 111, 124, 206, 212
Chesapeake College, 186
Chesapeake Publishing Corporation, 179, 180, 182, 235
Chesapeake Record, 124, 206, 212
Chester River, Md., 5
Chester River Press, 184, 221
Chestertown, Md., 3, 4, 12, 17, 21, 23-24, 25, 26, 40, 75, 103, 110, 121, 122, 128, 139, 142, 143, 150, 153, 179, 182, 183, 221-24
Chestertown Enterprise, 147, 148, 150, 164, 176, 221
Chestertown Gazette. See *Apollo; or, Chestertown Spy*
Chestertown High School, 184
Chestertown Telegraph, 26, 40, 45, 221, 224
Chestertown Transcript, 92, 93, 106, 109, 110, 150-51, 221-22, 223
Chincoteague, Va., 166
Chincoteague Bay, 256

Choptank River, Md., 176, 179
Christian, A. A., 246
Church Hill, Md., 111, 229
Church Hill Air Line, 229
Church Hill News, 229
Cincinnati, Ohio, 99
CIO, 167
Civil War, 62, 110, 120, 125, 131, 132, 139, 222, 236, 245
Claggett, Dr. Laurence G., 100, 242
Clark, Charles B., 47
Clark, William D., 252
Clarke, Edward J., 138-39, 141, 151
Clay, Henry, 41
Coburn, Joe, 99
Coleman, Thomas M., 66-67, 211
Comet. See *St. Michaels Comet*
Commodore Maury, 133
Communism, 164-65, 167
Confederacy, 82, 84, 85, 88, 92
Constitutional Convention of 1851, 61
Constitutional Union Party, 84
Cook, John H., 239
Coolidge, Calvin, 145
Cooper, George W. M., 121, 247
Corddry, George, 156
Cosby, Royal Gov. William, 7-8
Councell, William H., 88, 96, 121
County Record, 179, 186, 187, 189, 202, 204, 206
Courier, The, 247
Courier and Farmer, 203
Cowan, James, 10-21, 29, 35, 62, 119, 241
Cox, Ernest, 132
Crawford, R. Clay, 222
Crawford, William, 40-41
Crisfield, John W., 98, 110
Crisfield, Md., 110, 122, 123, 132, 134, 138, 142, 168, 231-32
Crisfield Leader, 111, 112, 231
Crisfield News, 231
Crisfield Post, 231, 234
Crisfield Times, 119, 123-24, 132-33, 134, 138, 164, 180, 182, 185, 231-32, 251
Crisfield Tribune, 230, 232
Crockett, Samuel M., 253
Croughan, William W., 85
Crumpton, Md., 111, 229
Crumpton Gazette, 125, 229

Crumptonian, 125, 229
Culp's Hill, 95
Cumberland Road, 59

Daily and Sunday Times, 247-48
Daily Banner, 118, 145, 154-55, 158-59, 174-75, 176, 180, 182, 185, 218, 245
Daily Banner and Cambridge Record, 218
Daily Times, 247
Davis, Green K., 155
Davis, Jefferson, 95, 98
Deep South, 56, 57, 74, 75
Delaware, 59, 61, 110, 134, 171, 182
Delaware State News, 228
Delmarva Farmer, 183, 235
Delmarva Peninsula, 160
Democrat, The, 235, 236
Democrat and Dorchester Advertiser, 56, 215, 218
Democrat and Herald, 215, 216, 218, 219
Democrat and News, 167, 218-19, 220
Democratic Messenger, 147, 148, 180, 185, 254
Democratic Party, 36, 45, 56, 72, 110, 127, 141-42, 235
Democratic-Republicans, 35, 36, 40, 45
Denton, Md., 14, 40, 42, 75, 98, 102, 110, 116, 128, 140, 151, 179, 182, 186, 187, 201-3, 204
Denton Journal, 25, 76, 91, 106, 110, 180, 187, 202-3
Deringer, H. Hurtt, 183, 184-85
Diary, 25
Dickinsen, Charles, 154
Dobson, Emory, 186, 187, 189
Dobson, H. Clay, 246
Dobson, Stewart, 186-87
Dorchester Community News, 219
Dorchester County, Md., 12, 40, 56, 69, 76, 111, 166, 174, 175, 214-20
Dorchester County Era, 219
Dorchester News (Cambridge), 182, 183, 218, 219, 220
Dorchester News (Hurlock), 149, 150, 179, 180
Dorchester Standard, 219
Douglas, Stephen A., 74, 77, 82
Dover, Delaware, 17, 180, 230, 231, 248
Downes, R. E. C., 229
Drummondtown, Va., 54
Duer, Robert F., 165
Duffy, Edmund, 159
Du Hamel, William, 229

Eagle of Freedom, 26
Eastern Shore, 9, 10, 11, 12, 18, 21, 26, 28, 33, 36, 38, 40, 41, 42, 45, 60, 61, 69, 70, 72, 76, 77, 82, 88, 89, 105, 106, 107, 110, 114, 134, 143, 145, 150, 156, 159, 165, 166, 176, 178, 183, 184
Eastern Shore Farmer, 235
Eastern Shore Journal, 125, 235
Eastern Shoreman (Pocomoke City), 42, 251
Eastern Shoreman (Salisbury), 111, 125, 230, 248
Eastern Shoremen, 16, 28, 30, 59, 62, 72, 98, 122, 124, 130
Eastern Shore News, 180
Eastern Shore of Maryland, The, 47
Eastern Shore Railroad, 60, 111
Eastern Shore Republican, 151, 230, 232
Eastern Shore Star, 46, 47, 235, 240
Eastern Shore Times, 182, 186, 250-51
Eastern Shore Times and Beachcomber, 251
Eastern Shore Whig and People's Advocate, 38, 42, 45, 46, 47, 49, 235-36
Easton, Md., 10, 11, 12, 15, 18, 23, 26, 27, 30-31, 32, 36, 40, 41, 54, 75, 102, 110, 114, 118, 125, 127, 134, 138, 144, 182, 183, 235-45, 246
Easton Democrat, 111, 112, 236, 240, 245
Easton Emergency Hospital, 135
Easton Enterprise. See *Enterprise, The*
Easton Gazette, 36, 59-60, 74, 76, 88, 90-91, 94-96, 110, 111, 112, 117, 119, 121, 128, 129, 130, 134, 136, 139-40, 151, 236-38, 242, 243
Easton Gazette, and Eastern Shore Intelligencer, 236
Easton High School, 184
Easton Hotel, 51
Easton Independent, 236, 238

Easton Journal, 96, 110, 205, 238-39, 242, 245
Easton Ledger, 111, 131, 238, 239-40
Easton Publishing Company, 134, 230
Easton Rotary Club, 135
Easton Star, 28, 61, 84, 86, 88, 90-91, 94, 95, 96, 110, 111, 112, 121, 125, 127, 128, 236, 238, 240-41, 245
Easton Star-Democrat, 241. See also *Star-Democrat*
Edison Company, 122
Elkton, Md., 54, 61, 64, 66, 75, 110, 111, 179, 182, 206-11
Elkton Appeal, 111, 210
Elkton Courier, 210, 212
Elkton Mechanic, 43, 210
Elkton Press, 40, 211
Elliott, Daniel J., 155-56, 161
Emerson, John H., 41-42, 83
Emory, Frederic, 97, 229
Enterprise, The (Easton), 241
Enterprise, The (Greensborough), 204
Enterprise (Lexington Park, Md.), 186
Era of Good Feelings, 40
Evans, Prentiss W., 168, 170
Evening Post Publishing Company, 180, 218, 245
Evening Times, 145-47, 248, 249

Farm and Home, 204
Farmers Branch Bank of Easton, 41
Fascist Italy, 170
Federalists, 16, 17, 34, 243
Federalsburg, Md., 111, 203-4, 220
Federalsburg Courier, 122, 151, 203
Federalsburg Times, 160, 179, 186, 187, 203-4, 220
Fifteenth Amendment, 127
Fillmore, Millard, 71
Foard, Edward L., 66
Footner, Hulbert, 132
Ford, John T., 246
Forman, Thomas M., 33
Fort Delaware, 92
Fort McHenry, 89, 92
Fort Sumter, 85, 86
Forwood, Amor T., 61, 64-67, 68
Foxx, Jimmy, 149

Frazer, Dr. J. H., 207
Frazier, John, Jr., 103-5
Freedmen's Journal, 128, 222
Freedom's Sentinel, 43, 228, 229
Free Press. See Greensborough Free Press
Free School of Annapolis, 5
Fremont, John C., 72
Friends School, 140

Galena, Md., 183
Garfield, James, 126
Gazette-Democrat, 236, 241, 243
General Advertiser, 241
Georgetown, Del., 54
Georgetown, Md., 183
Gerrish, George, 21, 24, 25-26, 221
Gettysburg (Battle of), 95, 96
Gibbs, Henry W., 243
Gibson, Jacob, 16-20, 21, 35, 62
The Glory and the Dream, 176
Gluckheim, Md., 111, 220
Godwin, Harold, 170
Goldsboro[ugh], Md., 110
Goldsborough, Phillips L., 219
Goldsborough, Dr. W. W., 206
Goodwin, Frank, 149, 184
Graham, Alexander, 36, 236
Graham, Joseph A., 249
Great Depression, 144, 151
Green, John D., 38, 39, 42, 78, 235
Green, Mrs. Rachel, 38, 39
Green, Sam, 82
Greensboro[ugh], Md., 110, 204
Greensborough Free Press, 111, 127, 204
Gregory, Dick, 174
Groome, William, 11, 51
Guiteau, Charles, 126
Gullett, Albert G., 91, 92
Gutenberg, Johann, 41

Haines, Charles, 211
Hamilton, Andrew, 3, 5-9
Hamilton, James, 5
Hamilton, Margaret, 5
Hammond, Nicholas, 34
Hand, John T., 228
Handy, Gordon M., 52
Harding, Warren G., 145

Harrington, Norman, 119, 171-74
Harris, Robert, 26
Harrison, Dr. Samuel A., 28, 30, 47, 102, 245
Hastings, Lawrence, 122
Hatcheson, Richard, 33
Havre de Grace, Md., 26
Henberry, 5
Herald, The, 232, 233
Herald and Eastern Shore Intelligencer, 241
Herrick, S. W., 229
Herring, Donald, 186
Hicks, Thomas Hollyday, 61, 62, 69
Highley, Reverend Burton S., 246
Hillsboro[ugh], Md., 40, 110, 204
Hines, J. K., 104
History of Cecil County, 67-68
History of Crisfield, 137-38
History of Queen Anne's County, 229
Holland, Charles F., 121, 247
Holland, Noah, 133
Hollyday, Henry, 59-60
Home Guards, 85, 89, 92, 97
Home Journal, 213
Hostetter, E. Ralph, 178-80, 181, 185
Hotchkiss, Bruce, 183
House of Representatives, The U. S., 41, 98
Houston, F. H., 245
Howard, Luke, 33, 34
Hughes, Gov. Harry, 183
Hurlock, Md., 149, 150, 203, 220
Hurlock Advance, 111, 220
Hutton, Bob, 187, 189

Impartial Reading Herald, 25
Independent, The (Denton), 201, 203
Independent (Easton), 114, 238
Independent Newspapers, Inc., 180, 230, 248
Index (Crisfield), 111, 231
Index (Trappe), 125, 245
Indianapolis Star, 186
Ingraham, Prentiss, 118
Inquirer, 43, 224
Intelligencer, The, 214, 219-20
Item, The, 220

Jackson, Andrew, 36, 40, 41, 45, 54, 55, 56, 154
Jackson, William H., 247
Jacksonian Democrats, 41, 45
Jackson Picket Guard, 43, 211
"Jacobins," 18
Jacobs, Col. C. W., 80
Jefferson, Thomas, 16, 28, 29, 32, 36
Jeffersonians, 41, 72
Johnson, Andrew, 127
Johnson, J. A., 239
Johnson, Joseph H., 218
Johnston, George, 67-68
Jones, William, 211
Journal, 203
Jump, John W. D., 134
Justice, John W. S., 232
Justice, U. S. Department of, 176

Keating, George, 213
Keating, Miss L. Parker, 97
Keating, Thomas J., 62, 78, 80, 97, 151, 227
Keene, Vachel, 36
Kemp, C. H., 247
Kennedy, Robert F., 176
Kent Bugle, 43, 45, 222, 223
Kent Conservator, 76, 84, 92, 93, 223
Kent County, Md., 3, 4, 5, 9, 17, 33, 34, 40, 76, 104, 106, 128, 139, 147, 150, 183, 184, 221-24
Kent County News, 45, 47, 76, 84, 85, 92, 98, 99, 102, 103, 104-5, 108, 110, 117, 121, 122, 123, 128, 139, 142-43, 151, 179, 182, 183-84, 221, 222, 223-24
Kent Independent, 224
Kent Island, 131
Kent News. See *Kent County News*
Kentucky, 186
Kerbin, William H., 185
Kiah, T. H., 164
Kimmelshue, Ed, 173
Kirby, Major William, 94
Kirby, William, 70
Know-Nothings, 69-71, 72, 73, 211
Koenig, Frederick, 41
Korea, 178

Lancaster, Pa., 54
Land of Legendary Lore, 118
Lanford, A. Lee, 249
Latimer, Thomas S., 219
Laurel, Del., 248
Ledger. See *Easton Ledger*
Ledger-Enterprise, 141, 251-52, 253
Lee, General Robert E., 107
Lee, Yuel, 155, 156, 158, 161
Leesburg, Va., 88
Leonard, Jonathan, 239
Lexington, Kentucky, 58
Libertyville, Md., 148
Lightbourn, A. W., 243
Lincoln, Abraham, 74, 77, 82, 83, 84, 85, 94, 97, 102, 104, 105, 106, 107, 109
Little Rock, Arkansas, 171
Lloyd, Edward, 18
Lockwood, Brig. Gen., 92
Locofoco Party, 72
Locust Grove, Md., 183
Lohmeyer, Richard V., 186, 250, 251
Lord Baltimore, 7
Louisville Courier, 59
Loveday, Charles T., 225
Lowe, Solomon, 51
Lynch, Md., 183
Lyons, Richard, 16
Lyric Theater, 124

Madison, James, 40
Malone, Col. Lemuel, 249
Manchester, William, 176
Manderville, H., 229
Manila, Philippines, 118
Manokin River, 132
Marion Station, Md., 128, 232
Marshall, Lindsay C., 218
Marshall Seminary, 14
Martin, Alexander, 28, 29
Martin, Thomas E., 62, 201
Martin, William A., Jr., 185-86
Martinsburg, W. Va., 185
Maryland Censor, 43, 241, 243
Maryland Citizen, 109, 110, 228
Maryland Coast Dispatch, 182, 250
Maryland Coast Press, 182, 186, 251
Maryland Constitution, 59

Maryland Courier, 111, 203, 204
Marylander, The, 128-29, 232, 233, 234
Marylander and Herald, 65, 132, 133, 159, 161, 162, 164, 165, 182, 186, 187, 188, 232-33, 234
Maryland Farm Bureau, 153
Maryland Gazette, 4, 12
Maryland General Assembly, 3-4, 5, 12, 54, 60
Maryland Herald and Eastern Shore Intelligencer, 12, 13, 14, 15, 16, 17, 18, 19, 20, 23, 28, 33, 119, 241-42
Maryland Historical Magazine, 122-23
Maryland Independent, 242
Maryland Journal, 25
Maryland News, 213
Maryland News-Courier, 213
Maryland Poultry Digest, 153
Maryland Press Association, 135
Maryland Pythian, 211
Maryland State News, 228
Maryland Sentinel, 227, 228
Maryland State Legislature, 20, 21
Maryland Tribune, 247, 248
Maryland Weekly Advertiser, 220
Matthews, Rives, 168-70
Maulin, Anna Catharina, 5
McCauley, Charles O., Jr., 211
McClellan, George B., 96, 105, 106, 109
McCoole, Mike, 99
McCord, John, 211
McDowell, Elijah, 51
McHurd, Jane, 10
McKeldin, Theodore, 154
McKnight, Paul V., 186
McMath, George N., 180, 182
McPhail, Marshal James S., 90-91
McPherson, William, 133
Mencken, Henry L., 158-59, 160, 161, 165
Mergenthaler, Ottmar, 119
Merrick & Kemp, 247
Merrill, Albert J., 252
Methodism, 51, 52, 122
Michie, Armistead R., 218
Middleton, Henry C., 51
Midland Journal, 209, 213
Mid-Shore Times, 238, 242-43

Miles, Hooper S., 249
Millington, Md., 183, 229
Mills, Michael, 186
Mississippi, 57
Model Printery, 204
Monroe, James, 34, 40
Moore, Jackie, 191
Morgan, R. Reese, 77-78, 247, 248
Morris, Gouverneur, 9
Moss, Harry, 124, 206
Mullikin, James C., 33, 117, 239
Mullikin, Percival, 246
Mullikin, Robert T., 246

Nanticoke River, 76
Natchez, 56
Nation, Carrie, 124
National Guard, 174
National Guard Armory (Salisbury), 162
National Recovery Administration, 165
Nazi Germany, 170
NBC, 170
Negroes, 56-57, 103, 104, 164-65, 174, 176
Nellie Pentz (steamer), 104
Nelson, Earl Lee, 133
New Comet, 246
New Era, 111, 248
New Farm, 205
News, The, 212-13
News & Farmer, 152-53, 154, 178, 182, 187, 205
News Letter, 205
News Publishing Company, 249
Newtown, Md., 111, 251, 252
Newtown Gazette, 111, 252
Newtown Record, 111, 252
New York, N. Y., 3, 4, 6, 7, 8, 9, 25, 99, 119, 143, 178, 180, 202, 204, 207, 209, 219, 223, 228, 230, 245
New York Evening Post, 18
New York Journal, 94
New York Herald, 86
New York Herald-Tribune, 180
New York Times, 132, 149, 175
New-York Weekly Journal, 7, 62
Nixon, Richard M., 176
North Carolina, 182

North Dorchester News, 219, 220
North East, Md., 111, 206, 207, 211-12
North East Advertiser, 151, 211, 212
North East Record, 124, 207, 212
North East River, Md., 98
North East Star, 111, 207, 212

Observer. See *Centreville Observer*
Oceana, 251
Ocean City, Md., 166, 182, 186, 250-51
Ocean City Post, 251
Ocean City Week, 251
Onancock, Va., 180
Once A Month, 243
Onley, Va., 180
Order of the Star-Spangled Banner, 69
Ordinance of Secession, 83
Owl Swamp, 140
Oxford, Md., 23, 111, 171, 245-46
Oxford Enterprise, 111, 245-46
Oxford Press, 124-25, 213

Page, Henry, 128-29
Page, James, 33
Parker, Samuel Q., 248
Parker, Thomas, 186
Parksley, Va., 124
Parsons, Levin A., 248
Patapsco Enterprise, 82
Patchett, S. Ellwood, 114
Pathfinder, 233
Pattison, John R., 165
Pattison, Richard, 219
Pearl, 42, 43, 201, 203
Peninsula Democrat, 243
Peninsula General Hospital, 156
Peninsula Ledger, 140-41, 251, 252, 253
Peninsula Patron, 111, 248
Peninsula Press (Crisfield), 232
Peninsula Press (Snow Hill), 254, 255
Pennington, William H., 213
People, The, 254
People's Monitor, 35, 36, 43, 62, 241, 243
People's Press, 43, 233
Perkins, Eben F., 221
Perry, Denise, 184
Perryville, Md., 111, 212
Perryville News, 151, 211, 212

INDEX

Perryville Record, 212
Philadelphia, Pa., 4, 5, 10, 11, 21, 47, 54, 99, 164, 166
Philadelphia Bulletin, 155, 166
Philadelphia Inquirer, 155
Philadelphia Ledger, 155
Philadelphia Minerva, 21
Philadelphia Record, 155
Phillips Packing Co., 167
Piatt, Col. Don, 103
Pinckney, Charles, 34
Piper, Michael, 5
Pliescott, Elwood J., Jr., 214
Plummer, James H., 103, 104, 128
Plummer, John Dukes, 127
Plummer, Risdon, 127, 204
Pocomoke City, Md., 111, 122, 125, 133, 140, 180, 185, 231, 251-53
Pocomoke City Times, 125, 252
Pocomoke Progress, 252
Pocomoke Record and Gazette, 252
Pocomoke Round Table Society, 140-41
Poe, Edgar Allan, 69
Poisal, Rev. William M., 118-19
Pokrandt, James E., Jr., 185
Polk, Richard, 186
Port Deposit, Md., 110, 111, 209, 212-13
Port Deposit Board of Trade, 213
Port Deposit Journal, 213
Port Deposit Rock and Cecil County Commercial Advertiser, 213
Portsville, 140
Press, The, 252, 254, 255
Preston, Md., 111, 152, 178, 182, 187, 204-5
Preston Echo, 205
Preston News, 152, 204, 205
Preston News and the Bay Country Farmer, 205
Preston Times, 204, 205
Price, William, 95
Princess Anne, Md., 54, 65, 76, 98, 110, 128, 129, 159, 161, 164, 165, 182, 186, 232-35
Prohibition Party, 122, 252
Protestant Episcopal Church of Easton, 135
Public Monitor, 243

Pulitzer Prize, 166, 167

Queen Anne's County, Md., 17, 35, 40, 76, 97, 149, 152, 225-31
Queen Anne's Journal, 180, 228
Queen Anne's News . . . and the Queenstown News, 229
Queen Anne's Record, 47, 152, 225, 226, 228
Queen Anne's Record-Observer, 45, 47, 152, 179, 182, 184, 186, 225, 228-29
Queen Anne's Record—the Centreville Observer, 228
Queen Anne's Telescope, 228, 229
Queenstown, Md., 111, 125, 229-30
Queenstown Bank of Maryland, 230
Queenstown News, 125, 126, 229-30
Quinn, Egbert, 138, 170
Quinn, Lorie C., 112, 119, 123-24, 137-38, 139, 142, 230, 251
Quinn, Lorie C., Jr., 138

Reagan, Ronald, 183
Record and Gazette, 122, 133, 252, 255
Reed Rifles, 104
Reese, James E., 141-42
Reese, William R., 112
Rehoboth Beach, Del., 166
Reisterstown, Md., 162
Republican Party, 72, 74, 110, 127, 128, 142, 209, 236
Republican Star, 235, 243-44
Republican Star; or, Eastern Shore General Advertiser, 243, 244
Republican Star; or, Eastern Shore Political Luminary, 17, 18, 19, 21, 26, 27, 28, 29, 30-32, 33, 34, 35-36, 37, 38, 39, 45, 46, 47, 130, 243-44
Republican Star; or, General Advertiser, 243, 244
Republican Star and General Advertiser, 243, 244
Resort Publications, Inc., 251
Ricaud, James B., 104
Richmond, Va., 96, 107
Richmond Dispatch, 88
Ricketts, Palmer C., 64-67, 68, 209
Rider, Thomas F. J., 250

Ridgely, Md., 205-6
Rimpo, Maurice, 175, 185
Rising Sun, Md., 111, 213
Rising Sun Commercial, 124-25, 213
Rising Sun Journal, 111, 213
Ritchie, Albert C., 161, 162, 165, 167
Rivers of the Eastern Shore, 132
Riverton, Md., 140
Robson, Thomas K., 61, 62, 94-96, 97, 121, 125, 128, 240
Rock Hall, Md., 183
Rogers, General, 92
Roman Catholics, 69, 71, 72
Roosevelt, Franklin D., 165, 176
Rosendale, Christopher J., 230
Rowlandville, Md., 178
Rowlenson, J. H., 228
Rowlenson, Nicholas S., 243
Royal Oak, Md., 118
Ruralist, The, 111, 220
Ruralist Company, 220
Russell, L. Bates, 222
Russum, George M., 62

St. John's College, 138
St. Louis Post Dispatch, 170
St. Mary's Beacon, 92
St. Michaels, Md., 111, 176, 246
St. Michael's Comet, 111, 118, 246
Salisbury Advertiser, 111, 117-18, 121, 122, 125, 180, 182, 248-49
Salisbury Advertiser and the Eastern Shoreman, 248, 249
Salisbury Advertiser and the Wicomico Countian, 249
Salisbury Advocate, 249
Salisbury Courier, 142, 249
Salisbury State College, 186
Salisbury Times, 111, 146, 147, 148, 154-56, 157, 158, 161, 162-65, 170, 174, 175, 181, 182, 184, 186, 189, 190, 191, 192, 247, 248, 249
Salisbury Times and Shoreman's Daily, 247
Salisbury Times and the Wicomico News, 247
Saunders, Robert, Jr., 21, 24-25, 26, 221
Schenck, Major Gen. Robert C., 103

Schneider, Jacob, 25
Sentinel, 76, 77, 78, 79, 249
Sequoia, 176
Shannahan, John H. K. II, 134
Shannahan, John, H. K. III, 134
Shannahan, Samuel E., 114, 134-37, 138
Sharp Shooter, 245
Sharpshooter, 99-102, 249
Sharptown, Md., 111, 250
Sharptown Herald, 140, 250
Sharptown Observer, 250
Sharptown Sporting Club, 140
Sheppard, J. C., 229
Sheppard, Will H., 91
Sherwood, George W., 45-46, 235
Sinepuxent Bay, 166
Smith, Ann, 46-47
Smith, George Wishart, 27, 33
Smith, H. Everett, 76, 93-94
Smith, Joseph, 54
Smith, Perrin and Margaret, 27
Smith, Thomas Perrin, 18, 19, 26, 27-33, 34-38, 41, 45, 62, 130, 243
Smith Island, 132
Smyrna, Del., 54
Snow, Walter T., 54
Snow Hill, Md., 51, 52, 54, 110, 122, 147, 155, 180, 184, 253-56
Snow-Hill Messenger, 40, 51, 255
Snow-Hill Messenger and Worcester County Advertiser, 255
Snow Hill Methodist Episcopal Church, 52
Social Journal, 245
Somerset County, 12, 40, 85, 129, 170, 231-35
Somerset Herald, 40, 52, 85, 87, 110, 233-34
Somerset Iris and Messenger of Truth, 43, 54, 55, 56, 234
Somerset Journal, 234
Somerset News, 168, 169, 234
Somerset Republican, 230, 232
Somerset Union, 62, 76, 85, 87, 88, 234
South, The, 74, 76, 84, 98
South Carolina, 82, 83
Southswell Communications, Inc., 251
Spencer, Jervis, 33

Spencer, William, 33
Spreet, Isaac, 143
Stafford, Capt. Andrew J., 97, 245
Stant, Alvert V., 230
Stant, William, 132
Star-Democrat, 45, 46, 47, 112, 114, 119, 134, 137, 140, 171-74, 175, 179, 180, 181, 182, 183, 184, 236, 240, 242, 245
State Rights Advocate, 43, 76, 78, 80, 228, 229
State Rights Advocate and Maryland Sentinel, 227
Steamboat'n' Days, 134
Stevensville, Md., 179, 182, 186, 230-31
Stewart Building, 242
Still Pond, Md., 183
Story of the Easton Star-Democrat, 33, 117
Stowe, Harriet Beecher, 82
Stowell Printery, 220
Straughn, Levin E., 214
Stuart, Dr. Alexander, 33, 34
Sudlersville, Md., 229
Sunpapers. See *Baltimore Sun*
Supreme Court, The U. S., 161, 171
Surprise (steamboat), 35
Sykes, Dr. James, 33

Talbot Banner, 182, 184, 245
Talbot County, Md., 10, 17, 18, 28, 45, 46, 47, 76, 84, 106, 118, 134, 171, 172, 174, 175, 180, 235-47
Talbot County Free Library, 135
Talbot County Record, 152, 245
Talbot Courthouse, 10
Talbot Times, 111, 245, 246
Tall, Reuben S., 70, 214
Tangier (police schooner), 132
Tangier Island, 132
Tawes, J. Millard, 154, 168-70
Taylorville, Md., 155
Telegraph, The, 222, 223
Telescope, and Eastern Shore Advertiser, 43, 224
Temperance, 54
Temperance Banner, 43, 211
Tevis, Lt. Col. Charles Carroll, 103-4
Thomas C. Nicols & Co., 243

Thomson Newspapers, Inc., 180, 247
Thornton, W. Thomas, 204
Tidewater Inn, 175
Tilghman Island, 166
Time Piece, 25
Times, The, 202, 204
Times and Advertiser, 229
Times and Public Advertiser, 227, 229
Times-Record, 182, 202, 203, 204
Timmons, Bill "Dink," 147-48
Toadvine, Melvin, 184, 185, 189, 193
Tolchester, Md., 143
Torbert, Henry, 127
Toronto, Canada, 178, 180, 247
Town of Hurlock and Easton Publishing Company, 220
Towson, Md., 155
Transchoptankiana, 165
Trappe, Md., 111, 113, 125, 246-47
Trappe Courier, 247
Trappe Enterprise, 246, 247
True Marylander, 65, 234-35
Truitt, Charles J., 146-47, 155, 156, 158, 160, 165-67
Truman, Harry, 154
Tubman, B. G., 70
Turner, John, 16
Tylor, Wilson M., 112, 117, 129, 135, 139-40, 141

Uncle Tom's Cabin, 81, 82
Underground Railroad, 82
Union (North), 74, 75, 76-77, 82, 84, 85, 88, 89, 96, 98, 103, 139, 209, 236
Union Hotel, 94, 102
Union Reformer, 43, 70, 211
University of Maryland, 184, 185, 186
University of Tennessee, 186
Upper Dorchester News, 203, 220
Usilton, Fred, 151
Usilton, William B., 103, 104, 123, 139
Usilton, William B., Jr., 123, 139

Vallandigham, James L., 54
Vanderford, H., Jr., 84, 109, 201, 228
Vandergrift, John S., 143
Vegetable Growers Messenger, 153
Village Herald, 65, 232-33

Vincent, Clarence L., 250
Vinton, E. P., 220
Virginia, 5, 76, 132

Wailes, Charles A., 248
War of 1812, 83
Warehime, D. Scott, 187, 205
Washington, D. C., 164, 176
Washington, George, 51, 70
Washington College, 138, 153, 184
Washington Post, 168, 175, 176
Washington Street (Easton), 29, 30, 32
Washington Times-Herald, 168
WASPs, 150
Watergate, 183
WBOC, 147
WBOC-CATV, 147
WBOC-FM, 147
Weekly Advertiser, 26
Weekly Phenix, 246
Weekly Post, 186
Weekly Sentinel, 228, 229
Weekly Sentinel and General Advertiser, 228, 229
Welch, J. W., 43
Wennersten, John R., 122-23
Western Shore, 59, 60, 61, 62, 185, 187
Wharton, Owen T., 248
Whig Party, 40, 41, 45, 46, 70, 209, 210, 213
White Citizens Committee, 171
Whitney Communications Corporation, 180, 182, 183, 202, 204, 207, 208, 219, 228, 230, 245
Wicomico Countian, 247, 248, 249
Wicomico County, Md., 40, 111, 146, 247-50
Wicomico County Grand Jury, 160
Wicomico High School, 184
Wicomico News, 111, 125, 142, 151, 247, 249-50
Wicomico Record, 111, 125, 248, 250
Wilkinson, Henry, 206
Williams, Gee, 186
Williams, Matthew, 156, 160, 161
Wilmer, L. A., 212

Wilmer, the Reverend James Jones, 26
Wilmington, Del., 61
Wilson, Woodrow T., 137-38
Wiltshire Manor, 154
Winchell, Walter, 152
Winters, Owen B., 152
Wollaston, Thomas A., 102
Worcester Advertiser, 255
Worcester Advocate, 255
Worcester Banner, 255
Worcester County, Md., 12, 40, 54, 61, 111, 139, 147, 186, 250-56
Worcester County, Maryland's Arcadia, 255
Worcester County Democrat, 254
Worcester County Messenger, 182, 184, 253, 254
Worcester County Shield, and Spirit of the Whig Press, 43, 255, 256
Worcester County Shield; Spirit of the Whig Press, 43, 255, 256
Worcester County Shield and Farmers' Manual, 51, 58, 62, 64, 72, 74, 76, 93, 110, 255-56
Worcester County Temperance Society, 52
Worcester Democrat, 138-39, 159, 180, 182, 185, 251, 253
Worcester Enterprise, 251, 252, 253
Worcester Palladium, 256
Worcester Sentinel and Farmers' and Mechanics' Shield, 43, 256
Worcester Shield, 256
Worcester Shield, and Spirit of the Whig Press, 256
Worcester Spy, 256
World War I, 120
World War II, 144, 147, 151
Wright, Gustavus W. T., 35, 36
Wright, Robert, 35

"XYZ, Mr.," 34

Zenger, John Peter, 3-5, 6-9, 10, 62, 168
Zieber, John S., 233